The China Boom

CONTEMPORARY ASIA IN THE WORLD

CONTEMPORARY ASIA IN THE WORLD

DAVID C. KANG AND VICTOR D. CHA, *EDITORS*

This series aims to address a gap in the public-policy and scholarly discussion of Asia. It seeks to promote books and studies that are on the cutting edge of their disciplines or promote multidisciplinary or interdisciplinary research but are also accessible to a wider readership. The editors seek to showcase the best scholarly and public-policy arguments on Asia from any field, including politics, history, economics, and cultural studies.

The China Boom

WHY CHINA WILL NOT RULE THE WORLD

Ho-fung Hung

COLUMBIA UNIVERSITY PRESS   NEW YORK

COLUMBIA UNIVERSITY PRESS
Publishers Since 1893
New York   Chichester, West Sussex

cup.columbia.edu
Copyright © 2016 Columbia University Press

Library of Congress Cataloging-in-Publication Data

Hung, Ho-fung.
  The China boom : why China will not rule the world / Ho-Fung Hung.
    pages   cm. — (Contemporary Asia in the world)
    Includes bibliographical references and index.
    ISBN 978-0-231-16418-4 (cloth : alk. paper) — ISBN 978-0-231-54022-3 (e-book)
  1. Economic development—China—History. 2. Capitalism—China—History. 3. China—
Economic policy—1949- 4. China—Foreign economic relations. 5. China—Foreign
relations—1949- 6. China—Economic conditions—1949- 7. China—Social conditions—1949-
I. Title.

    HC427.9.H896   2015
    330.951—DC23
                                                                    2015009582

Columbia University Press books are printed on permanent and durable acid-free paper.
This book is printed on paper with recycled content.
Printed in the United States of America

c 10 9 8 7 6 5 4 3 2 1

COVER DESIGN BY CHRIS SERGIO; COVER IMAGE © SHUTTERSTOCK
BOOK DESIGN BY VIN DANG

TO MY MOTHER

Contents

Illustrations
and Tables

TABLES

Preface

IN 1769, French philosopher Voltaire wrote that "in China, everything is decided by the great tribunals, subordinate to one another, whose members are admitted only after several stringent examinations. . . . It is impossible under such an administration for the emperor to exercise an arbitrary power. . . . Now if there has ever been a state in which the life, honor, and welfare of men has been protected by laws, it is the empire of China. . . . What should our European princes do when they hear of such examples? Admire and blush, but above all imitate." From today's perspective, Voltaire's idealization of imperial China seems ludicrous. In the Enlightenment, such a distorted view of China was not restricted to its admirers but could be found among other philosophers who were contemptuous of China. For example, Kant remarked that "the concept of virtue and morality never entered the head of the Chinese," and Hegel once asserted that "Chinese are interested only in highly tasteless prescriptions for cult and manners."[1]

These romanticized or racist views of China from some of the best minds in Enlightenment Europe cannot be attributed solely to the lack of information about China at the time because early accounts of China by travelers, merchants, and missionaries were not without accurate information. Some of those accounts are still regarded as serious sources on imperial China. The Enlightenment thinkers' distorted images of

China show more about their politics in Europe. They used China, which enjoyed an economic prosperity and internal peace that fascinated Europe during the age of *chinoiserie*, as a polemical tool. Voltaire was a keen supporter of enlightened despotism and saw absolutist monarchs, such as his patron Frederick the Great, as progressive forces that warranted the eradication of aristocratic privileges. He portrayed China as the most successful model of such benign absolutism. But more radical Enlightenment philosophers who believed in popular sovereignty attacked absolutism by portraying a dark China where society and culture rotted under despotism.

Even though much information about China is available for global consumption nowadays, popular and scholarly writings on China, whose rising economic and political clout in the world attracts wide attention in the West, are still often distorted by the authors' political dispositions in their home countries. Whereas some use the image of a mighty, impeccable, and radically distinct China to support their critique of the allegedly corrupt and inefficient Western economic and political systems, some are keen to see China as the last stand of Communist dictatorship waiting to be swept away by free-market and liberal democracy.

What Voltaire and Hegel wrote about China as an exotic other had little direct effect on development within China (though some of these writings were later used to justify Western imperialist encroachment). In today's more interconnected world, where Western hegemony in the world system of knowledge production persists, Western accounts of China are instantly accessible in China despite government censorship there, generating significant effects on China's self-conception. Conservative forces in China are never shy of employing Western praise of the "China model" to defend the status quo, and quite a few dissident intellectuals uncritically adopt Western contempt of China to support their call for "total westernization," even to the point of hailing Western intervention as a liberating force.

Fostering a balanced, undistorted, and holistic account of the development of China that brings China's full complexity to readers is therefore very important. Doing so would facilitate more sensible and well-informed policies toward China among Western governments and would also contribute positively to critical, progressive discourses within China. Authors writing about China are inevitably predisposed to different perspectives and judgments, but constructing a balanced and undistorted account of the current Chinese economic boom is not the same as pretending to have no personal take on any of the issues involved. Yet no reasonable account can allow the writer's opinions and politics to interfere with the selection and analysis of the evidence.

As a U.S.-based scholar born and raised in Hong Kong, I certainly have my own views and aspirations about China. My familial and personal histories are tied closely to the development of the People's Republic of China. My maternal grandfather was an intellectual who fought in the resistance against the Japanese invasion. With high expectation of the nascent Communist regime, he took his family, including my newborn mother, from Hong Kong to Guangzhou in 1949 to participate in the construction of a new socialist country. But beginning in 1957, he was persecuted as a rightist because of his untimely criticism of Soviet domination during the Hundred Flowers and so spent most of his life in the countryside thereafter, passing away not long after his "rehabilitation" under Deng Xiaoping. My mother moved back to Hong Kong alone in the aftermath of the Great Leap Forward, staying with her relatives active in the pro-Communist unions in the British colony. My uncles and aunts stayed on the mainland and were inevitably caught up in the Red Guards movement. I always feel that my grandfather's passion for justice and knowledge has passed down to me through my mother.

I came of age in late-colonial Hong Kong in the 1980s and 1990s, and my intellectual outlook was shaped by the many stories from the maternal side of my family, my mother's nostalgic recollection of her childhood in 1950s Guangzhou, the intellectual and cultural vibrancy in China during the 1980s, the Tiananmen revolt in 1989, and the local student movements that sought democracy and autonomy for Hong Kong on the eve of the 1997 sovereignty handover. In the meantime, my former Red Guard and anticolonial relatives were on the way to becoming the beneficiaries of the China boom, seeing their gains as compensation for what they lost during their turbulent youth.

My personal and familial histories rendered me anxious, curious, and concerned about the past, present, and future of China and other Asian societies that are living under China's giant shadow. Combined with my training in sociology, which lends me the conceptual and analytical tools to understand the world for the sake of changing it, these histories led me to the two main research projects that have defined my intellectual agenda so far. In the first, I aim to delineate the origins and particularities of political modernity in China by way of protests from early-modern to contemporary times. One result of that project is the book *Protest with Chinese Characteristics* (2011). In the second project, I aim to trace the origins, unveil the core dynamics, and assess the global repercussions of China's economic resurgence in the world. This monograph has developed from it.

I started to investigate the political economy of the China boom during my days at Indiana University. The start of this endeavor benefited greatly from the insights provided by my distinguished China studies colleagues there, Scott Kennedy and Ethan Michelson in particular. Exchanges with my mentors and colleagues at Johns Hopkins University, including the late Giovanni Arrighi, Joel Andreas, Tobie Meyer-Fong, Bill Rowe, Beverly Silver, and Kellee Tsai, help me greatly in anchoring my analysis in historical and comparative contexts.

Parts of this project have been presented in different venues, including sociology colloquiums at the University of Maryland–College Park, the University of California–Berkeley, State University of New York–Binghamton, *Academia Sinica* in Taiwan, and the National University of Singapore; a seminar at the University of California–Los Angeles Center for Social Theory and Comparative History; Harvard University's Workshop on History, Culture, and Society; Northwestern University's Asia Pacific Politics Colloquium; the Comparative Research Workshop at Yale University; the Colloquium on the Economies and Societies of India and China at the New School; the International Relations Department and Socio-Economic Center colloquium at the Universidale Federal de Santa Catarina, Brazil; the "Year of China" colloquium at Watson Institute at Brown University; a seminar at the French Center for Research on Contemporary China, Hong Kong; a seminar at the National Tsing-Hua University, Taiwan, "The State of the Chinese Economy" conference at the University of Southern California; the "Global Asias" conference at Penn State University; the "China Rising" conference at the University of Bristol, Britain; the "Global Capitalist Crisis" conference at York University, Toronto; the "India–China Comparison" international seminar at the Institute of Development Studies Kolkata in the University of Calcutta, India; the BRICS seminar organized by IBASE in Rio de Janeiro, Brazil;

and the Gaidar Forum at the Russian Presidential Academy of National Economy and Public Administration, Moscow. Comments and suggestions from the audience at these presentations helped me to polish my arguments. I also thank the vital intellectual atmosphere at the University of Chicago Beijing Center and the Asian Research Institute of the National University of Singapore. They made the writing and revision of the manuscript during my visit to Renmin University in the summer of 2013 and to Singapore in the summer of 2014 much more pleasant and fruitful.

I thank especially Perry Anderson, Robbie Barnett, Bob Brenner, Robert Buckley, Amiya Bagchi, Michael Burawoy, Gordon Chang, Nitsan Chorev, Patrick Chovanec, Jose Mauricio Domingues, Deng Guosheng, Arif Dirlik, Prasenjit Duara, Feng Shizheng, Mark Frazier, Edward Friedman, Eli Friedman, Thomas Gold, Jack Goldstone, Jeff Henderson, Huang Ping, Bill Hurst, Bob Kapp, Elisabeth Koll, Patricio Korzeniewicz, Ching Kwan Lee, Daniel Lynch, Jim Mahoney, Ka Chih-Ming, Leo Panitch, Michael Pettis, Sidney Rittenberg, Murray Rubinstein, Mark Selden, Victor Shih, Dorothy Solinger, Sebastian Veg, Jeff Wasserstrom, Wen Tiejun, and Zhao Dingxin for their insights while I developed this project. I appreciate very much the suggestions and research assistantship provided by Zhan Shaohua, Wang Yingyao, Lily Murphy, and Huang Lingli. Anne Routon, my editor at Columbia University Press, was invariably efficient and supportive throughout the project. This project, like my previous one with Columbia, has benefited a great deal from her intellectual taste and editorial suggestions. I also thank Amy Vanstee and Annie Barva for copyediting the manuscript.

Many ideas in the book evolved with the publication of a number of articles over the years. Part of chapter 1 is a rewritten version of a section of the article "Agricultural Revolution and Elite Reproduction in Qing China: The Transition to Capitalism Debate Revisited," *American Sociological Review* 73, no. 4 (2008). A few pages in chapter 3 updated some analyses from "America's Headservant? PRC's Dilemma in the Global Crisis," *New Left Review*, no. 60 (2009), and from "Beijing and the Banks: Paper-Tiger Finance," *New Left Review*, no. 66 (2011). Some of the data in the first section of chapter 5 are included in "China: Savior or Challenger of the Dollar Hegemony?" *Development and Change* 44, no. 6 (2013). Part of chapter 6 comes from rewriting and updating some of the content of "China and the Global Overaccumulation Crisis,"

Review of International Political Economy 15, no. 2 (2008), and "China's Rise Stalled?" *New Left Review* no. 81 (2013).

As always, Huei-Ying, my intellectual and life companion, offers me the most important encouragement, confidence, and critique that drive any progress I make in my work. She is always the irreplaceable reminder of the initial compassion that took me to critical social science. Any gaps and naïveté in my arguments can never escape her critical eyes. Our children, Henry and Helia, have been growing fast alongside the development of this project. Their increasing zeal for knowledge and urge to analyze creates immense pressure for me to stay curious and incisive so as not to lag behind. I hope they will feel proud of this book, which they inadvertently contributed to.

State Making and Capitalist Development in China

16TH TO 21ST CENTURIES

1581 With the influx of Japanese and American silver through trade and with the rise of silver as the principal medium of domestic bulk commercial transaction, the Ming government unified taxes into a single silver tax. This unification further enhanced the silverization and commercial growth of the economy.

1592–1598 Hideyoshi, a warlord who unified Japan, challenged China's centrality in Asia's international order by invading Korea. Ming China sent in troops to repel the Japanese force from Korea.

1635 The Tokugawa government of Japan started the seclusion policy, forbidding foreign trade. This prohibition stemmed the export of Japanese silver to China. Cut off from the Japanese silver supply, China came to rely solely on Europeans traders, who brought American silver to purchase Chinese products at such Asian colonial ports as Manila, Macao, and Batavia (today's Jakarta).

1644 Peasant rebels toppled the Ming dynasty (1368–1644). The Manchus, a militant ethnic group originating in China's northeastern border, invaded and swiftly took over all of China, founding the Qing dynasty (1644–1911).

1661–1683 The Qing government imposed an evacuation policy to depopulate most of the southern coastal area as a scorched-earth tactic to cut off supplies to the remaining Ming loyalists holding the Island of Taiwan, which had become a commercial hub of trade between Chinese and European merchants. The policy cut off foreign trade and the flow of

American silver into China, fostering a contraction of the market economy. Maritime commerce revived in 1683, when all trade restrictions were revoked in the wake of the surrender of the Ming loyalists and the Qing incorporation of Taiwan.

1757   The Qing government decreed that all foreign trade had to be conducted in the port of Guangzhou.

1796–1804   Millenarian sects in Southwest China launched the White Lotus Rebellion. The incompetent imperial army was unable to contain it for nearly a decade despite the vast financial resources the state mobilized to fund the pacification campaign. In the aftermath of the rebellion, the Qing state was substantially weakened.

1839–1842   To stem the massive outflow of silver caused by China's purchase of opium that the British grew in South Asia, the Chinese government banned the opium trade. Britain responded by initiating the Opium War in the name of defending free trade. After China was defeated, the Nanking Treaty was signed, which opened up Shanghai and other coastal cities for free trade. Hong Kong was ceded to the British as a colony.

1850–1864   Millenarian sectarians claiming to have received a revelation from Jehovah launched the Taiping Rebellion, which swept across southern and central China, subjugating some of the most prosperous commercial cities, including Suzhou and Hangzhou. The Qing state suppressed the rebellion with foreign support and local militarization, but the imperial state was further weakened in its wake.

1861–1895   The ailing Qing state initiated the self-strengthening movement that sought to foster state-financed and imported-technology-based industrial enterprises, including military industries. The movement ended in 1895 when the Japanese navy crushed the Chinese navy, built as part of the movement's achievement, in the Sino–Japan War of 1894–1895. Taiwan became a Japanese colony.

1911   The Republican revolution toppled the Qing dynasty, but the revolutionaries were too weak to form a new centralized state. Provincial military strongmen, who had prospered in the last years of the Qing dynasty, took over and fought with one another, leading post-Qing China into an unstable period dominated by these rival warlords.

1921   The Chinese Communist Party (CCP) was founded in Shanghai. Under Soviet supervision, the CCP formed a united front with the Republican revolutionaries, who established the Nationalist Party (Kuomintang, KMT) to prepare a military offensive against the warlords.

1927   When the KMT–CCP united front, with the Soviet Union's military and financial support, was about to win national power and subordinate warlordism, the KMT started an anti-Communist purge, eliminating

CCP organizations in major cities. When CCP members were rounded up in coastal urban centers, the CCP turned to the countryside and organized the peasant-based Red Army. The KMT–CCP civil war began.

1937   Japan invaded China proper. The second KMT–CCP united front was formed against Japan.

1945   Japan surrendered. The Soviet army swiftly took over Japan's military-industrial base in China's Northeast, handing over the industrial facilities and heavy weaponry there to the CCP's Red Army, which had so far been made up of no more than poorly equipped rural guerillas. The KMT–CCP civil war resumed.

1949   The CCP defeated the KMT in the civil war, driving the latter to Taiwan, which the United States has protected from a Communist takeover ever since. The CCP founded the People's Republic of China in mainland China. The Communist governments' first major initiative was land reform, which broke down large landholdings and redistributed them to peasant households.

1950–1953   The Korean War broke out. China entered the war, and the United States led other nations on its side in the Cold War to impose an embargo on China.

1953–1956   The Chinese government initiated the Socialist Transformation campaign to nationalize most urban enterprises and integrated peasant households into rural collectives. Under Soviet financial as well as technical support, the CCP sought rapid state-led industrialization.

1958–1961   Mao launched the Great Leap Forward campaign, in which large-scale People's Communes were formed and became the only legitimate economic and social organizations in the countryside. Peasants were mobilized through the Communes to build local furnaces for steel making. The ill-coordinated campaign and the wasting of the vast labor force to make substandard steel led to a large-scale famine. During this period, Soviet–China relations deteriorated as China aspired to greater independence from the Soviet Union.

1966–1969   Mao, sidelined in the aftermath of the famine, staged a comeback by launching the Cultural Revolution, mobilizing youth Red Guards to seize power from allegedly corrupt bureaucrats. By 1969, most opponents of Mao in the CCP had been purged, and the whole government came to be staffed by Mao loyalists. Mao disbanded Red Guard organizations and sent the former Red Guards to the countryside to be "reeducated" by the peasants.

1969   The Soviet–China split escalated into border military conflict between the two countries.

1972   Nixon visited China in order to forestall Soviet expansion while the United States was losing the Vietnam War. China was motivated to end the international embargo against it and to seek new allies against the Soviet Union. After the visit, China's relations with the United States moved toward normalization, and China's trade with the U.S. side of the Cold War accelerated.

1976–1980   Mao died in 1976. After a brief intraparty struggle, Deng Xiaoping became the top leader of the CCP in 1978. The CCP started to adopt market reform by dismantling the People's Communes. Though the state still owned land, peasant households obtained the "right to use" on small plots of land from the government and could sell their products on the market. The peasant economy and the market economy revived in the countryside. Township and villages enterprises, nominally owned by local governments, took off in rural areas. Special Economic Zones were set up in 1980 to attract foreign direct investment, mostly from Hong Kong initially.

1984–1989   With the success of market reform in the rural areas, the CCP started urban reform, which consisted of price liberalization and a reform of urban state-owned enterprises. Unchecked inflation and rampant corruption erupted in the cities.

1989   Inflation and corruption fueled the spread of urban discontent. Growing inequality and falling living standards in cities, coupled with diffusion of liberal thoughts among students, culminated in widespread urban revolts in 1989. The revolt started among the students who occupied Tiananmen Square in Beijing in early summer, but it also spread to workers and many other cities across the country. The revolt ended in a bloody crackdown by the People's Liberation Army in Beijing. In the aftermath of the crackdown, Deng made Jiang Zemin the CCP's new top leader while maintaining his own leadership behind the scenes.

1992   In response to the comeback of the old guard, who resisted further market reform after the Tiananmen crackdown in 1989, Deng Xiaoping traveled to major cities in southern China and praised their achievements in economic liberalization. He made several speeches during his tour to assert that market reform must go on. His speeches unleashed a new surge of market reform and commercial expansion. Local governments and private enterprises alike raced to invest, and state banks opened the floodgate of easy loans. These acts overheated the economy, causing inflation, fiscal deficit, and current-account deficit.

1993–1994   The government adopted a series of policies to cool down the economy and to resolve the fiscal and current-account deficits. They included drastic devaluation of the renminbi to boost exports, fiscal reform that made local governments surrender a larger portion of revenue to the central government, and a tightening of bank credits.

1998   Zhu Rongji became premier. He deepened the reform of state-owned enterprises. A large number of these enterprises were privatized, though in many cases the government continued to be the sole or majority stakeholder. Massive worker layoff from state enterprises started. Housing reform was also begun, privatizing apartments that used to be rationed by state enterprises and local governments. An urban private-housing market was created.

1999–2000   The economic overheating and investment boom, followed by credit tightening in the mid-1990s and the fallout of the Asian financial crisis of 1997–1998, led to a slowdown of the economy. A rapid rise in nonperforming loans in the banking system ensued. In response, the government bailed out the troubled banks by creating four asset-management companies, which took over bad loans from the four big state banks (Bank of China, China Construction Bank, Industrial and Commercial Bank of China, Agricultural Bank of China). Having unloaded their most toxic assets onto these companies, the banks expanded or were listed overseas one after the other.

2001   China gained accession to the World Trade Organization. China's trade surplus has soared ever since. China invested a majority of its foreign exchange reserve in U.S. Treasury bonds.

2002   Hu Jintao became head of the CCP.

2006   Agricultural taxes were abolished as part of the initiative to improve development prospects and living standards in rural China and in response to escalating antitax unrest there. Other policies developed at this time include increasing government investment and available credits in rural areas.

2008   The new Labor Contract Law came into effect. The law made it more difficult for firms to fire workers and ensured that firms would contribute to workers' social security accounts. The legislation also reflected the central government's intention to move China away from labor-intensive manufacturing, to increase the wage share in the economy, and to stem mounting labor unrest.

2008   China surpassed Japan to become the largest foreign holder of U.S. Treasury bonds.

2008–2009   In response to the global financial crisis triggered by the collapse of Lehman Brothers in the fall of 2008, the Chinese government introduced a sizeable stimulus, which was made up of fiscal and financial stimulus via state bank lending. The stimulus sped up and expanded infrastructure constructions. It enabled China to rebound swiftly from the initial fallout of the global crisis, which had made its export engine stall.

2011–2012   The stimulus started to lose steam, and local government's heavy indebtedness resulting from the stimulus began to hamper economic growth.

2012   Xi Jinping became head of the CCP. The new leadership suggests that it will revive the economy by speeding up urbanization and financial liberalization.

The China Boom

INTRODUCTION

Sinomania and Capitalism

AFTER THE COLLAPSE OF LEHMAN BROTHERS in September 2008, which unleashed a global financial crisis, China's export sector crashed at the turn of 2009. In a few months, however, the Chinese economy rebounded strongly into double-digit growth, where it largely had been since the 1980s. At a time when the global economic status quo seemed to be crashing, more than three decades of vibrant economic growth experienced in China—still ruled by the Chinese Communist Party (CCP)—induced excitement and even fantasy about the world's future among writers on both the left and the right.

To be sure, left-leaning intellectuals and the business elite have different reasons for their euphoria about China, which Perry Anderson calls "Sinomania" (2010). For corporate CEOs, the rise of China and its apparently strong recovery from the crisis represent a vast, new, and limitless frontier for profit, just when business profitability in the advanced capitalist countries is seeing less and less room for expansion. For example, the business-school professor and veteran hedge-fund trader Ann Lee's best-selling book *What the U.S. Can Learn from China: An Open-Minded Guide to Treating Our Greatest Competitor as Our Greatest Teacher* (2012) has drawn wide applause from business presses and consultants. The billionaire Donald Trump, who accused China of "stealing" American jobs during his entertaining bid for president in 2012, is in fact an admirer of how business is conducted in China, as he noted at an international hospitability conference in New York in 2008: "In China, they fill up hundreds of acres of land, constantly dumping and dumping dirt in the ocean. I asked the builder, did you get an environmental impact study? He goes, 'What?' I asked, 'Did you need approval?' No, the Chinese said. And yet if I am the last guy to drop one pebble in the ocean here in this city [New York], I will be given the electric chair" (qtd. in Heyer 2008).

In the meantime, for some intellectuals, the rise of China represents the emergence of an ultimate challenge to Western domination. Others assert that China's experience points to a "Chinese model" of capitalist development that is grounded in active state intervention (e.g., Ramo 2004). They see this "model" as a progressive and superior alternative to neoliberal capitalism, which is premised on unregulated free-market forces and has prevailed ever since Ronald Reagan's and Margaret Thatcher's free-market reform in the 1980s. State-directed "Chinese capitalism" is hailed for its supposedly better handling of economic crises and its greater effectiveness in sustaining uninterrupted rapid growth and poverty alleviation.

China's apparent success even leads some to question the viability of the Western democratic system and ponder the virtue of an authoritarian government. For example, the *Time* magazine article "Why China Does Capitalism Better than the U.S." suggests that "one of the great ironies revealed by the global recession that began in 2008 is that Communist Party–ruled China may be doing a better job managing capitalism's crisis than the democratically elected U.S. government" (Karon 2011). Martin Jacques, the former editor of *Marxism Today*, the organ of the Communist Party of Great Britain, goes so far as to celebrate "the birth of a new global order" and "the end of the Western world," seeing the 2008 financial crisis as "the beginning of the Chinese world order," as described in his book *When China Rules the World* (2009). This book stayed on best-seller lists in the United States and the United Kingdom for many months and was featured favorably in major financial presses. This is not the kind of treatment that a leftish author usually gets.

Just as the eighteenth-century European Sinomania among Enlightenment intellectuals was grounded in partial and sometimes deliberately distorted information about an exotic China (Hung 2003), the latest celebration in the Western world of the Chinese miracle and of its robust recovery from the recent global financial crisis often has been informed by a biased and selective understanding of the underlying dynamics of China's capitalist boom. China is a large economy, the development of which hinges on complex interaction between private and state-owned sectors. The economy is also driven by three main engines: domestic consumption, fixed-asset investment, and export. The interconnections among and relative weights of these sectors are mediated by the legacies and paths of China's long quest for modernity since the Qing dynasty was defeated by European gunboats in the mid–nineteenth century. As such, any account that lacks holistic and historical perspectives is inadequate for a full understanding of capitalist development in China.

The first goal of this book is to outline the historical origins of China's capitalist boom and the social and political formations in the 1980s that gave rise to this boom. It addresses why capitalism did not emerge spontaneously in eighteenth-century China, which was the most prosperous and admired market economy in the early-modern world; how and why state builders in the nineteenth and early twentieth centuries failed to foster state-directed capitalism, as Japan did; and how the rural-agrarian and urban-industrial developments in the Mao period laid the foundation for the capitalist boom in the 1980s. It also discusses the regional, global, and sociopolitical contexts at the turn of the twenty-first century that have made such a boom possible.

As Michel Aglietta (1997, 1998) suggests, capitalism in any particular country is not fundamentally different from capitalism elsewhere (see also Aglietta and Bai 2012; cf. Nee and Opper 2012). The underlying principle and basic dynamics of capitalism as an economic system are universal, though capitalism is always enmeshed in historically and nationally specific sociopolitical structures that enable the release of its productive forces at some times and fetter its reproduction at other times. There is no such thing as "Chinese capitalism" that is fundamentally different from "American capitalism," "Japanese capitalism," or "German capitalism." But this does not mean that the rise of capitalism in China is a simple replication of its rise elsewhere and will produce no distinct effects. On the contrary, capitalism in China is combined with China's particular social relations, state institutions, and geopolitical interests to present a particular face and to bring particular consequences to the global order. For example, many China observers have noticed the weight of state-owned enterprises (SOEs), a legacy of the Mao period, in China's capitalist development and have debated how it has contributed to China's economic growth and what lesson other developing countries can draw from this contribution (e.g., Y. Huang 2008; Acemoglu and Robinson 2012). Frederic Jameson once remarked metaphorically that "the [capitalist] system is better seen as a kind of virus . . . and its development as something like an epidemic" (1998: 139–40). It follows that even if the capitalist virus is fundamentally the same everywhere, the infected hosts' responses and behaviors will still diverge depending on the preconditions and characteristics of their bodies. This book is not another attempt to unveil a nonexistent "Chinese capitalism." Instead, it is meant to decipher how capitalism adapts to, thrives in, and falters under the Chinese conditions.

This book's second goal is to explore the global effects of China's capitalist boom and the limit of that boom. I focus on four common conceptions about how China is reshaping the world and evaluate them against reality. The first conception is that, given the weight of the state-owned sector in the Chinese economy, China is challenging the free-market ideology and global free-market or neoliberal order that the United States has been promoting since the 1980s. The second conception is that China is reversing the long-term trend of income polarization between the industrialized West and the industrializing rest by raising the income level of the vast population of the poor within China. China is also thought to constitute a new model and opportunity for developing countries in their efforts to catch up with developed countries. The third conception is that China is challenging or even replacing the political domination by the West in general and by the United States in particular, thus radically changing the existing world order. The fourth conception is that amid the global crisis that originated in and affected mainly the United States and Europe, China is rescuing the global economy by becoming the most powerful driver of growth.

This book offers a thorough examination of the historical origins, global effects, and imminent demise of China's recent capitalist boom, constructing a lens through which we can assess the prospect of China's capitalist development in a more sanguine, comprehensive, and well-informed manner. These four conceptions, which in my view overestimate

China's transformative impact on the global political economy and the sustainability of the China boom, are critically examined one by one in chapters 3 to 6. In contrast to popular opinion, I show that China is rising as a major, competitive capitalist power implicated in the world market that it is no different from other capitalist powers such as the United States, Japan, and Germany. The China boom has been dependent on the global neoliberal order, which is based on expanding, unfettered transnational flow of goods and capital, and it is in China's vested interest to maintain the status quo, though China might seek to change the balance of power within this arrangement. More, China's own imbalanced developmental path is a key source of rather than the solution to the global economic imbalance that led to the global financial crisis. Just like booms in all other capitalist powers, the China boom, which is the product of a specific concatenation of historical processes and global forces, cannot last forever. Therefore, China is more a foundation of the global status quo and its contradictions than a challenge and solution to it. Its boom is destined to be smashed sooner or later under the weight of imbalances it has created.

Existing accounts of capitalism in China, their insights notwithstanding, are often limited by a casual and sometimes confusing concept of what capitalism is and how capitalism as an economic system is related to the state and society. Any solid analysis of China's capitalist boom has to be grounded on a rigorous conceptualization of capitalism, as outlined in the next section.

A Brief Theory of Capitalism

In *The Protestant Ethic and the Spirit of Capitalism* ([1930] 1992), Max Weber put forward a concept of capitalism that still resonates today. To Weber, what is characteristic of a capitalist economic system is the dominant capitalist spirit, in which the urge to accumulate money for the sake of accumulating more money in a rational and methodical manner overrides all other imperatives. Benjamin Franklin described this spirit many years earlier: "Remember, that money is of the prolific, generating nature. Money can beget money, and its offspring can beget more, and so on. Five shillings turned is six, turned again it is seven and three pence, and so on, till it becomes a hundred pounds. The more there is of it, the more it produces every turning, so that the profits rise quicker and quicker" (qtd. in Weber [1930] 1992:50). However, as Weber points out, this logic is contrary to that of most if not all existing religious-moral systems preceding modern times:

> In fact, the summum bonum of this ethic, the earning of more and more money, combined with the strict avoidance of all spontaneous enjoyment of life, . . . is thought of so purely as an end in itself, that from the point of view of the happiness of, or utility to, the single individual, it appears entirely transcendental and absolutely irrational. Man is dominated by the making of money, by acquisition as the ultimate purpose of his life. Economic acquisition is no longer subordinated to man as the means for the satisfaction of his material needs. This reversal of what we should call the natural relationship, so irrational from a naive point of view, is evidently as definitely a leading principle of capitalism as it is foreign to all peoples not under capitalistic influence.   ([1930] 1992, 53)

This unusual capitalist logic could not emerge by itself because of the widespread hostility toward it among preexisting religious orders from Catholicism to Islam, which condemned the pursuit of profit in one way or another. But once capitalism emerged and prevailed, it broke free of these sanctions and brought sweeping changes all over the world. Capitalism is like the spirits in Pandora's box. It had been carefully encased, but once it was accidentally released, it brought about a widespread, profound, and irreversible transformation of the world.

Certain contingent extraeconomic forces helped clear the way for the initial release of the capitalist force in some parts of early-modern Europe. To Weber, one of these forces was the Calvinist conception of predestination, wherein the anxiety to have a glimpse of God's grace urged Calvinist merchants to accumulate wealth for the sake of accumulating wealth and to see the size of their wealth as an indicator of such grace. Though many scholars have rejected Weber's cultural explanation of the rise of capitalism, his definition of capitalism as a system with the "ceaseless accumulation of capital" as its modus operandi can be found in many works by contemporary theorists of capitalism, including Immanuel Wallerstein and Giovanni Arrighi.

Wallerstein (1974, 1979) concurs with Weber in seeing the rise of capitalism in Europe as an unusual world-historical event. To him, capitalism emerged in sixteenth-century Europe out of the medieval "crisis of feudalism." It brought forth an international division of labor among core countries (specializing in high-value-added products), periphery countries (specializing in low-tech and raw-materials export), and semi-periphery countries (specializing in both high-value-added and low-value-added products). The genesis of such an international division of labor was driven by the rise of the logic of ceaseless accumulation of capital. This logic created and sustained exploitative unequal exchanges between core and periphery. It also induced the system's geographical expansion to incorporate new periphery zones through colonialism. Most of Wallerstein's work is about how the international division of labor developed, but it says little about how exactly the logic of ceaseless capital accumulation was set free against all odds. Arrighi (1994, 2007; Arrighi and Silver 1999) fills this gap with his analysis of the long history of capitalism, which combines insights from Karl Marx and Fernand Braudel, the French economic historian who delineated the origins of capitalism in his three-volume classic *Civilization & Capitalism: 15th–18th Century* (1992).

For Marx, in a market exchange, or what he calls "generalized commodities exchange," laborers produce things that they are good at producing in order to exchange them for other things they want, with money as the medium. This activity can be represented by the formula C-M-C, where C is commodity and M is money. In such an activity, money is just a tool of exchange, and the acquisition of a useful commodity is the end. Though generalized commodity exchange is an indispensable precondition for capitalism, it is not capitalism itself. Capitalism, to Marx, is the activity of using money to pursue a larger sum of money, an activity that turns the original sum of money into capital. Capitalism can therefore be represented by the formula M-C-M′, in which M′ equals M plus an increment, or ΔM. In such an activity, the commodity involved is just a medium in the pursuit of increasing monetary wealth. Here Marx agrees with Weber in seeing the pursuit of profit for the sake of making more profit as the defining characteristic of capitalism. Unlike Weber, however, Marx also suggests that the origin of the increment in capital, ΔM, must come from exploitation of value produced by waged laborers as surplus value.

Whether ΔM originates from surplus value in the labor process is a topic of debate. What is more important but neglected by Marx and many other analysts inspired by him is how exactly market exchange (C-

M-C) and capital accumulation (M-C-M') are related. Are they linked logically and naturally, with the latter being a spontaneous, inevitable outcome of the former? In *Capital*, Marx seems to suppose so. But if we look back at history across civilizations, as Braudel did, we readily find many cases—such as the Ottoman, Mughal, and Qing Empires—in which an advanced market economy did not lead to a spontaneous rise of capitalism (see also Pomeranz 2000 and the discussion in chapter 1). The puzzle becomes under what conditions capitalism could emerge out of a market economy.

For Braudel (1992), the market and capitalism are not to be confused and should be examined as two distinct patterns of economic activities. Whereas a market economy is grounded on exchange and competition among small producers, concerned more about livelihood than profit, capitalism is driven by profit maximization and wealth accumulation that historically required state support and monopolistic economic organizations, as exemplified by chartered companies in early-modern Europe, vertically integrated corporations fomented by antitrust regulations in the twentieth-century United States, and state-sponsored transnational corporations from such emerging powers as Brazil, Russia, and China today. The difference between market and capitalism is tantamount to the difference between a local farmers' market and transnational grocery chains. Though there were always urges in a market economy for some to pursue endless accumulation of monetary wealth, these urges had been repressed by political and cultural forces before modern times.

Arrighi traces how capitalism was set free and thrived in early-modern Europe by arguing that the unusual interstate system there, which was plagued by frequent military conflict, urged state makers to compete for internationally mobile capital to finance their war efforts, thus forging a state–capital alliance unseen anywhere else. Under such an alliance, capitalists supported state expansion by purchasing government bonds and submitting taxes, and the state offered military and political protection crucial to capitalists' accruing and securing of resource bases and trade routes. According to Arrighi, it was this state–capital exchange in early-modern Europe's unique geopolitical environment, rather than the Protestant ethics emphasized by Weber, that enabled capitalism to break free of the straitjacket of traditional moral hostility to it and rise to dominance.

After the first round of capital accumulation, or the "primitive accumulation," which was usually conducted through coercion and violence that concentrated scattered economic resources into capitalists' hands, such as during the European plundering of overseas colonies and the Enclosure in England, the accumulation became self-sustaining. The capital initially accumulated was continually reinvested in improving the economy's productivity, technology, and infrastructure. Such continuous improvements eventually fostered the Industrial Revolution at the turn of the nineteenth century (Braudel 1992: vol. 3; Arrighi 1994). In this light, all late industrialization in late-coming capitalist countries, China at the turn of the twentieth century included, was essentially a struggle to jump-start primitive accumulation and bring about the rise of self-perpetuating and self-aggrandizing capital.

Chapter Outline

With this concept of capitalism in mind, this book is divided into two parts. The first traces the rocky path of the historical rise of capitalism in China from the eighteenth century to the present, deciphering the origins of the contemporary capitalist boom. The second part explores the impact of the China boom on the global political-economic order and the demise of the boom.

In chapter 1, I discuss how the massive influx of American silver into seventeenth- and eighteenth-century China fueled a commercial revolution that made China the most advanced market economy in the early-modern world. Because eighteenth-century China was governed by a centralized paternalist state constantly fearful of social and political unrest stemming from rising inequality, merchant activities were circumscribed within the realm of market exchange, and the expansion of capital-accumulation activities was contained by a state that saw such activities as disruptive to social stability.

Chapter 2 describes the ordeal in which generations of Chinese state builders attempted to follow in the footsteps of late industrializers such as Germany, Japan, and Russia to foment state-directed industrialization as a response to Western imperialism from the mid–nineteenth century onward. After the Qing Empire was defeated by the industrial empire Great Britain, the Chinese elite devised a state-sponsored industrialization program aimed at appropriating and concentrating surplus from the countryside to foster the first generation of industrial capital. But because of the vicious cycle of rebellions and declining state capacity, the Qing state failed to accomplish this task. Following decades of chaos and warfare after the collapse of the Qing Empire in 1911, the Chinese Communist Party came to power in 1949. It followed a variant of the Soviet model, resorting to rural collectivization to extract rural surpluses and redirect them to feed rapid industrialization in the cities. This primitive accumulation of capital, although carried out in the name of socialism, was a success. By the late 1970s, China was equipped with a network of state-owned industrial capital and infrastructure.

Chapter 3 shows how the contemporary rise of capitalism in China is, on the one hand, a continuation of Cold War East Asian capitalism by the Asian allies of the United States—Japan, South Korea, Taiwan, Hong Kong, and Singapore—and, on the other hand, built on the foundation laid in the Mao period, including a large, healthy, and educated rural surplus labor force and an extensive network of state-owned capital. It discusses how China's decentralized authoritarian state emerged and fueled the capitalist boom. We see that the post-Mao market reform can be organized into two phases, with the 1980s focused on the revival of the market economy and rural growth and then the 1990s concentrated on the transformation of SOEs into profit-oriented capitalist corporations, many of which were aided by Wall Street financial firms and capitalized in overseas stock markets such as New York and Hong Kong. Chapter 3 also shows how the dominance of the export sector was subsidized by resources extracted from the rural hinterland. Given the transformed state enterprises tightly connected to the global financial circuit and the centrality of the export sector in the economy, the China boom is dependent on global free trade and investment flow. This assertion challenges the conception that China constitutes an alternative to the global neoliberal order.

In part II, chapter 4 discusses how China's capitalist boom reshaped the pattern of global inequality. It shows that although inequality has been growing rapidly in China, even the most backward and poorest segment of the population has been seeing per capita income growth at a rate higher than average worldwide growth. China has been contributing to the reduction in global inequality during the past three decades, reversing the long-term trend of global income polarization between the West and "the rest" since Europe's Industrial Revolution. But once China attains a per capita income level higher than world average, this reversal will diminish, and inequality may once again grow. Whether the unprecedented reduction in global inequality will continue depends on whether other developing countries follow in China's footsteps to attain rapid economic growth. Although China's appetite for natural resources has helped many developing countries achieve rapid growth in recent years, its export-oriented manufacturing is putting pressure on other developing countries that are similarly reliant on labor-intensive export manufacturing. If the opportunities and threats that China brings to other developing economies do not cancel out each other, the resulting net benefits or net impediments to development will vary from country to country. It is possible that the developing world as a whole will not benefit at all from the China boom and that the reversal of global income polarization brought about by the China boom is no more than a temporary aberration in the long term. This chapter questions the conception of China as a great equalizer in the world economy.

Chapter 5 disputes the idea that China's rise is at the expense of U.S. global power and is speeding up the decline of U.S. global dominance. Although the U.S. share of the global economy and its political influence around the world have been dwindling since the 1970s, its residual geopolitical dominance has been sustained by the continuous hegemonic status of the U.S. dollar in the international monetary system. This continuing status enables the United States to borrow internationally at low interest rates so that Americans are able not only to live but also to fight beyond their means. The perpetuation of the dollar's hegemony since the abolition of the gold standard in 1971 has been supported by the U.S. military's global supremacy. This dollar–military nexus has never been broken because all contending capitalist powers since the 1970s, such as Germany and Japan, have lacked geopolitical autonomy from the United States as a provider of military protection. China is the first rising capitalist power to stand outside the U.S. global military umbrella, so it should have the potential to end the twin dominance by the dollar and the U.S. military. But through its addiction to U.S. Treasury bonds, China has been following in Japan's footsteps in providing significant support to the dollar hegemony and thus to the residual U.S. global dominance.

China's immense purchase of U.S. debt is not a result of voluntary generosity but a consequence of China's export-oriented model, which led to an influx of U.S. dollars into China's central bank, the People's Bank of China. China cannot achieve genuine economic and geopolitical autonomy unless it successfully rebalances its economy and reduces its reliance on exports. This chapter also shows how China helps increase developing countries' bargaining power vis-à-vis wealthy countries and how China has started to be perceived as a neocolonial power in the developing world at the same time. It argues, however, that instead of ushering in a new world order, China is at best a new power in an old order.

Chapter 6 discusses how the particular pattern of capitalist growth in China, characterized by a decentralized and authoritarian structure of governance and a fiscal squeeze of the countryside, has been precipitating a greater economic imbalance marked by overinvestment and underconsumption during the past two decades. China's economic imbalance has been a significant contributor to the global imbalance that precipitated the Great Crash of 2008. Although China's immense stimulus program in 2009 successfully generated a strong rebound by means of lax lending to hasten investment projects and export-boosting measures, it only exacerbated China's internal imbalances and indebtedness, which will severely inhibit its growth in the years to come. Given the prospect of a sustained economic slowdown, the need to rebalance the Chinese economy is more urgent than ever. Such rebalancing must focus on making household consumption and income a larger share in the national economy. Attaining this balance, therefore, requires a serious redistribution of income and capital, which in turn requires a difficult and unpredictable reshuffling of the social and political order that has prevailed since the Tiananmen crackdown in 1989. In contrast to the conception of China as a savior to the global economy in crisis, this chapter argues that China is in fact a major source of global economic imbalances and crises and that the China boom is set to fade.

PART ONE

Origins

ONE

A Market Without Capitalism

1650–1850

IMPERIAL CHINA has long been portrayed in Eurocentric historiography as a plainly agrarian and inward-looking empire in contrast to the commercially dynamic and maritime-oriented Europe. Mark Elvin and others reject this image, arguing that China experienced a golden age of vital commercial expansion and growing maritime trade from the twelfth to the thirteenth century (Shiba 1970, 1983; Ma 1971; Elvin 1973; Abu-Lughod 1989: 316–40; Braudel 1992: 3:32). These trends were terminated abruptly in the fifteenth century, when the famous Zheng He expedition ended and China's capital city was moved from Nanjing in the south to Beijing in the north. China subsequently turned away from the ocean and was caught in a "high-level equilibrium trap" (Elvin 1973), lagging behind Europe economically and technologically, which paved the way for China's humiliation by European gunboats in the nineteenth century (see also Wallerstein 1974: 53–63; Abu-Lughod 1989: 340–48; Braudel 1992: 3:32).

This revisionist image of China is not much of a departure from the traditional view as far as the four centuries between the Ming retreat from the sea and the Opium War (1839–1842) are concerned. It is challenged, however, by a more recent wave of research illustrating a renaissance of maritime trade and internal commerce in China beginning in the sixteenth century. The enormous demand for Chinese products such as silk and ceramics in the world market transformed China into a "sink of silver" that absorbed most of the bullion originating in the Americas and circulating in the world economy at that time (see, e.g., Atwell 1977, 1982, 1998; von Glahn 1996: 113–41; Frank 1998; Pomeranz and Topik 1999; Pomeranz 2000). This absorbed silver fueled a commercial prosperity in China from the seventeenth century to the eighteenth century. In early-modern times, living standards in China reached, if not surpassed, the level of the standards in western Europe. In retrospect, therefore, the contemporary economic ascendancy of China, as Joseph Nye notes, is not a "rise" but a "renaissance" because China is simply regaining the economic prosperity it once enjoyed in early-modern times (2002, 19). This U-shaped change in China's economic fortune from around 1800 is illustrated by a comparison of China's and the West's shares of global gross domestic product (GDP) per capita in this period, as shown in table 1.1.

In this chapter, I examine the form and extent of China's commercial revolution before the nineteenth century and why such a commercial revolution did not develop into capitalist transition and industrial revolution in the nineteenth century, as it did in western Europe. Starting in the early nineteenth century, China's economy deteriorated, whereas Europe took off under industrial capitalism and employed its new industrial-military power to subjugate China. This is the backdrop against which all examinations of China's quest for capitalist-industrial development in the twentieth century must be viewed.

Commercial Revolution in Ming–Qing Times

Eighteenth-century China is known to historians as a golden age of long-lasting peace and prosperity. Many attribute this prosperity to the massive influx of American silver (Quan 1987, 1996b; von Glahn 1996; Frank 1998: 108–11, 160–61). Though American silver (together with Japanese silver before the Tokugawa Seclusion in the 1630s) began to flow into China in large quantities in the late sixteenth and early seventeenth centuries, during the last decades of the Ming dynasty (1368–1644), the amount then was insubstantial compared to the amount imported during the eighteenth century. Most of the silver absorbed by China came from European traders. By the early eighteenth century,

TABLE 1.1   China's and the West's Share of Global GDP and
GDP per Capita (%), 1500–2008

YEAR	1500		1820		1940		2008	
	GDP	*GDP per capita*	*GDP*	*GDP per capita*	*GDP*	*GDP per capita*	*GDP*	*GDP per capita*
China	24.9	1.1	33.0	0.9	6.4	0.3*	17.5	0.9
United Kingdom	1.1	1.2	5.2	2.6	7.3	3.5	2.8	3.1
Western Europe	15.5	1.4	20.4	1.9	27.5	2.5	14.5	2.9
United States			1.8	1.8	20.6	3.6	18.6	4.1
World	100	1	100	1	100	1	100	1

* Data from 1938 used for China's share of GDP per capita in 1940.
Source: Maddison n.d.

China's transition to a silver standard, under which government taxes and bulk transaction were paid in silver, had been completed. In the late sixteenth and seventeenth centuries, the bullion influx's contribution to economic growth was more or less neutralized by the turmoil of state breakdown, civil war, and dynastic transitions. It was only after the consolidation of the Qing dynasty (1644–1911) that the silver could contribute to a full-fledged commercial expansion. The extraordinary increase in the quantity of silver circulating in the Chinese economy led to long-term modest inflation, or what is known as the "Chinese price revolution" of the eighteenth century (Quan 1996a, 1996c, 1996d). During that century, the general price index of China increased by 300 percent. This inflation was not distributed evenly, however, hitting mostly the economically advanced lower Yangzi valley and southeastern coastal areas (which were closely linked to the export market) (Marks 1991; Quan 1996d). Such a differential inflation rate fostered a regional division of labor across the empire. High inflation and high wages brought urbanization and proto-industrialization to the central and southeastern coast. Meanwhile, vast areas of inland regions with less inflationary pressure were transformed into peripheral zones, supporting the development in the coastal core regions by supplying them with foodstuffs (principally rice) and other raw materials (such as timber) (Atwell 1977, 19–20; P. Smith 1988; Chao 1993, 40–42; Marks 1996, 1998; J. Fan 1998; Rowe 1998; Xu T. 1999).

In the lower Yangzi region, specialization in growing mulberry and cotton bushes as well as skyrocketing rice prices made the region dependent on food imported from Hunan, Shandong, and Sichuan (Li B. 1986). Raw silk and cotton production was turned from a sideline (complementing rice cultivation) to a major economic activity among the peasants. Weaving of silk and cotton textiles was increasingly separated from the realm of household production and concentrated in urban workshops (Li B. 1986; Chao 1993: 41). There were also merchants who organized mass production of textiles and porcelains specifically targeted at the foreign market (Chao 1993: 41–42; He 1996: 52). In the biggest cities of the region, such as Hangzhou and Suzhou, factories hiring from a couple hundred to a thousand workers were not uncommon. Class conflicts between the workers and factory owners became an emergent pattern of urban life (Fang X. et al. 2000; Fang Z. et al. 2000; Wu 2000).

In Fujian and Taiwan, large-scale sugar plantations appeared in the late Ming period, and the sugar-processing industry developed simultaneously (Chen X. 1991: 70–77). Just as mulberry growing displaced rice cultivation in the lower Yangzi region, sugar plantation increasingly displaced rice cultivation in Fujian and Taiwan, which came to rely on other provinces for their food supply (Chen X. 1991: 69–70). Starting in the eighteenth century, the mountainous Fujian province became a major tea-producing region of China as well.[1] "Raw tea leaves were collected by wholesale merchants, then processed in workshops set up in the market towns or cities in the vicinity of the tea production sites. The processed tea was sold across the domestic market or to European traders in Guangzhou, the only port open for foreign trade in the mid-Qing period" (Chen C. 1982: 48).

The commercialization of Guangdong was relatively slow in the Ming period. Only after the Qing government instituted policy in 1757 dictating that all foreign trade had to be conducted in Guangzhou, the provincial capital of Guangdong, did Guangdong's development take off. Before 1757, Guangdong silk was less welcomed by foreign merchants because of its inferior quality compared to Yangzi silk. After that, however, more peasants abandoned rice cultivation and shifted to mulberry growing in the region (Ye and Tan 1984; Marks 1991, 1996). At the same time, the city of Foshan (near Guangzhou) developed into a national center of ironware production, manufacturing agricultural and industrial instruments that were marketed to all corners of the empire via domestic trade routes (Lo 1994: 46–66).

During the eighteenth century, the Qing government actively intervened in the agrarian economy of the rice-exporting provinces. Aggressive irrigation and reclamation projects were launched in the peripheral zones (such as Guangxi next to Guangdong and Sichuan at the upper Yangzi River) so that more rice could be produced and exported to the economically advanced, rice-deficient provinces (P. Smith 1988; Marks 1991, 1996; Gao 1995; Xu T. 1999). Accompanying the reclamation projects was a massive state-planned migration program that resettled the population from certain overcrowded provinces to the newly reclaimed agricultural land in the periphery. Besides these endeavors, the government was keen on improving empire-wide networks of rivers, canals, and roads, which were essential to long-distance, interregional trade of bulk goods. It is not an accident that French physiocrats in the eighteenth century regarded China, based on descriptions from Jesuits missionaries and other travel writers, as the model of an unfettered and advanced market economy (Hung 2003).

The Curious Case of China–Europe Divergence

Given China's commercial advancement in the eighteenth century, it is puzzling why industrial capitalism emerged spontaneously in late-eighteenth-century Europe but not in China. This question has in fact been puzzling generations of historians and sociologists since Marx and Weber. Most classical social theories about Europe's transition to capitalism stipulate that the key to such a transition is how and why a group of urban bourgeoisie managed to break away from the feudal order to become an autonomous and then a dominant social group (Weber 1958, [1930] 1992; Marx [1848] 1972; cf. Hilton 1978). Whether the theories focus on the role of dynamic class struggle, medieval urban institutions, or Protestant asceticism in fostering a distinct and intact community of entrepreneurs, they mostly agree on the urban origins of modern capitalism. These urban-origin theories were overshadowed in post–World War II social sciences by the "agrarian origins" school, which sees industrial capitalism in England as first and foremost the result of England's early-modern Agricultural Revolution. According to this school of thought, the revolution not only freed up a large amount of labor to be absorbed by expanding industries but also generated large agrarian surplus in the form of the rural elite's elevated income, which was then invested in the urban-industrial sector to fuel the Industrial Revolution.

Studies of capitalist transition in Japan and of the nontransition in China have been influenced heavily by the agrarian-origin theories of Europe's transition. For example, many studies explain Japan's successful capitalist-industrial takeoff in the nineteenth century in terms of an agricultural revolution in the Tokugawa period (1603–1867). They find that the endogenous forces that can lead to capitalist takeoff were ripe by the time imperialist intrusion forced the Japanese state to struggle for survival by promoting capitalist industrialization from above (T. Smith 1959; Collins 1997). The most prevalent theories about China's nontransition to capitalism are equally influenced by the agrarian-origin school. For example, the "agricultural involution" thesis suggests that unchecked demographic growth in early-modern China led to a continuous diminishing per capita agricultural productivity and a lack of incentive in innovating labor-saving technology because of the abundant supply of zero-cost labor (P. Huang 1985, 1990; cf. Elvin 1973). With a stagnant or even deteriorating agrarian sector, a capitalist-industrial takeoff was simply out of the question.

But this agrarian-origin approach is challenged by new evidence about China's early-modern economy, as outlined in the previous section. The sweeping commercialization of the economy led to the dissolution of the coercive agrarian order based on manorial estates and the rise of a peasant economy grounded in free alienation and transaction of land and labor (Jing 1982: 169–81; P. Huang 1985: 97–105; von Glahn 1996; Rowe 1998, 2002: 493–502). Continuous innovations in farm management and production technologies by free peasant producers, in addition to the practice of checking population growth (through such means as infanticide), enabled long-term growth in agricultural productivity, rural income, and peasants' standard of living in the empire's economic core (Lee and Campbell 1997; Li B. 1998; Lee and Wang 2000). It is noted that net return on peasants' labor increased by 20 to 50 percent from 1600 to 1750 in the most advanced region, which entailed "highly impressive gains for peasant households who enjoyed high incomes and apparently voluntary leisure" (Goldstone 2003: 29). The socioeconomic indicators given in table 1.2 show that China was not at all behind England at the turn of the nineteenth century.

Despite this homegrown agricultural revolution, industrial capitalism did not emerge spontaneously in eighteenth-century China, as it did in England, nor did it take root under the government's conscious promotion of it in the nineteenth century, as it did in Japan. These inconvenient new findings unsettled the agrarian-origin school and triggered a new wave of scholarship to look for a new explanation of industrial-capitalist transition in Europe and China.

The new explanation that attracts the most attention is Kenneth Pomeranz's (2000) ecological argument. Pomeranz asserts that the divergence of developmental patterns between England and China did not occur until the turn of the nineteenth century. Before that, both economies were experiencing impressive growth in commerce, population,

TABLE 1.2   Select Indicators of Economic Performance and Living Standards in Early-Modern China and Europe

	LAND PRODUCTIVITY (£/ACRE)[a]	LABOR PRODUCTIVITY (D/DAY)[a]	AVERAGE NUTRIENT INTAKE (CALORIES PER MALE ADULT PER DAY)[b]	AVERAGE LIFE EXPECTANCY (EXPECTED LIFE AT BIRTH)[c]	ANNUAL GRAIN TRADE VOLUME (MILLION TONS)[d]
China	26.18	51.3	2,651	35–39.6	2.6
Europe	3.30	60.9	2,000–3,500	31–34	0.22

[a] Data based on English Midlands c. 1806 and Yangzi Delta c. 1820, with constant price level at 1820 (Allen 2009: table 5) (d = pence).

[b] Data based on nineteenth-century England and nineteenth-century China (Pomeranz 2000: 39).

[c] Data based on mid-eighteenth-century England and select economically advanced regions in mid-eighteenth-century China (Pomeranz 2000: 36–37).

[d] Data based on figures for all major trade routes in eighteenth-century China and the eighteenth-century Baltic trade, which accounted for 80 percent of the total European long-distance grain trade (Shiue and Keller 2007: 1191–92).

and agricultural productivity. Toward the end of the eighteenth century, development in both regions reached the limit that the available and diminishing ecological resources, such as timber and cultivable land, could allow. Whereas Chinese development was trapped, however, England successfully circumvented the ecological constraint and leaped forward to industrial revolution. The single most important factor that allowed England to overcome this constraint was its access to vast resources in the Americas, such as raw cotton and sugar.

This explanation is neat, but it is problematic in three ways. First, it does not clarify why England did not capitalize earlier on its easy access to American resources to foster capitalist-industrial development. Second, the availability of American resources to England versus their unavailability to China is not accurate. American resources in eighteenth-century England were far from inexpensive. Many of these resources were in fact sold to England at higher-than-average world-market prices (Vries 2001). It would not have been difficult for China, possessing a huge silver reserve originating in several centuries of trade surplus, to purchase New World resources from the world market if need arose (see Goldstone 2004: 279). Third, Japan had no direct access to American resources initially, but it industrialized successfully in the nineteenth century by purchasing most of its essential raw materials from the world market (Howe 1996: 90–137).

Therefore, Pomeranz's ecological factors may have contributed to the nonemergence of capitalism in China, but they are not the whole story. One crucial factor missing in eighteenth-century China was a strong, urban, entrepreneurial class capable of concentrating the agrarian surplus to foster a capitalist-industrial takeoff. Recent studies of the Industrial Revolution in England have highlighted the crucial role of such an elite in siphoning the agrarian surplus brought about by the Agricultural Revolution to facilitate the industrial technological breakthrough.

Jack Goldstone (2000, 2001, 2002, 2004; see also Carroll 2006) stipulates that the key to England's capitalist-industrial takeoff at the turn of the nineteenth century was the popularization of a unique engineering culture, which motivated entrepreneurs to turn preexisting scientific knowledge to practical improvement of commercial venture. A question to follow is, Who was the primary impetus behind the rise and diffusion of this engineering culture in England? According to Robert Allen's (1983) theory of "collective invention," the application of abstract scientific knowledge to innovative practical use during the Industrial Revolution was always conducted through recurrent and costly experimentation by capital-intensive firms and the mutual diffusion of the subsequent knowledge among these firms. This argument is reaffirmed by Richard Lachmann's observation that a process of "forced draught," which drastically centralized the vast economic surplus from the agrarian economy in the hands of urban entrepreneurs, was necessary to turn the gains of the Agricultural Revolution into the fuel of industrial investments and innovations that finally led to the "spontaneous combustion" of the Industrial Revolution. This centralization was carried out via various routes, such as landowners' investment in urban companies and urban–rural commercial exchange with the terms of trade in the former's favor (2000: 199–203).

In other words, collective invention or diffusion of an engineering culture in production is impossible without a critical mass of resourceful entrepreneurs who are capable of concentrating the vast surplus from the agricultural sector and using this to execute the costly trial-and-error development of productive technology. In England, the first generation of industrial entrepreneurs was far from a group of self-made men. Many of them were the offspring of established entrepreneurial families who relied on their families' accumulated wealth and resource networks for their initial investment (Brenner 1993: 51–91; Rose 2000: 66–79; Grassby 2001).

The lack of such a preexisting urban entrepreneurial elite who could accumulate capital over generations accounts for the absence of a spontaneous capitalist-industrial takeoff in China despite the large agrarian surplus there: the surplus remained dispersed among the peasants instead of being centralized to fuel urban-industrial growth (Hung 2008). To discern why there was no such strong entrepreneurial elite in China, we need to look into the Qinq Empire's class structure and political institutions.

Where Had All the Capitalists Gone?

During Qing times (1644–1911), the state elite and the rural gentry elite constituted the two major elite groups in China. After the Manchus

secured their rule over China in the mid–seventeenth century, the Man-
chu emperor reestablished a centralized bureaucracy more rationalized
than bureaucracies of earlier dynasties (Zelin 1984; Marsh 2000). The
state elite class was composed of bureaucrats appointed by the emperor
and were mostly high-level degree holders emerging from the imperial
examination (Ho P. 1962; Elman 2000). The gentry elite were lower-level
degree holders not eligible for bureaucratic posts. They usually stayed in
their home areas and served as informal leaders in local communities
(Jing 1982).[2]

The gentry elite, who enjoyed tax privileges on their landed property and could therefore easily expand their holdings, became the dominant landholders, living on fixed rents collected from tenants. During
the eighteenth century, lay landlords, who held no imperial degree and
therefore no gentry status, increased in number and occupied an ever
larger proportion of the whole landholding class (Li W. and Jiang 2005:
369–88). But most lay landlords owned small tracts of land, and they
depended on the local gentry for communication with the government
and many other services, such as rent collection. Many of them even registered their land under the name of local gentry to partially enjoy the
gentry's tax privileges. They were therefore in a subsidiary position and
never constituted a major elite group (Brook 1990). The state and gentry
elite were generally collegial and intertwined, similar in their ideologi-
cal outlook and linked by kinship or other social ties. Local bureaucracies, usually understaffed, heavily relied on the local gentry's collabora-
tion for a wide range of government functions, such as arbitration of disputes and tax collection. In return, the gentry secured, on top of their tax
privileges, a share of the local government's revenue as remuneration for
their services (Chang C. 1962: 43–73, 197; Ch'u 1962).

Besides these two major elite groups, a nascent group of entrepreneurial elite emerged in concert with the rapid commercialization of the
economy. These elites normally operated in merchant groups bounded
by native-place identities and shared dialects. Upon the webs of native-place associations, these merchants constructed commercial networks all over the empire to conduct their profitable long-distance trade
and financial affairs, thus facilitating the circulation of grains, salt, textiles, and other goods across the empire (Hamilton 2006: 43–47, 56–70,
93–126). The mercantile elite were most commonly lay peasants or landlords who diverted their savings to commerce (Ye 1980).

In contrast to the traditional view that the Qing government was always hostile to mercantile activities and eager to curb commercial growth because of the Confucianist loathing of commerce, recent studies converge on the view that "the Qing seems perhaps the most pro-commercial regime in imperial Chinese history" (Rowe 1998: 185). By the eighteenth century, the tenet that, in addition to agriculture, "industry and commerce are also the pillars of the world" (*gongshang yiwei ben*) as well as the conviction that merchants' property rights (*ye*) should be protected against official abuses and other menaces had replaced the anticommercial variant of Confucianism as the dominant ideology among the state and gentry elites (von Glahn 1996: 215–24; Rowe 2001: 155–287; Zelin, Ocko, and Gardella 2004).

In the 1720s, a pivotal decade for the centralization of the Qing state (Zelin 1984), the emperor even declared in an edict that "both merchants and other commoners were like children in the empire as a family . . . and they should be treated equally" (qtd. in Shen 2007: 85). This favorable disposition toward commerce is consistent with the bureaucracy's increasing dependence on private merchants to secure a local grain supply, complete infrastructure projects, and even procure logistical supplies for military campaigns (Rowe 1998; Perdue 2005: 315–406). Many officials and rural gentry families saw commerce as an opportunity to diversify their sources of income. Covert or open investment by these elite families made up a large portion of the operating capital of many successful urban commercial ventures in Qing times (Pomeranz 1997). Because the state and gentry elites supported or even overlapped with the emergent entrepreneurial elite, one would expect the latter to expand and strengthen continuously. In reality, however, the reproduction of the entrepreneurial elite was severely limited, and they never became a major and independent group on equal footing with the state elite and gentry elite.

Throughout Qing times, a number of conspicuous merchant groups monopolized the most profitable business sectors. The most outstanding case was the Anhui merchant group, which originated in Anhui province. It thrived on the production of and trade in salt, textiles, tea, and other items in the economically advanced metropolises along the Yangzi River, such as Yangzhou, Suzhou, and Hankou. They always operated their businesses under the blessing of state officials, who were happy to see their contribution to the stable supply of consumer goods and to benefit from their tax contribution as well as from bribes. Despite the prominence of these merchant groups at large, they were mostly no more than decentralized networks constituted by individual merchant families that rose and fell successively. These families rarely thrived over generations. The common pattern was that after a certain successful entrepreneurial family accumulated sufficient initial fortune, they pulled out from commerce and turned themselves into gentry or state elite by investing their wealth in preparing their younger generations for imperial examination (Wang Z. 1996: 1–57; Hamilton 2006: 43–47, 56–70).

This pattern among China's merchant families is exemplified by the Pan family, one of the wealthiest Anhui merchant families in the seventeenth and eighteenth centuries. As a member of the Anhui merchant group, the Pans thrived in the salt and condiment trade in the seventeenth century. Late in that century, they moved from their native place in Anhui to Suzhou, the wealthiest city of early-modern China, to expand their business. But after this resettlement, the family started shifting their resources from commercial investment to education. They established schools and hired prestigious literati to educate the younger members of the family. By the late eighteenth century, only one minor household in the extended family remained in the family business, which had already shrunk substantially. Most of the Pans managed to obtain different levels of imperial degrees and become the leading gentry and state elite in the Suzhou area. Some of them even became high-ranking officials in the central government. Their political power was so overwhelming that their mercantile origin was eventually nearly forgotten (Xu M. 2004: 195–246). The same pattern can be found among the wealthiest Anhui salt merchant families based in Yangzhou (Ho P. 1954; Wang Z. 1996). In eighteenth-century Hankou, the Anhui merchant families even pooled together their financial resources to found a nationally known academy dedicated to preparing their offspring for the imperial examination (Li L. 2002).

With the recurrent departure of the most successful members of the merchant class from commerce, capital accumulation and further expansion of these merchant networks were limited, though the sustenance of the network at large was guaranteed by the continuous entry of new members from modest backgrounds. This history stands in contrast with that of the powerful business families growing over generations in early-modern Europe and to a lesser extent in Tokugawa Japan. In England, many of the first industrialists in the late eighteenth and early nineteenth century originated from or were financed by these established entrepreneurial families such as the Rothschilds (Crouzet 1985; Braudel 1992: 3:585–94; Brenner 1993: 51–91; Rose 2000: 66–79; Grassby 2001).

In China, successful entrepreneurial families' propensity to transform themselves into gentry and state elite, together with the gentry and state elite's relatively low propensity to transform themselves into entrepreneurs, limited the growth of the entrepreneurial elite's size and power. As a result, the Qing commercial economy was marked by "weak firms in strong networks" in contrast to the "firm-based economy" grounded on enterprises operated by business dynasties in eighteenth-century England and nineteenth-century Japan (Reddings 1991; Hamilton 1999: 16–25). With the lack of a strong entrepreneurial elite who accumulated their financial and organizational capacity over generations, China was short of an agent competent in centralizing the abundant agrarian surplus and diverting it to costly and risky productive innovation.

Considering that the state and gentry elite in Qing China were in fact supportive of commerce and that the anticommercial variant of Confucianist ideology among the elite had been replaced by a pro-commercial variant in Qing times, it is puzzling why the entrepreneurial elite did not grow into a stronger group in Qing China. The answer to this puzzle lies in the empire's peculiar class politics.

The Paternalist State Against Capitalism

Influenced by the Confucianist conviction of benevolent rule and paternalist protection of the weak, the Qing state was lenient toward tenant peasants and actively protected their livelihood against "rich but not benevolent" (*weifu buren*) landlords (Brenner and Isett 2002; Gao 2005: 17–76, 147–69), just like a loving father protects the younger siblings from the older ones' bullying. The Qing state showed the same paternalist disposition when handling urban class conflict. For example, Qing officials stepped in to defuse the conflicts between workshop owners and workers who demanded wage increases by pressuring the owners to compromise with the workers. The government's approach in containing such conflicts in textile workshops in Suzhou—the most prosperous commercial and production center of the Qing Empire—is illustrative.

Anhui businessmen controlled major cotton textile workshops operating in the city of Suzhou. These workshops were highly profitable because Suzhou's textile industry commanded a colossal share of the empire-wide textile market (Fan 1998: 276–79; Li B. 2000: 80–85). But the industry was also plagued by recurrent conflicts between factory owners and workers (Yuan 1979). After several instances of large-scale labor unrest in the seventeenth and early eighteenth centuries, the local government intervened more often in resolving labor disputes. In adjudicating these disputes, government officials frequently invoked the metaphor of landlord–tenant relations. The workers' duty of timely submission of finished products to the owners was compared to tenants' duty of punctual rent payment. But at the same time local officials often reminded workshop owners of their obligation to provide stable employment to their workers, just as rural landlords should protect their tenants' tenure and never expel them at will. When conflict seemed imminent, the local government attempted to preempt the outbreak of labor unrest by urging workshop owners to make concessions, such as raising wages and shortening the work day (Chiu 2002).

This conflict-containment strategy unintentionally increased the transaction cost that workshop owners had to bear if they attempted to attain economy of scale by hiring a greater number of workers. This heightened cost constituted a constraint that discouraged workshop owners from expanding their business into large-scale factory production. It gave them no other choice than to depend on a decentralized putting-out system grounded on peasant household production for most of the production process despite the existence of favorable conditions for large-scale manufacturing, including available technology, abundant labor power, and the existence of an empire-wide mass market for Suzhou textiles (Xu T. 1999; Chiu 2002; cf. Li 2000).

The Qing government's paternalistic and accommodating approach to labor unrest stood in sharp contrast with the approach taken by the eighteenth-century English state, which was ever more aggressive in aiding the nascent industrial entrepreneurs by repressing labor unrest. Eric Hobsbawm notes that "as the [eighteenth] century progressed, the voice of the manufacturer increasingly became the voice of government," and state support enabled the "innovating entrepreneur . . . [to] succeed in imposing himself" despite "the bulk of public opinion against him" (1952: 66–67). Since the mid–eighteenth century, the state had helped early industrial capitalists to enforce labor discipline by penalizing workers who refused to work as long as their employers wished and by regularly raiding workers' homes to look for evidence of embezzlement (Marglin 1974; M. Mann 1993: 92–136).

The Qing state's paternalistic sympathy for the underprivileged is also epitomized by its handling of many food riots that troubled urban centers, where commercialization of essential food items often led to local residents' looting and attacking of food merchants. The typical strategy employed by Qing officials in handling this unrest was to crack down on the rioters but also to force the merchants to lower food prices as a long-term remedy to prevent future riots. This strategy was used to deal with a large-scale riot against Anhui merchants in the entrepôt city of Hankou near the central Yangzi River in 1740.

Encountering a shortage of salt in many parts of Hubei province in early 1740, the provincial governor adopted a merchant-friendly policy that encouraged Anhui salt merchants in Hankou to export part of their abundant stock to the neighboring regions hit hardest by the shortage in order to stabilize salt prices in those regions and enhance the traders' profit at the same time. But the traders' exporting activity pushed up local salt prices in Hankou and unleashed a riot. Thousands of angry citizens encircled and smashed major salt houses in the city. They held a number of leading merchants hostage and forced them to sell their stocks locally and at lower prices. Despite the scale of disorder, the government ordered no suppression or arrest. The emperor, in an edict about how to pacify the rioters, simply referred to them as "stupid people" (*yumin*) who "were not patient enough to wait for the proper handling of the situation by the authority" (*bu jingting banli*). He instructed local officials to console the angry citizens and to make them "content with their lot" (*ge'an benfen*) as well as to urge the merchants to lower their sale price so that "both the merchants and the people could get a fair deal" (*liangde qiping*). The final investigation report by the central government did not blame the rioters for the incident but did blame the merchant-friendly provincial governor for his incompetence. After demoting that governor, the central government devised a series of measures to lower salt prices and cut merchants' profit margins as a means to prevent future conflicts (QSL-QL n.d., juan 117:7, 117:20–21, 118:6–7, 120:28, 122:16–17, 123:5–7, 137:15–16).

The Qing government's handling of the Hankou salt riot is emblematic of its commitment to protecting the lower class's right to subsistence during acute food crises. Similar food riots in which contenders looted local grain traders' stock or forced them to sell their stock at lower prices became recurrent nuisances of city life during the eighteenth century (Wong 1997: chap. 9). Although in better times the Qing government often rewarded merchants' contributions to the securing of food supplies with measures that favored the merchants, such as low commercial taxes and low-interest government loans, in the midst of a food crisis the same government never hesitated to persuade or press local grain merchants to sell their stock at discounted prices. The grain merchants sometimes protested against these price-control measures, but their protests were mostly futile (QSL-QL n.d., juan 193:13–14, 273:26–28; see also Rowe 2001: 180–81; Hung 2004, 2011; Dunstan 2006: chaps. 1–3).

Food crises and riots were not limited to China. They also proliferated in eighteenth-century England in the context of rapid commercialization of the food supply and demographic expansion (Thompson 1971). But the way English authorities handled food crises diverged significantly from the way they were handled in China. In the early eighteenth century, local governments in England, like the Qing state, were sympathetic with the rioters. They often urged merchants to lower food prices to soothe the angry contenders. But as commercialization of the food supply and centralization of the state advanced during the century, the central English government increasingly marginalized paternalist local authorities and relentlessly repressed food riots to defend merchants' "legitimate right" to make a profit at the expense of people's right to subsistence (Thompson 1971; Wong 1997: 222–29; cf. Tilly 1975).

The urban entrepreneurial elite in eighteenth-century England benefited from *absolute* and *unconditional* support from the state, which shielded them against resistance from below. This support was justified by the increasingly dominant ideology of classical political economy (Perleman 2000; Somers and Block 2005). This ideology conceptualized the unrestrained free market as a natural order and claimed that the state was obliged to defend this order by protecting entrepreneurs. The dominance of this ideology can be understood against the backdrop of Europe's interstate conflict that urged state makers to ally with capital in building up its military capacity, as discussed in the introduction. The entrepreneurial elite in eighteenth-century China, in contrast, enjoyed only *relative* and *conditional* support from the state. It is true that the Qing state elite never saw the mercantile elite as their antinomies and were diligent in facilitating their business and helping them secure their property rights in merchant–merchant or merchant–official disputes (Zelin, Ocko, and Gardella 2004). But when it came to managing conflict between entrepreneurial profits and subsistence of the poor, the state elite often favored the latter at the expense of the former.

Taking into consideration that the Confucianist state viewed merchants and other commoners as children who deserved equal grace from the state as a metaphorical patriarch, state protection of the poor from the excess of merchants' profiteering activities was tantamount to the paternalist protection of a younger sibling from a bullying older one. In light of the insecurity that the contentious lower class caused the mercantile elite and the lack of political protection against this insecurity, the entrepreneurial elite's propensity to transform themselves into gentry or state elite over generations becomes more comprehensible.

To be sure, not all entrepreneurial elite families ended up taking the path to gentry and state elite status. Some members of the entrepreneurial class, particularly those from such coastal provinces as Fujian and Guangdong, chose to migrate to the colonial port cities that European powers had been setting up in Asia since the sixteenth century: Portuguese Macau at the tip of Guangdong's Pearl River Delta, Spanish Manila, Dutch Batavia (today's Jakarta), and so on. They continued their entrepreneurial activities over generations by facilitating Europeans' purchase of Chinese goods and the Chinese import of American silver. This diasporic group of Chinese capitalists continued to thrive into the nineteenth and early twentieth century and contributed significantly to the late-twentieth-century China boom, which I turn to in chapter 3. Over the eighteenth century, however, the Qing state carefully separated these overseas Chinese merchants from domestic merchants, and the former could barely set foot in China, let alone influence the empire's domestic political economy (Hung 2001; Wang G. 2002; Kuo 2009, 2014: chap. 1).

Even as the Qing state's paternalist disposition prevented the commercial revolution from fomenting the rise of a strong domestic capitalist class within China, its capacity declined precipitously in the late eighteenth century. In contrast to the early-modern European states' expansionary budgets and reliance on merchants' purchase of public debt (Arrighi 1994), the Qing government had established a rigid fiscal regime in the eighteenth century. To guarantee social stability by preventing the recurrence of massive social unrest caused by heavy tax burdens during the late Ming period, the Kangxi emperor, who ruled the Qing Empire from 1661 to 1722, promised that the Qing government would never increase the peasants' burden and raise land taxes—which had been the major source of government income—in the early eighteenth century. His descendants closely kept this promise. At the same time, however, the government did not seek new sources of revenue. As a consequence, the central government's tax income remained more or less the same throughout the eighteenth century, which constrained the growth of government expenditure. Limited increase in expenditure meant limited increase in salary for government officials and budgets for maintaining public infrastructure, such as the irrigation systems and canals (Guo 1996: 13–14).

The policy worked fine initially, but when the inflationary pressure picked up, the state's capacity eroded rapidly. By the end of the eighteenth century, the general price index had risen threefold, and the government budget on payroll and infrastructure maintenance had shrunk concomitantly in real terms. Underpaid officials then resorted to extorting bribes to maintain their luxurious lifestyles, while local governments at the brink of bankruptcy resorted to illegal levy of extra taxes to pay their bills (Guo 1996: 14–15). The state's fiscal distress was aggravated by the extraordinary population expansion resulting from the long-standing peace and prosperity throughout the century.

The state's falling capacity, reemergence of local tax bullies, bureaucratic corruption and paralysis, and rising population pressure, brought the Qing Empire to a standstill in the late eighteenth century. The empire had thus been weakened considerably long before the Opium War began in 1839 (Zelin 1984: 307–8).

The most notable event signaling the Qing's decline was the White Lotus Rebellion of 1796–1804, which was initiated primarily by overburdened peasants and landless vagrants. The rebellion swept the empire's heartland, and tremendous resources were used to put it down, further drying up the state's treasury. The state's fiscal crisis was also deepened because of China's successive wars with Western imperial powers, starting with the Opium War of 1839–1842 (Zelin 1984: 264–301), in which the British successfully used gunboats to force the Qing court to open up China's market to free trade. This opening aggravated the social dislocation and disintegration of the Qing state, which was finally overthrown by Republican revolutionaries in 1911. In the course of this nineteenth-century imperial decline, an expanding group of Chinese state elite, facing pressure from Western imperial powers, started to look for ways to jump-start a capitalist-industrial takeoff, but to little avail. The difficulty they encountered was attributable to the elite classes' failure to build a coherent, strong state machinery necessary for surplus centralization and state-led industrialization in the nineteenth and early twentieth century.

TWO

Primitive Accumulation

1850–1980

ALEXANDER GERSCHENKRON points out in his classic work *Economic Backwardness in Historical Perspective* (1962) that only early industrializers such as England could develop industrial capitalism through spontaneous activities by the nascent capitalist class. As late industrializers from Germany to Russia to Japan faced an increasingly competitive world economy, they required an ever higher level of state intervention to direct and concentrate essential financial resources for a quicker start in capital accumulation. This argument meshes with Immanuel Wallerstein's (1979, 1990) view that both the state-directed capitalism in Japan beginning in the late nineteenth century and "actually existing socialist countries" in the twentieth century were backward countries' efforts to move up from the world system's peripheral zone by harnessing state power to speed up the primitive accumulation of private capital (as in Japan) or state capital (as in socialist countries).

Corresponding to the ordeal of imperial collapse, war, revolution, and socialism from 1850 to 1980 in China were the state-building elite's attempts to erect a strong state to induce capitalist-industrial takeoff in response to the intense economic and military encroachment by Western imperial powers after the Opium War of 1839–1842. Whereas the Qing state, which had already been weakened by the vicious cycle of peasant revolts and local militarization since the late eighteenth century, failed to bring about this takeoff and collapsed in 1911, the Communist Party, which came to power after three decades of revolutionary war, managed to build a strong and autonomous state capable of concentrating disperse economic surplus from the countryside to construct a network of state-owned industries and infrastructure, laying the groundwork for the capitalist boom at the turn of the twenty-first century.

Limited Industrialization and Imperial Collapse

As seen in chapter 1, the advanced market economy in mid-Qing China did not lead to the spontaneous rise of industrial capitalism because the reproduction of the urban entrepreneurial elite was constrained by the lack of the state's unconditional support of the elite against contentious popular classes. The insecurity of urban entrepreneurs only worsened in the nineteenth century amid the state's deteriorating fiscal crisis. Besides intermittent urban riots, the nineteenth century also witnessed a tide of protracted and violent heterodox religious uprisings. These uprisings were inspired mostly by the White Lotus religion or its variants, which originated circa 1100 c.e. and prophesized the total destruction of the corrupt world and the coming of a utopian one. These millenarian sects, despite assiduous repression by the Qing state, never ceased to grow illicitly in the eighteenth century. They grew rapidly by recruiting the swelling rank of landless vagrants displaced by commercialization and demographic pressure (Kuhn and Jones 1978; Harrell and Perry 1982; Hung 2011: chap. 4).

Sporadic religious rebellions during the eighteenth century were usually put down swiftly. Toward the end of that century, nonetheless, the frequency, scale, and intensity of these uprisings escalated when the Qing state's capacity to maintain social order declined and when the strength of heterodox sects grew with the expanding class of landless vagrants. These uprisings culminated in the White Lotus Rebellion of 1796–1805, heralding a century of recurrent large-scale rebellions, including the Taiping Rebellion of 1851–1864, which would have toppled the Qing state had it not been for Western participation in its repression (Kuhn 1978; Hung 2005). These rebellions further constrained the reproduction of China's entrepreneurial elite, both directly and indirectly. The sectarian rebels, with a strong egalitarian impulse, earnestly confiscated accumulated wealth and executed the rich along the way. The intense battles between the imperial army and the rebels always interrupted local commercial and agricultural activities, hence destroying much of the surplus generated in the agrarian economy in the affected area.

The indirect impact of these rebellions on the entrepreneurial elite was equally devastating. Finding the large, corrupt, and immobile imperial army unreliable in the eradication of heterodox rebels during the White Lotus Rebellion, the Qing state opened the Pandora's box of local militarization, encouraging gentry elite to collaborate with bureaucrats to organize local militias. Amid growing social disorder, these militias proliferated in all corners of the empire during the nineteenth century. In the midst of the Taiping Rebellion, many of them even merged to become larger and more formal military structures, leading to the post-Taiping rise of provincial armies autonomous from the imperial center (Kuhn 1970).

Short on financial support from the central government, these military organizations financed themselves by levying heavy special taxes on local commercial centers and agricultural producers (Kuhn 1970: 87–92; S. Mann 1987). The gentry elite, the main agents of local militarization, reaped handsome profits from the process because they usually appropriated 20 to 30 percent of all funds raised for military purposes as their remuneration. Militia operations had become the single most important source of their government-service income by the late nineteenth century (Chang 1962: 69–73). Even some merchant families jumped onto this lucrative bandwagon by abandoning their original businesses to turn themselves into militia organizers (McCord 1990). The militarization process entailed the transformation of members of the gentry, state, and mercantile elites into a military-predatory elite.

The protection offered by the military-predatory elite did not match the extraordinary tax burden that they imposed on the entrepreneurial elite, who were already suffering from financial losses incurred by the upheaval itself. For instance, the Taiping Rebellion constituted a dramatic turning point that portended the demise of the Anhui merchant network. The battles—which were fought mostly in the middle and lower Yangzi area, where most of Anhui merchants' businesses were concentrated— and the massacres of the rich in cities captured by the rebels physically annihilated many prominent Anhui merchant families. Many of those who survived went broke as a result of the heavy tax burden they were forced to bear to finance counterinsurgency campaigns and the decade-long disruption of their businesses (Ye 1982; Zhou 1996).

At the same time that nineteenth-century China still lacked any vibrant entrepreneurial elite capable of concentrating the agrarian surplus to bring forth a capitalist-industrial takeoff, the new military-predatory elite siphoned vast surpluses off the economy, not for productive investment but for the accumulation of means of violence. In the 1860s, the Qing state initiated a top-down industrialization program to foster an array of state-sponsored industrial enterprises as a response to the series of humiliating defeats by Western industrial powers. But this industrialization effort was hampered by the ever-expanding military-predatory elite, who consumed a large portion of the economic surplus that the central government could otherwise have mobilized to finance the growth of new industrial firms. It is not surprising that the success of the industrialization program was limited. At most, it achieved nothing more than to create a few isolated "pockets of growth" scattered across the empire (Perkins 1967; Wright 1981).

A comparison of the capitalist-industrial takeoff in nineteenth-century Japan and the retrogression to an agrarian-coercive order in China is telling. In the early nineteenth century, the advantages and limitations of Japan's economy were similar to, if not worse than, those of China's economy. Subsequent to the agricultural revolution in the Tokugawa period, the Japanese economy's agrarian surplus was decentralized among peasant cultivators (T. Smith 1959; Collins 1997). Japan was not short of a resourceful mercantile elite, but such merchants were far from securely dominant. They were also checked, at least in part, by growing popular contention from below when the commercialization process increasingly jeopardized commoners' subsistence (Vlastos 1986: 92–141). After the Meiji Restoration of 1868, however, the energetic Meiji reformers built a highly centralized state that effectively and brutally repressed all kinds of popular contention, clearing the path for the entrepreneurial elite (Bix 1986: 189–214). The state managed to centralize vast economic resources into its hands through heavy agricultural taxes. It employed these concentrated resources to construct infrastructure, ranging from railroads to telegraph systems, necessary for industrial growth. It also channeled a substantial portion of its revenue into the financing of large, vertically integrated, private corporate conglomerates known as *zaibatsu*, with Mitsubishi and Mitsui as well-known examples (T. Smith 1959: 201–13; Westney 1987; Howe 1996: 90–200; Hamilton 1999: 18–25).

This pro-capitalist, centralized state, which was effective in concentrating and channeling the substantial agrarian surplus to jump-start a capitalist-industrial takeoff, was simply nonexistent in nineteenth-century China. Whereas the expanding military-predatory networks in China eroded the state's financial capacity and thwarted its effort to cultivate a vital and self-expanding urban entrepreneurial elite from above, a formidable, state-sponsored strata of corporate elite took shape in Meiji Japan. The relative geographical isolation of Japan also made that country less vulnerable to the worst imperialist encroachment, contributing to the Meiji state's success (Moulder 1977). The state-directed development of a capitalist class in Japan further strengthened the centralized state's capacity, bringing Japan into a virtuous cycle of capitalist expansion and rising state power. In the meantime, in China the continuous difficulties posed to the rise of a strong capitalist class, the fragmentation of the imperial state into local predatory-military warlords, and imperialist invasion dragged the empire into a vicious cycle of state breakdown and economic chaos that led to the final collapse of the Qing dynasty in 1911, which was followed by decades of civil war and imperialist domination in the early twentieth century.

The Resilient Peasants

The decades between the fall of the Qing dynasty in 1911 and the founding of the People's Republic of China in 1949, known as the Republican period, were plagued by waves of revolution, civil war, and war with imperialist powers. It is noteworthy that most modernizing elites of the period—including the military strongmen who dominated much of China in the warlord period, the Nationalist Party (Kuomintang, KMT), and the Chinese Communist Party (CCP)—did share a similar vision of building a strong, autonomous, and centralized state to seek state-led urban-industrial development after the model of Germany, Japan, or Soviet Russia, where a centralized state extracted and concentrated scattered rural surplus to fuel primitive accumulation of industrial capital.

In many other peripheral countries subjugated by Western powers through formal or informal colonization, colonizers often reorganized local agriculture by creating capitalist plantations or establishing capital's vertical control over family farms. In this reorganization, the local rural sector specialized in cultivating a single crop or a few commercial crops (such as raw cotton, sugar, and rubber), which were sucked out of the local economy to facilitate industrial expansion at the colonizers' home countries. Cases in point are British India, where the local textile handicraft industry was destroyed by the colonial administration and its diversified indigenous agriculture was replaced by raw cotton export monoculture, and Japanese Taiwan, where the local economy was turned into an agricultural hinterland providing the Japanese empire's industrial and commercial centers with raw sugar and rice (see, e.g., Bujra 1992; Ka 1998; Williamson 2008). Many scholars find that such colonial reorganization of local agriculture was a source of underdevelopment after the end of colonialism because the landowning elite, who were empowered in this structure and were entrenched in an export-oriented monoculture economy, resisted diversification and capitalist-industrial development. Their path dependency helped perpetuate the economy's reliance on raw-material exports to core countries with unfavorable terms of trade, which hindered the transfer of rural surplus into indigenous capitalist-industrial growth (Friedmann 1999; McMichael 2011: 26–45; see also Mahoney 2010).

China stands apart from these typical cases in the sense that no single foreign imperialist power fully penetrated into and reorganized its agrarian economy from the 1850s to 1949 because it was never formerly colonized by a single core power. Moreover, the Chinese peasants tenaciously resisted the restructuring of the rural economy. Foreign industrialists' failure to establish control over the raw cotton supply as well as the audacity of rural handicraft production of cotton cloth are telling indications of the autonomy of the Chinese countryside.

In the eighteenth century, although the English East Indian Company (EIC) aggressively marketed cotton cloth from England in China, the Chinese were not interested in it at all. On the contrary, China itself was an exporter of cotton cloth to Europe. After 1730, the EIC gave up on selling English cotton to China and began to purchase large quantities of "Nankeens," the cotton cloth made in the lower Yangzi region, especially

Jiangsu (Li B. 1986: 12; Carteier 1996: 257–58; Quan 1996e: 638–39). The EIC sold the Nankeens in Java, England, and other European countries and found it a profitable trade, though its profit was not as large as the profit from the trading of Chinese tea (Greenberg 1951: 179–80; Johnson 1993: 179).

Jiangsu was traditionally a base of production of cotton cloth for China's national market beginning in the fourteenth century (Li B. 1986; Carteier 1996: 253–54). Into the seventeenth and eighteenth centuries, the cotton-spinning and weaving industries in northern and northwestern China also grew, while national and foreign demand for Chinese cotton cloth mounted (Li B. 1986). Cotton was grown, spun, and woven in peasant households. The Nankeens for export were grown and spun mostly in peasant households in the Songjiang prefecture. They were then sent to the more sophisticated urban workshops in Songjiang city, Shanghai, and Suzhou for dyeing and finishing (Johnson 1993: 177).

The export of the Nankeens brought prosperity to the cities, towns, and villages involved in the cotton textile supply chain in the lower Yangzi region, and the making of Nankeens also spread to Guangdong province. China's cotton industry soon became so large that the supply of local raw cotton became insufficient, and the industry started to import Bengal cotton yarns or raw cottons. The Nankeens exported through the EIC grew continuously throughout the late eighteenth and early nineteenth century (Li B. 1986; Carteier 1996: 257).

It was commonly held that after the British won the Opium War and became free to market their cotton in large quantities and low prices in the treaty ports, the local cotton textile industry in China declined, just as the Indian textile industry did after colonization there (Quan 1996e: 643–44). But evidence shows that this is not the case. After the Opium War and the opening of treaty ports for free trade, British cotton textiles did flood the Chinese market. These imported textiles, manufactured by power looms, were of higher quality, and they did take part of the Nankeens market. Nonetheless, the resulting deindustrialization in China was never as smooth and complete as it was in India. Though the British textiles were successful in replacing the Nankeens in coastal cities, striking a blow to urban workshops, they were less successful in displacing the cotton cloth produced in the peasant households and later in rural industries in China's inland market (Xu X. 1992: 116–17). Foreign cotton cloth, mainly the English product, was regarded as a luxury consumed mainly among the urban middle class (Xu X. 1992: 155–56). The peasants and other rural consumers did not like the English cotton because it was too delicate, thin, and nondurable. In contrast, Chinese cloth would not wear out for many years and was thick enough to withstand the harsh winter. In 1861, the cotton merchants in Tianjin lowered the price of foreign cloth to half that of Chinese cloth in a futile attempt to compete with locally made cotton cloth (Xu X. 1992: 155–57).

The household producers' persistence was another important factor in the failure of imported textiles. For the peasant households, especially those in the lower Yangzi region, where specialization of agriculture was most extensive, weaving textiles was a matter of life and death, and they refused to abandon the weavers even when profits fell to subsistence level. Such small-scale household weaving activity continued into the Republican period (Dikotter 2006: 116). After all, the British in China did not directly control the countryside as they did in India, where they could restructure rural society and economy at will through taxation and other administrative means. In 1936, less than half of all cloth production in China came from power looms rather than from hand looms (Dikotter 2006: 194). The reason for the persistence of peasant household production of cotton cloth in the Republican period in the first half of the twentieth century is the same as the reason for its persistence in the nineteenth century: "Machine-made cloth did not simply displace an inferior hand-woven cloth: while the former was cheaper per square yard, the latter was thicker and could outlast it in the long run. . . . Well-to-do farmers continued to buy hand-woven cloth, even at a premium of 50 per cent, because they found it profitable for the reasons of durability" (Dikotter 2006: 194–95).

The peasant economy was even more productive in grain production. In the century after Western industrial and imperialist powers subjugated China, China's peasant-based agriculture remained intact. The traditional historiography that prevailed in China and in Western academia until the 1970s portrayed this peasant economy as stagnant and associated with poverty and bare subsistence. A spate of studies beginning in the 1970s, however, found that in many regions of Republican China peasant-based agriculture actually experienced considerable growth in per capita output and income in this period (Myers 1970;

Brandt 1989; Rawski 1989; Little n. d.). For example, Thomas Rawski indicates that between the late Qing and the early Republican period up to the full-scale outbreak of the Sino–Japanese War in 1937, China's average annual agricultural growth was at 1.5 percent, which was 0.5 percent higher than annual population growth (1989: 268). In a similar vein, Loren Brandt calculates that the growth in agricultural labor productivity over the same period was about 40 to 60 percent (1989: 132). Such gradual improvement in the peasant economy, as the argument goes, was grounded on continuous commercialization as well as on improving infrastructure and transportation networks in the countryside. Just as in the eighteenth century, the fragility of capitalist industrialization in early-twentieth-century China was a result not of the lack of rural surplus but of the lack of effective actors who could channel the rural surplus to fuel industrial growth.

To be sure, not everybody in the countryside could benefit from such agricultural growth. The war among warlords in the 1910s and 1920s, the war between the KMT–CCP alliance and the warlords in the late 1920s, the war between the KMT and the CCP in the 1930s, and above all the anti-Japanese war after 1937 disrupted agricultural production in many regions and exacerbated the expansion of the landless vagrant class. Rapid growth of sectarian rebel groups and bandit organizations in the countryside begun in the late eighteenth century continued into the Republican period. These recalcitrant groups, composed of the expanding marginal rural population, were crucial building blocks of the CCP's Red Army, particularly after 1927, when the KMT forced the CCP's urban organizations to leave big cities and to regroup in the countryside (Perry 1980; Hung 2011: chap. 4).

In the end, the CCP, with support from the peasants and aid from the Soviet Union, ousted all other power contenders and built a stable, centralized state capable of mobilizing and concentrating rural surplus to fuel rapid urban-industrial growth. Although such growth after 1949 occurred in the name of socialism, what the Communist government did was to construct an effective state-controlled collective agriculture to appropriate the vast rural surplus and centralize it in the state's industrialization program, achieving what many generations of state builders had failed to do since the late nineteenth century. This effort was a state-directed, compressed primitive accumulation of capital.

State Socialism on Peasants' Backs

As a prominent political economist in China asserts, "The contemporary reform in China . . . should be seen as a redistribution of the billions in state capital accumulated during the Mao era. . . . This redistribution of state capital is the foundation of the [current] accumulation of private capital" (Wen 2004: 36). The market reform after Mao, in this light, is as much an outgrowth of the Maoist path of development as a break from it. The regime of accumulation in the Mao era, an accumulation whose primary agent was the state rather than private entrepreneurs, shares many similarities with but also manifests significant differences from the generic Soviet model. From the consolidation of the Communist regime in the early 1950s to the advent of market reform in the late 1970s, China's socialist state shared the Soviet priority of rapid industrialization, which was led by heavy industries and grounded on an unequal exchange between agricultural and industrial sectors under the so-called price scissor. The Chinese Communists were no less harsh than the Soviet Communists toward the peasants during their pursuit of rapid industrial growth, though their seizure of power had been enabled largely by the peasants' support.

In the early years of the People's Republic, the Communist party-state did reward the peasants' support through land reform, breaking down large landholdings into smaller ones to be distributed evenly among peasant households (Hinton 1966). The Communist government also revamped rural infrastructure and promoted rural cooperatives to help the peasants pool together resources for agricultural investment. But upon the completion of land reform in the mid-1950s and after a few years of rapid economic growth during the recovery from the civil war, the party–state encountered the problem that had held back China's development since late imperial times: the difficulty in concentrating the decentralized rural surplus and directing this surplus to the urban-industrial sector.

Peasants' tax resistance resurfaced in the mid-1950s when the government redoubled resource extraction in the countryside to speed up industrial development (Li H. 2006). The government scheme to promote urban industries by pushing sales of farm tools such as iron ploughs made in the cities hit a wall when the peasants adamantly clung to traditional means of farming (Wen 2013: 37–38). Peasants also kept most of the products they made for household consumption or local marketing rather than selling them elsewhere, thus constraining urban-rural exchanges as an important channel for agriculture-to-industry surplus transfer. Worse still, with the stabilization and recovery of the urban economy, surplus labor in the countryside started migrating to the cities en masse to seek jobs (Cheng and Selden 1994). In this context, economic growth slowed significantly in the mid-1950s, when the recovered urban-industrial sector could not maintain its post–civil war high-speed growth owing to the insufficient supply of rural surplus.

Facing growth slowdown, the Communist government could devise no creative solution other than to follow the Soviet path of radical rural collectivization on top of tighter state control of industries through expansion of state ownership in the cities. In a matter of a few years, peasant households all over China surrendered their land and other means of production (such as ploughs and cattle) to large-scale collectives known as the People's Commune. All agricultural production was transferred into the framework of factory-like rural communes controlled and managed by the party with a military-like top-down command structure. The state annihilated rural markets, claimed all Commune outputs, and sold fertilizers and agricultural machineries from the urban-industrial sector at elevated prices. The state's extraction of resources from the countryside was larger than its investment in it. China's rural collectivization process was no less violent than that of Soviet collectivization. The violence was not conducted directly through massive execution of noncompliant peasants as in the Soviet Union but indirectly through the horrendous famine in the wake of the hastily executed and sloppily coordinated collectivization campaign known as the "Great Leap Forward" in 1958–1961. This regime of agriculture-to-industry surplus transfer resulted in a persistent and even enlarging disparity between the rural and urban standards of living (Schurmann 1966: 442–96; Shue 1980; Vermeer 1982a, 1982b; Friedman, Pickowicz, and Selden 1991; Selden 1993; Yang 1996: 21–70; cf. Ka and Selden 1986).

The price that the countryside was forced to pay under the collective agriculture system enabled rapid industrialization. A recent estimation shows that between 1953 and 1978 the total amount of surplus

transferred from agriculture to industry through the unequal exchange
between agricultural and industrial products was about 600 to 800 billion yuan or renminbi (RMB) (Wen 2000: 177). It was 374 billion yuan
according to a more conservative estimation (see table 2.1). According
to that conservative estimation, the agriculture–industry surplus transfer via the "price scissors" as a percentage of total agricultural output
jumped from less than 10 percent in the early 1950s to more than 20 percent in the 1960s and 1970s (Kong and He 2009; Wen 2013: 12). This was
no small percentage, given that agricultural output was not far from subsistence level in the Mao era.

The Communist regime thus managed to achieve what earlier industrializers in China had failed to achieve since 1850: to capture and centralize the scattered rural surplus and direct it to fuel urban-industrial
growth. From the 1950s to the 1970s, despite all economic fluctuations
and interruptions by political campaigns, the industrial share of GDP
rose from 20.9 percent in 1952 to 47.9 percent in 1978 (Chinese National
Bureau of Statistics n.d.). Industrial labor productivity grew by 236.7
percent over the same period. In contrast, the concurrent agricultural
labor productivity growth was only 25.5 percent (Kong and He 2009: 6).
This industrial growth would not have been possible had it not been for
the strong Communist state's draconian policies.

The most crucial feature of China's collectivization process not found
in the Soviet Union or in most other socialist countries was the spatial
segregation system that prohibited migration of peasants to cities. In
the Soviet Union, rural collectivization was accompanied by an urbanization process through which millions of peasants migrated to cities
and became industrial workers. In contrast, frightened by the scale of
rural–urban migration in the early 1950s and the prospect of a revival
of large-scale unemployment as well as urban social disorder caused by
swelling migrant population in the cities, the Chinese government imposed the household registration (*hukou*) system at the height of the collectivization campaign in 1958 to prevent the peasants from fleeing their
home villages. Under this system, all Chinese peasants were chained to
the land. They did not have access to jobs or social rights to education,
medical care, and housing in any place other than their registered birth-
place. Changing one's household registration from one place to another

TABLE 2.1   Amount of Rural–Urban Surplus Transfer
Through the "Price Scissor" in Mao's China

YEAR	TRANSFER AMOUNT (IN BILLION YUAN)	TRANSFER AS % OF AGRICULTURAL OUTPUT
1952	3.5	9.2
1953	5.1	11.8
1954	4.6	10.3
1955	6.6	13.5
1956	5.8	11.5
1957	8.6	16.5
1958	-12.1	-36.8
1959	5.0	11.4
1960	10.1	22.8
1961	7.4	14.3
1962	10.3	18.4
1963	12.5	19.9
1964	14.9	20.9
1965	17.3	20.8
1966	19.6	21.7
1967	17.5	19.6
1968	16.3	18.2
1969	18.0	19.5
1970	20.1	20.0
1971	20.7	19.9
1972	20.8	19.9
1973	23.5	20.4
1974	22.9	19.4
1975	24.5	20.0
1976	21.4	18.0
1977	24.0	20.1
1978	25.8	20.1
TOTAL	374.7	

Source: Kong and He 2009: 7.

was extremely difficult, leaving peasants with no other choice than to provide labor to the Communes (Cheng and Selden 1994; Wang F. 2005).

Not only did the People's Commune system facilitate primitive accumulation of urban-industrial capital by squeezing rural surplus out of the countryside, but it also served as a shock absorber during three economic crises in the socialist cities, according to a recent groundbreaking study (Wen 2013). The Chinese economy under Mao, like all other economies driven by the process of capital accumulation, did not escape the periodic crises of overproduction that brought plummeting profits to the state industrial sector, deteriorating government fiscal conditions, and urban unemployment. In each of these crises, however, the state alleviated urban unemployment by mobilizing the youth to join the People's Communes. This approach resulted in three waves of "down to the countryside" campaigns in the early 1960s, the late 1960s, and the mid-1970s. Without the tightly controlled countryside as a shock absorber, urban unrest in Mao's China would have been much more severe during downtimes in the economic cycle.

As compensation for the draconian restriction on migration and the squeeze of rural surplus, the party–state invested in agricultural infrastructure, basic education, and health care in the Communes, creating a compact between the peasants and the state. Life expectancy at birth in China rose dramatically from 43.5 years in 1960 to 66.5 years in 1978, according to World Bank data (World Bank n.d.). This was due mostly to improvements in the rural areas. The "barefoot doctor" public-health program installed in the countryside in the 1960s contained the spread of contagious diseases, reduced infant mortality, and brought other improvements, as a U.S. medical delegation observed in rural China in 1973:

> Before the establishment of the People's Republic of China in 1949, the health problems in China were as staggering as they were notorious. . . . The incidence of infectious diseases . . . caused death rates that were as high as any in the world. Sanitation was virtually unknown in the rural areas where the great majority of the people lived. Most of the scientifically trained medical personnel were in the cities. . . . The picture today is dramatically different . . . there has been a pronounced decline in the death rate, particularly infant mortality. Major epidemic diseases have been controlled . . . nutritional status has been improved [and] massive campaigns

of health education and environmental sanitation have been carried out. Large numbers of health workers have been trained, and a system has been developed that provides some health service for the great majority of the people. (P. Lee 1974: 430–31; see also World Health Organization 2008)

The efforts toward primitive accumulation under Mao rendered China a fairly industrial nation based on its economic output but an agrarian nation based on its demographic structure. In the advent of market reform in the late 1970s, less than 25 percent of the Chinese population was urban, though output in the industrial sector had reached 47.9 percent of GDP, as we have seen. This industrial-agrarian configuration in China was in sharp contrast to that of the Soviet Union, where more than two-thirds of the population was urban by 1980.

This developmental outcome of the Mao era left China with a huge reserve army of rural labor with good health and a high level of literacy (in comparison with the labor force of most other developing countries). This army of labor, when released through the loosening of the rural–urban segregation system in the 1980s and 1990s, became an important resource that accounted for China's attractiveness to foreign industrial capital. In addition to this large labor force, the bulk of state capital, which included industrial SOEs run by different levels of the government and an extensive network of infrastructure, also contributed to China's attractiveness to foreign capital. Many preexisting SOEs have become the foundation of joint-venture projects through which foreign manufacturers have established their foothold in China. Public infrastructure—ports, telecommunication networks, transportation systems—built on the foundation laid in the Mao period became an indispensable facilitator of the movement of capital, labor, and goods within China and across its border.

In addition to these two structural legacies, the Maoist path of development bequeathed China a policy environment in which the government could make decisions about market-reform strategy with high autonomy (Friedman 1999; So 2003). Because the Maoist state relied almost solely on surplus extracted from the countryside for the primitive accumulation process and refused to rely on external borrowing, as many other socialist and developing countries did in the 1970s, the Chinese state was much less burdened with external liabilities, while many other developing countries fell prey to dictation by their creditors when the international debt crisis hit in the 1980s.

In the 1970s, skyrocketing oil prices led to an immense pool of petrodollars that ended up in many offshore banks outside U.S. and U.K. regulation. These banks offered low-interest loans to governments in the developing world. When the global interest rate on the dollar peaked above 20 percent in the early 1980s as a result of Washington's effort to fight inflation via tightening the money supply, many externally indebted developing countries and socialist countries suddenly became severely indebted as the heightened interest snowballed into the principal. The resulting international debt crisis led to lost decades of development in many Latin American, African, and Southeast Asian states (e.g., see Stallings 1995). The heavily indebted countries that relied on the World Bank and the International Monetary Fund (IMF) for rescue lost their economic sovereignty when these two financial institutions forced them to adopt radical economic liberalization reform as a condition for their loans.

In comparison, China did not borrow much from foreign creditors in the 1970s. When its relations with Western capitalist countries warmed up and its trade with these countries resumed after Nixon visited in 1972, its trade deficit deteriorated as a result of waves of importation of foreign machines (Selden 1997; Chen D. 2004; Wen 2013: 70–76). The temptation to rely on low-interest loans from foreign banks at that time should not be underestimated. But China did resist this temptation, in part because of the domination of the Maoist ideology of self-reliance.

China's relatively low level of external indebtedness throughout the 1970s enabled it to emerge unscathed from the international debt crisis that started in the early 1980s and wreaked havoc on many developing and Soviet bloc economies (see table 2.2). The Chinese state, therefore, did not have to rely on emergency credit from the World Bank and the IMF for rescue, which meant it could maintain its autonomy vis-à-vis the United States and experiment with market reform gradually rather than undergo the shock therapy that the World Bank and IMF applied to most of their debtors amid the debt crisis.

By the late 1970s, when the state-directed primitive accumulation of urban-industrial capital had reached its limit and the economy had entered a prolonged slowdown (see figure 2.1), China was already endowed

TABLE 2.2   China's External Debt in
            Comparison with the Debt of
            Selected Developing and Socialist
            Countries as of 1981

COUNTRY	STOCK OF DEBT AS % OF GROSS NATIONAL INCOME
China	2.99
Latin America	
Argentina	46.6
Bolivia	52.6
Brazil	32.4
Mexico	32.7
Africa	
Algeria	42.6
Sudan	67.4
Nigeria	19.6
Asia	
India	11.8
Indonesia	25.5
Malaysia	37.3
Eastern Europe	
Poland	44.2

Sources: World Bank n.d. For Poland, Boughton 2001:
320–21; IMF n.d.b.

with a network of state industries and infrastructure; a large, educated,
and healthy rural labor force; and a state autonomous from foreign governments and international financial institutions. These legacies of the
Mao period, regardless of the high cost that the Chinese people had paid
for them, laid the foundation for the success of the subsequent market
reform. The reform not only ended the economic stagnation of the late
1970s but also enabled China to follow in the footsteps of Japan and the
Four Tigers, experiencing three decades of capitalist boom.

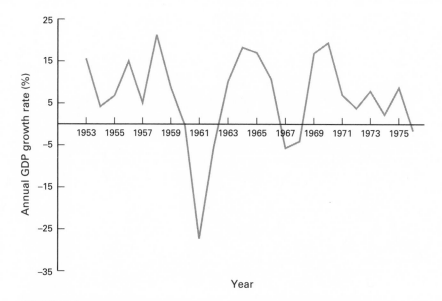

FIGURE 2.1

Annual GDP growth rate of Mao's China, 1953–1976. *Sources*: China Data Online n.d.; Chinese National Bureau of Statistics n.d.

THREE

The Capitalist Boom
1980–2008

THE CONTEMPORARY CAPITALIST BOOM in China is built on the industrial foundation laid in the Mao period. At the same time, such a boom is linked to the earlier booms in Japan and the Four Tigers—South Korea, Taiwan, Hong Kong, and Singapore—which lasted roughly from 1950 to 1990. We cannot fully understand the dynamics of the China boom without understanding those of the earlier Asian Tigers.

Many scholars explain the ascendancy of Japan and the Four Tigers as formidable exporters of manufactured goods to the Global North after World War II in terms of endogenous forces within these economies, most notably the institutions of a centralized economic governing bureaucracy, known as the developmental state, that directed precious resources to strategic industrial sectors (Amsden 1989; Wade 1990; Arrighi 1996; Hung 2009b). But at the same time it would not have been possible for these endogenous conditions to bring about rapid economic growth had there not been the all-encompassing Cold War geopolitics in East Asia. During the Cold War period, what was being fought in East Asia was actually a hot war because, from the U.S. perspective, Communist China's support of rural guerrillas in Southeast Asia and its involvement in the Korean War and the Vietnam War led the region into a permanent state of emergency. Washington regarded the region as the most vulnerable link in the containment of communism and considered its key Asian allies—that is, Japan and the Four Tigers—too important to fail. This consideration accounts for Washington's generous offer of financial and military aid to these East Asian governments to help them jump-start and direct industrial growth. Washington also kept the U.S. and European markets wide open to East Asian manufactured exports, another advantage that other developing regions rarely enjoy. Without this openness in the Western market for their goods, it is simply un-imaginable how these Asian exporters could have any chance of success. Viewed in this light, the rapid economic growth of East Asia was far from a "miracle against all odds." Instead, the growth of Japan and the Tigers was consciously cultivated by the United States as part of its effort to create subordinate and prosperous bulwarks against communism in East Asia.

In the meantime, starting in the 1970s economic crisis in the Western capitalist world urged manufacturers there to outsource labor-intensive parts of the production process to lower-wage countries to cut costs and revive profits, and the East Asian Tigers, which had already achieved ex-port-oriented industrialization, became the largest recipients of such industrial relocation (for more on this topic, see chapter 6; see also Arri-ghi 1994: epilog, and Brenner 2003) The rise of the Asian Tigers was also a culmination of three centuries of Chinese diasporic capitalism in Asia. As we saw in chapter 1, some Chinese coastal entrepreneurial families, with their cross-generation class reproduction constrained by the Qing imperial state, chose to migrate to European colonial outposts in Asia to become the middlemen of Europe–China trade as early as the seven-teenth century. These Chinese traders rapidly advanced their fortunes, global networks, and entrepreneurial capabilities in the age of high imperialism at the turn of the twentieth century. In the postwar years, these overseas Chinese capitalists constituted the economic backbone of the export-oriented industrialization in Singapore, Hong Kong, and Taiwan (Hui 1995; Arrighi 1996; Hamilton 1999; Cochran 2000; Katzen-stein 2005: 60–69; Kuo 2009, 2014).

Organized under a multilayered subcontracting production network spearheaded by Japan, different East Asian manufacturers occupied different segments of the value chain, and each of them specialized in exporting goods to the Western world at a particular level of profitability and technological sophistication. While Japan specialized in the most high-value-added items, the Four Tigers specialized in middle-range products, and the emerging Tigers in Southeast Asia specialized in low-cost, labor-intensive ones. This famous "flying-geese formation" among the Asian exporters constituted a network of reliable suppliers of consumer products to the world market (Cumings 1984; Ozawa 1993).

Beginning in the 1980s and accelerating in the 1990s, China's market reform turned it into a late-coming Asian exporter, absorbing a great amount of manufacturing investment from Japan and the Four Tigers, particularly from Chinese diasporic capitalists in Hong Kong and Taiwan. On the one hand, the export-dependent and investment-heavy path of economic growth in China resembles the earlier Asian Tigers' pattern of development. On the other, the Chinese authoritarian state's strength and resilience, China's intact networks of SOEs that originated in the Mao era, and the country's deep surplus-labor pool in the countryside contributed to its divergence from its Asian neighbors. China's capitalist boom is tantamount to an explosion ignited by the mixing of the Maoist legacies and East Asian capitalism, each developed separately on opposing sides of the Cold War in Asia.

Decentralized Authoritarian Development

To recapitulate, the previous chapter showed how the Communist party–state managed to extract and concentrate scattered rural surplus and build up an extensive network of state-owned urban industrial capital through rural collectivization and the "price scissors" between agricultural and industrial products during the Mao period (Friedman, Pickowicz, and Selden 1991; Selden 1993; Wen 2000: 141–271). Though the peasants were chained to their villages by the household registration system, which restricted migration from their birthplaces, their life expectancy and literacy rate improved significantly as a result of state investment in rural elementary education and public health (Hesketh and Zhu 1997; Ross 2005: 1–13). The Maoist path of development fostered a high GDP growth rate over most of the period until the mid-1970s, when the growth momentum generated by the central-planning system was exhausted and the economy came to a standstill. But it also left China with a bulk of state capital and a vast pool of healthy and educated surplus laborers in the countryside. China developed a strong state less burdened by external debts in comparison with other developing and so-cialist countries. These developmental outcomes laid a solid foundation for market reform, launched by post-Mao leaders in the late 1970s as a remedy to overcome economic stagnation (Naughton 1995: 55).

The market reform started with decollectivization and restoration of a peasant economy in the countryside in the early 1980s, followed by urban state-enterprise reform and price reform in the late 1980s. In the 1990s, SOE reform accelerated, and the transformation of these enter-prises into profit-oriented capitalist corporations emerged as the core agenda of reform. Throughout these stages, the main thrust of the re-form was to decentralize the authority of economic planning and regu-lation and to open up the economy, first to Chinese diasporic capital in Asia and then to transnational capital from all over the world.

The process of "transferring power to lower levels [of government] and allowing lower levels to gain more profits" throughout the 1980s was a conscious effort by the reformist leaders at the center to create a "bureaucratic constituency of market reform" among local cadres as a counterweight to the conservative old guard (Shirk 1993: 334–35), who favored a command economy and had a vested interest in the centrally controlled industries, though the power base of this old guard in the central-planning establishment had been loosened during the Cultural Revolution (see also Andreas 2009). Cut off from subsidies from the cen-tral government and lured by the opportunities for profiteering activi-ties, local governments with different preexisting resource endowments devised diverging strategies of capital accumulation. Some directly ran collective township-and-village enterprises (TVEs) or turned public en-terprises within their jurisdiction into profit-oriented units (this mode of local development is known as "local corporatism" or "local state en-trepreneurialism"; see, e.g., N. Lin 1995; Walder 1995b; Duckett 1998; Oi 1999). Some assumed the role of "referees" instead of direct "play-ers" in the local economies. They promoted local development through such classical developmental state measures as making discrimina-tory rules and constructing appropriate infrastructure to facilitate the growth of select industrial sectors on which they relied for tax revenue (for a discussion of "local developmental state" in China, see Blecher and Shue 2001; Segal and Thun 2001; Wei 2002; Zhu J. 2004). Some relied on outright predation on local societies' preexisting wealth and on public assets through tax bullying, corruption, and selling of state-owned resources for private gain (Lu 1999, 2000a, 2000b; Sargeson and Zhang 1999; Bernstein and Lu 2003; Yu 2003; Guo and Hu 2004). The three local strategies of accumulation as described here are ideal-typical rather than empirical entities. They were in reality combined differently in different localities (Tsai 2002: 254; see also Baum and Shevchenko 1999; Xia M. 2000; Shevchenko 2004).

Lacking technical and management know-how as well as marketing networks in overseas markets, most local developmental or entrepreneurial states depended heavily on labor-seeking transnational capital, in particular Chinese diasporic capital from within East Asia, to jump-start and sustain economic growth. Though foreign direct investment (FDI) is not a major part of China's continental-size economy in quantitative terms, it played a significant role in driving China's labor-intensive and export-oriented industrial growth (see G. Lin 1997, 2000; Hsing 1998). As of 2004, almost 60 percent of Chinese exports were manufactured in foreign-funded enterprises, and this percentage was even higher for higher-value-added products. That figure is startlingly high in comparison with the figures for other Asian Tigers at a similar stage of take-off: 20 percent for Taiwan in the mid-1970s, 25 percent for South Korea in the mid-1970s, and 6 percent for Thailand in the mid-1980s. Measured in terms of the ratio between FDI and gross capital formation, China's FDI dependence has been among the highest in East and Southeast Asia since the 1990s (Huang Y. 2003: 4–35; Gilboy 2004; Hughes 2005).

The bulk of state capital accumulated in the Mao era became an attraction to foreign investors, who could simply connect themselves into the preexisting network of production by establishing joint ventures or multilayered subcontracting networks with local SOEs or collective enterprises. For example, foreign giants such as Boeing, Volkswagen, and Toyota started their businesses in China by collaborating with existing state-owned aircraft or automobile enterprises (Chin 2003). The "unlimited" supply of healthy and educated labor from the countryside, another legacy of the Mao era, persistently kept wage levels in China much lower than the international standard. China's attractiveness to global capital was further enhanced by the competitive pressure among local states, which raced with one another to achieve high GDP growth by offering the most favorable terms possible to foreign investors, ranging from tax breaks to free industrial land.

A consequence of economic decentralization was the weakening of the central government's authority. With local states becoming the leading agents or direct regulators of capital accumulation, the central government became an indirect player that specialized in devising the macroeconomic backdrop, such as interest rates, exchange rates, and preferential policy toward certain regions and sectors against which local states pursue development. Because of the central government's weakening power vis-à-vis that of local governments in direct economic management, some analysts have characterized China's political economy as "fragmented authoritarianism" (Lieberthal 1992).[1]

During the 1990s, the central government attempted to reinvigorate the power of the center in the area of administrative regulation, financial regulation, and commodities management. The 1994 fiscal reform ensured a larger share of revenue by the central government vis-à-vis local governments. But the recentralization went at best only halfway because the reform mostly recentralized bureaucratic power from the county and township level to the provincial level, but not from the provincial level to Beijing. In exchange for a smaller share of government revenue, provincial governments were granted larger autonomy in the pursuit of economic and income growth. In the end, the centralizing reform further empowered provincial governments vis-à-vis the central government and ironically aggravated the phenomenon of "perverse federalism" (Mertha 2005). The momentum of continuous empowerment of local states vis-à-vis the center is not easy to reverse, for this process is integral to market reform itself.

Under market transition, the old social compact in Mao's time, which was based on free health care, education, life-long employment, and other basic social services provided by SOEs and rural communes, was shattered. Before the late 1980s, the dissolution of this social compact was compensated by rising income offered by new market opportunities in the countryside and the shift from a scarcity to a consumer economy in the city. In the first stage of reform up to the mid-1980s, "everybody [won]" because most segments of the population benefited (Wang S. 2000: 37–39).

The social dynamics of the reform shifted dramatically when urban reform accelerated after the mid-1980s. The focus of this urban reform was to turn SOEs into autonomous profit-making units by hardening these enterprises' "soft-budget constraint," which warranted government subsidies and government absorption of losses. The reform also intended to replace fixed, centrally planned prices of key commodities with floating market prices. Under the new pressure to make profits, many SOEs started eliminating welfare packages for workers and replacing lifelong employment with short-term contractual work. Industrial workers' falling income and weakening job security were coupled with runaway inflation and rampant corruption unleashed by price reform. The price reform, which started with a "dual-track system" that allowed the coexistence of fixed planning prices and floating market prices for such key commodities as gasoline, cement, steel, and other materials in short supply, enabled government officials and state-enterprise managers to purchase these commodities at low prices through governmental channels, to stockpile them, and then to resell them at skyrocketing market prices to the emergent free market. Through this rent-seeking activity, many cadres or their kin and protégés amassed enormous private wealth and turned themselves into the first generation of China's "cadre-capitalist class" or "bureaucratic capitalists" in a matter of a few years (Sun 2002; Wen 2004: 37; So 2005). Inflation, corruption, and class polarization reached crisis proportions in 1988, paving the way for the large-scale unrest in 1989 (Hartford 1990; Saich 1990; Baum 1991; Selden 1993: 206–30; Naughton 1995: 268–70; Zhao 2001: 39–52; Wang H. 2003: 46–77).

During the democratic movement in 1989, students and liberal intellectuals diagnosed the economic chaos and corruption as having originated in the mismatch between courageous economic reform and timid political reform. They believed that political liberalization could redress the corruption and abuses generated by the reform. The demands made by nonstudent participants in the movement, in contrast, were more social than political. They called for an end to official profiteering and protection of workers' rights in the reforming SOEs. Whereas protesting students employed Western-style language and symbols of liberal democracy—such as the *Goddess of Democracy* statue erected in front of the Mao portrait in Tiananmen—to articulate their demands for a more complete end to the socialist system, many worker participants ironically held up the portrait of Mao Zedong to express their opposition to the dissolution of the very same system (Unger 1991; Calhoun 1994: 237–60; Wang H. 2003: 57–58).

In contrast to the protestors' disunity was the increasing unity in the party–state during the upheaval. The CCP's once sidelined old guard, who detested market reform, regained their influence amid the chaotic price reform. They adamantly defended the central-planning system and advocated relentless repression of the 1989 unrest to uphold one-party rule. The free marketeers, Deng Xiaoping included, and the nascent cadre-capitalist class, intimidated by the protestors' attack on their privileges, threw their support behind the old guard despite their disagreement with the old guard on economic issues. After the various factions in the party–state acted in unison to quell the unrest, market reform stalled when the old guard were back in charge. But the free marketeers soon displaced the conservatives again under the blessing of the ailing but still unchallengeable Deng Xiaoping, who took a surprising southern tour in 1992 to reenergize the local cadres' effort to further liberalize the economy. A new political consensus based on uncompromising authoritarian rule combined with equally uncompromising marketization was put in place, setting the tone of China's developmental path in the 1990s and beyond (Naughton 1995: 271–308; Wang H. 2003: 62–72).

In the end, the 1989 crackdown not only closed off the path to political liberalization but also accelerated the neoliberal attack on urban workers' rights. To break the international isolation of China resulting from the bloodshed in Tiananmen, Jiang Zemin and Zhu Rongji, the post-1989 CCP leaders originating in Shanghai and chosen by Deng, pursued an aggressive neoliberal economic agenda throughout the 1990s, conscientiously following the Washington consensus and advice from U.S. financial capital. This approach provided the cover and incentive to the Clinton administration in the United States to set aside all doubts about the CCP regime in the aftermath of Tiananmen and to adopt an engagement policy toward China in the name of promoting human rights improvement through U.S.–China economic exchanges.

In the 1990s, the liberalization of the economy and the subsequent social polarization advanced with far greater ferocity than in the 1980s. Massive layoffs of workers in SOEs, which were transformed into profit-oriented enterprises or underwent outright privatization, and complete dissolution of the welfare system embedded in public enterprises swept all major cities, creating a swelling urban underclass. Privatization of SOEs in the 1990s opened up new opportunities for senior cadres and their associates to snowball their wealth through "insider privatiza-tion," heralding the formation of a new class of oligarchs (Li and Rozelle 2000, 2003; Walder 2002b, 2003; Wang H. 2006). Had it not been for the post-Tiananmen authoritarian state's firm grip on society, the polariz-ing yet upheaval-free liberalization of the economy would have been im-possible, at least not at the pace witnessed.

Capitalism was firmly in place in China by the 1990s. The new rich—in-cluding the cadre-capitalist class, self-made businessmen, middle-class professionals, and the like—were the main beneficiaries of the party's new political consensus of the 1990s and became the party's new social base. Departing from the recruitment policy that discriminated against professionals with a high education in the Mao era, the CCP began in the 1990s to shore up its recruitment of young college graduates, who now constitute the backbone of China's new middle class (Walder 2004). In 2001, the party opened the door wider by allowing private entrepreneurs to become card-carrying party members. These beneficiaries of market reform are more antinomies than pioneers of political reform. Recent large-scale surveys consistently find that most middle-class profession-als and entrepreneurs in China are sternly opposed to political liberal-ization out of fear that it will unleash increasing social demands from below that will threaten their private gains (see, e.g., A. Chen 2002; Li et al. 2005; Tsai 2007). In this manner, China's party–state has reticently transformed itself from a socialist authoritarian state, which upheld the planned economic system and facilitated the accumulation of state cap-ital, to a capitalist authoritarian state, which defends the private accu-mulation of capital in a market system among the privileged and keeps at bay grassroots resistance to this accumulation process.

The intense competition among local governments for foreign in-vestment as well as the pro-capital authoritarian state's efforts to keep the laboring classes' demands at bay contributed to the attractiveness of China to global capital, in particular manufacturing capital, which had developed in Japan and the Asian Tigers during East Asia's postwar takeoff. Between 1990 and 2004, investment from Hong Kong, Taiwan, South Korea, Japan, and Singapore altogether constituted 71 percent of the stock of FDI flowing into China (China Profile 2011; Chinese Minis-try of Commerce 2011; Chinese National Bureau of Statistics n.d.). Many of these investments were export oriented, transforming China into the "workshop of the world." They underline the continuity between the Chinese economic miracle and the earlier East Asian miracles, and they tie China into the East Asian network of production. They are also the main sources of the Chinese economy's dynamism and profits. Before we examine the foreign-capital-driven and export-oriented engine of the Chinese economy, let us first look at the transformation of state enterprises that originated during the Mao era into profit-oriented corporations that remain at the commanding heights of the Chinese economy.

Capitalist State Enterprises and Neofeudalism

One aspect of the Chinese economic reform in the 1990s that stands apart from the 1980s is the priority of turning the myriad SOEs into profit-oriented corporations. Huang Yasheng, for example, distinguishes China's capitalist development into two stages in his widely acclaimed book *Capitalism with Chinese Characteristics* (2008). First, there was an entrepreneurial capitalism in the 1980s, when the driving force of growth were rural private enterprises and rural collective enterprises, many of which were private ones in disguise. Entrepreneurial capitalism was then followed by state-led capitalism in the 1990s and beyond, when large, urban-centered SOEs displaced and subjugated the private sector. The SOEs, no less driven by the profit motive than private enterprises, expanded under fiscal, financial, and policy favors offered by the party-state. As shown in table 3.1, SOEs dominated most major sectors in the Chinese economy.

The reform of SOEs in the 1980s never went beyond hardening their budget constraints and increasing their productivity through bonus incentives to workers, and the job security and welfare benefits that the SOEs provided to workers were not altogether abolished. Into the 1990s, aggressive reform of SOEs, which the government saw as a fiscal burden on central and local governments, was meant to turn these enterprises into profitable capitalist enterprises, whether they were still under state ownership or not. To turn the SOEs into internationally competitive corporations after the model of American corporations, the CCP invited U.S. investment banks to restructure some of the biggest state companies and sought to let these companies float in the newly created Chinese stock markets or in the markets of Hong Kong and New York.

TABLE 3.1   Total Assets of Chinese State-Owned/State-Holding Enterprises and Private Industrial Enterprises, National Total and Major Sectors, as of 2012

SECTOR	STATE-OWNED AND STATE-HOLDING ENTERPRISES (100 BILLION YUAN)	PRIVATE ENTERPRISE (100 BILLION YUAN)
National Total	312.1	152.5
Mining and washing coal	31.4	4.7
Extracting petroleum and natural gas	16.6	0.03
Mining and processing ferrous metal ores	3.9	2.6
Processing food from agricultural products	2.0	8.5
Manufacturing tobacco	7.0	0.02
Manufacturing textiles	1.0	9.0
Processing petroleum, coking, processing nuclear fuel	11.9	4.1
Manufacturing raw chemical materials and chemical products	15.9	11.4
Manufacturing nonmetallic mineral products	7.0	12.5
Smelting and pressing ferrous metals	29.8	11.0
Smelting and pressing nonferrous metals	12.1	5.4
Manufacturing automobiles	19.3	5.3
Manufacturing railway, ship, aerospace and other transport equipment	10.6	2.8
Manufacturing electrical machinery and apparatuses	6.2	11.3
Manufacturing computers, communication equipment, and other electronic equipment	8.4	4.3
Producing and supplying electric and heat power	83.1	1.3

Source: Chinese National Bureau of Statistics n.d.

In the words of Carl Walter and Fraser Howie, two veteran investment bankers who participated extensively in the transformation of China's SOEs, "Goldman Sachs and Morgan Stanley made China's state-owned corporate sector what it is today" (2011: 10). In 1993, Vice Premier Zhu Rongji boasted in a central-government speech that Morgan Stanley was planning to pour large investment into China; he conveyed the news as a boon to the troubled economy (Zhu R. 2011: 384).

The creation of China Mobile, which is among the few "National Champions" companies in China and is on the *Fortune* Global 500 list for 2014, illustrates what SOE reform in the 1990s was about. Before the 1990s, China's telecommunication services were provided through a patchwork of state-owned facilities operated by provincial governments. In the early 1990s, Goldman Sachs "aggressively lobbied Beijing" to create a national telecommunication company and succeeded (Walter and Howie 2011: 159). Under the auspices of international bankers, accountants, and corporate lawyers, China Mobile was created as a new company that represented the consolidation of previously provincially owned industrial assets. After years of American bankers' efforts in building its international image, China Mobile completed its initial public offering in Hong Kong and New York in 1997 despite the Asian financial crisis, raising U.S.$4.5 billion. As Walter and Howie point out, China Mobile's valuation was not based on an "existing company with a proven management team in place with a strategic plan to expand operations" but on projected estimates of the future profitability of the consolidated provincial assets as compared to performance of existing national telecom companies operating elsewhere in the world (2011: 161). International bankers, as minority stakeholders of the company, and China's central government, as a majority stakeholder, thus made huge fortunes by creating a "paper company." This is just one example of many similar operations that turned government assets into profit-oriented state companies. To be sure, these paper companies turned real once they floated in the stock market, and they are projected to become profitable soon.

Nowadays China Mobile is the world's largest mobile-phone operator, with 776 million subscribers and more than 60 percent of China's wireless market (*Forbes* 2014). Though it is a corporation capitalized on the New York Stock Exchange, its monopoly status in the telecommunication sector is a result of state policy and its path of creation. When the central government merged all telecommunication assets of different levels of government to create China Mobile, it fostered a monopoly corporation shielded from serious competition. To be sure, not all SOEs turned capitalist corporations enjoy monopoly status in their respective sectors as China Mobile does. Many SOEs are owned and operated by local governments and compete intensely with SOEs owned by other local governments or by the central government in the same sector. For example, in the automobile industry Shanghai Automotive Industry Corporation is a public company that originated as an extension of the Shanghai municipal government. The Shanghai government still owns 75 percent of it (Thun 2006: 103). It is one of the largest three automakers in China, but its market share in the Chinese auto market was a mere 23 percent as of 2013 (*Wall Street Journal* 2013b). It competes with other Chinese state-owned automakers such as Chang'an Motors in Chongqing, Sichuan, and the FAW Group in Changchun, Jilin. The Shanghai Automotive Industry Corporation, like other state-owned car makers, has relied heavily on its joint-venture operation with global leading automakers, such as Volkswagen (since 1984) and GM (since 1997), in making competitive vehicles (Thun 2006; Ahrens 2013).

At the aggregate level, SOEs, enjoying monopoly status or not, have been trailing the private sector in profitability. This is demonstrated consistently even in government data (see table 3.2). Their inferior performance is more remarkable if we take into consideration their size and the financial as well as policy support they receive from the government. Since the 1990s, large SOEs have been expanding with the virtually unlimited financial resources from state banks. Like other reforming SOEs, major state banks, having undergone the same internationalization and reorganization following the model of U.S. corporations, continue to be in the CCP's tight grip. The Achilles heel of this financial structure is that the party "tells the banks to loan to the SOEs, but it seems unable to tell the SOEs to repay the loan" (Walter and Howie 2011: 43).

State banks' lax lending to unprofitable SOEs and the latter's difficulty in repaying the loans led to a pileup of nonperforming loans (NPLs). The first wave of NPLs was created in the late 1990s. A few years after the Deng Xiaoping Southern Tour of 1992, which ignited the fever of debt-financed investment by local governments and SOEs, the economy cooled, partly as a result of the central government's effort to contain inflation

TABLE 3.2   Profit Rate in Various Types of Industrial Enterprises,
2007 and 2012

TYPE OF ENTERPRISE	TOTAL ASSET (BILLION YUAN)		PROFIT (BILLION YUAN)		PROFIT RATE (%)*	
	2007	2012	2007	2012	2007	2012
National Total	35,304	76,842	2,716	6,191	7.69	8.06
State-owned and state-holding enterprises	15,819	31,209	1,080	1,518	6.83	4.86
Private enterprises	5,330	15,255	505	2,019	9.5	13.2
Enterprises funded by Hong Kong, Taiwan, Macao, and other foreign investment	9,637	17,232	753	1,397	7.8	8.1

* Profit rate = total annual profits/total assets.
Source: Chinese National Bureau of Statistics n.d.

and partly as a consequence of the Asian financial crisis of 1997–1998, which hit China's export sector severely. This cycle of overheating and cooling resulted in exploding NPLs in the major state banks' books. This surge of NPLs was in the end resolved by a government bailout. In 1999, four asset-management companies (AMCs) were created to serve as the "bad banks" that would absorb most NPLs from the troubled banks, which thus became "good banks" after this loan-transfer operation. Each of the AMCs took up the NPLs from each of the four leading state banks. The bailout saved the big four, which eventually floated in international markets at good prices. But the AMCs were not as sufficiently capitalized by the government (and hence by taxpayers' money) as many supposed. Although capitalization from the Ministry of Finance for the four AMCs amounted to 40 billion RMB, the other 858 billion of their capitalization came from ten-year maturity bonds that they issued to the rescued big four banks (Walter and Howie 2011: 54–55). The continuous exposure of the big banks to the NPLs because they held AMC bonds means that the bailout was tantamount to creative accounting that merely postponed an NPL-induced financial crisis for ten years.

The bailout was supposed to be a time-buying device for the SOEs and state bank reform to march on. The idea was that after the transfer of NPLs to the AMCs, the major state banks would continue to improve their transparency and governance following their flotation in overseas financial markets. These banks would then become accountable to the market, and they would avoid repeating the mistakes of lax lending to well-connected SOEs. Meanwhile, the SOE reform was supposed to deepen, and the SOEs would finally become profitable and capable of re-paying most of their loans transferred to the AMCs.

However, contrary to the plan, SOEs and state bank reform started to lose momentum after 2003, when the Jiang Zemin–Zhu Rongji govern-ment was replaced by the new leadership, Hu Jintao and Wen Jiabao. The thrust toward reform was totally pulled back in 2005, when the Hu–Wen regime completed its consolidation of power. Despite Hu and Wen's ap-parently more left-leaning ideology, as expressed in their stated empha-sis on alleviating inequality, the termination of SOE reform did not re-vive the system of socialist enterprises that guarantee full employment and workers' welfare. Instead, the state sector was "caught somewhere between its Soviet past and its presumably . . . capitalist future." The SOEs "grew fat, wealthy and untouchable as they developed China's own domestic markets and always with the unquestioning support of a com-plaisant financial system" (Walter and Howe 2011: 21, 213). They became "cash machines" of the neofeudal elite controlling the party state: chil-dren or grandchildren of the founding leaders of the People's Republic of China who came to be known as the "princelings" in China. A diplomatic cable allegedly originating from the U.S. embassy in China, according to WikiLeaks, even details how major economic sectors in China have been divided up among the families of the Politburo members through their control of state enterprises, suggesting a feudalization of the economy (*Telegraph* 2010).

By the end of the first decade of the twenty-first century, these SOEs have become the dominating enterprises in China, overshadowing the private ones. Though SOEs' share in gross industrial output dropped from 83.1 percent in 1980 to merely 7.9 percent in 2011, and the total number of state-owned and state-holding industrial enterprises is less than one-tenth of the total number of private industrial enterprises in 2011, SOEs' total assets are 2.2 times larger than all private enterprises' total assets. Whereas each private industrial enterprise owns an average of 71 million RMB worth of assets, each state industrial enterprise owns 1,652 million RMB worth of assets on average (China Data Online n.d.; Chinese National Bureau of Statistics n.d.). There is a more than twentyfold difference in their average size. SOEs in China are thus mostly gigantic dinosaurs. In fact, among the eighty-five Chinese enterprises included in the 2013 *Fortune* Global 500 list, which ranks corporations around the world by their revenues, 90 percent are SOEs (*Caixin* 2013). Among the top-ten Chinese corporations listed in 2014, all except one are state owned (see table 3.3).

Their reform terminated halfway, SOEs continued to be unprofitable and incapable of repaying their lingering loans to the AMCs. As of 2006, the AMCs had recovered only about 20 percent of the bad loans, and the cash thus generated could barely pay for the interest on the AMC bonds

TABLE 3.3   Top-Ten Chinese Companies by Revenue in 2014 Global Fortune 500

COMPANY	OWNERSHIP	GLOBAL 500 RANK
Sinopec Group	State owned	3
China National Petroleum	State owned	4
State Grid	State owned	7
Industrial and Commercial Bank of China	State owned	25
China Construction Bank	State owned	38
Agricultural Bank of China	State owned	47
China State Construction Engineering	State owned	52
China Mobile Communications	State owned	55
Bank of China	State owned	59
Noble Group	Incorporated in Bermuda, headquartered in Hong Kong	76

Source: *Fortune* 2014.

that major state banks held. In 2009, it became clear that the AMCs could not repay their maturing bonds to the big banks (the bonds constituted up to 50 percent of bank capital among the four big banks [Walter and Howie 2011: 51]). As a remedy, the government extended the AMC bonds' maturity for ten more years. This extension, however, is no more than another postponement of a financial crisis. In ten years' time, China's financial system will be much more vulnerable as a large portion of the massive loans created in the emergency "Great Leap Forward Lending" (Walter and Howie 2011: 69) of 2009–2010 in response to the global financial crisis is destined to explode, creating a tsunami of NPLs in the future (for more on this impending crisis, see chapter 6).

When government facilities and socialist enterprises were transformed into profit-oriented state companies, a large number of state workers were laid off because the new companies, accountable to their stockholders domestically and internationally, no longer saw the maintenance of full employment and workers' standards of living as one of their missions. As a result, the SOEs jettisoned their function to provide housing, medical care, and many other social benefits to workers. Although the export sector, which started to boom in the 1990s (which I turn to later in this chapter), helped expand manufacturing employment, the expansion was not as big as the loss of manufacturing employment brought about by the SOEs' reform. As a consequence, China ironically experienced a net loss in manufacturing employment throughout the 1990s just as it was becoming the "workshop of the world" (Evans and Staveteig 2008). The attack on SOE workers' preexisting rights and social security triggered widely documented waves of worker resistance in the 1990s (Pun 2005; C. Lee 2007; Hurst 2009). Such resistance escalated and culminated in a massive protest by retired and laid-off workers in the old industrial bastion of SOEs in the Northeast in 2002. This resistance, though unable to stop the process of de facto privatization of SOEs, did force the government to increase spending in this industrial region to stimulate local economic growth and to compensate for the job losses caused by SOE reform. The resistance also urged the government to redouble its effort to introduce social security and a medical insurance system, however unevenly distributed they might be, to make up for the destruction of the SOE-based welfare regime.

Whereas the Chinese economy and government finance have been dominated and burdened by inefficient state enterprises thriving mostly on subsidies, financial favor, and protection by the state, the soaring liquidity in the financial system that fuels the orgy of the state sector's investment rests on the foreign-exchange reserves generated in the export sector. It is the export sector, dominated by domestic or foreign private enterprises, that is the foundation for China's capitalist boom, driving the expansion and increasing international competitiveness of the economy at large.

Rise of the Export Machine

In the 1990s, when the SOE reform was in full force, export-oriented manufacturing also started to take off. Though the export sector had emerged in the 1980s, thanks to the beginning of the inflow of Hong Kong manufacturing capital, it did not go far because most surplus labor in the countryside was retained in the TVEs and the booming agricultural sector. The one-off devaluation of the RMB against the dollar by 33 percent in January 1994, followed by a peg to the dollar, was a deliberate boost to China's export manufacturing as a remedy to the trade-deficit and balance-of-payment crisis in 1993–1994 (Wen 2013: chap. 3, part 4). The Clinton administration's decision to delink annual renewal of China's Most Favored Nation status from any human rights consideration in 1994 and its signing of a landmark trade agreement with China in 1999, which permanently lowered trade barriers for all kinds of Chinese goods, as well as the opening of the Chinese market in exchange for the opening of the U.S. and European markets to Chinese products during China's bid for accession into the World Trade Organization (WTO) (which became reality in 2001) contributed to the growth of China's export engine. But one indispensable fuel for China's export-oriented success has been the protracted low-wage labor released from the countryside since the mid-1990s.

Many argue that China's wage competitiveness originates from a demographic windfall that gave China an exceptionally huge rural surplus labor force, allowing China to develop under the condition of an "unlimited supply of labor" and to enjoy the advantage of a low wage for much longer than other Asian economies (figure 3.1) (Cai and Du 2009). But when we look carefully, this condition is not solely a natural phenomenon driven by China's demographic structure. Instead, it is a consequence of the government's rural-agricultural policies that intentionally

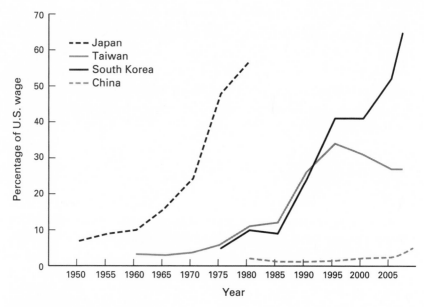

FIGURE 3.1

The hourly manufacturing wage in East Asia as a percentage of the hourly manufacturing wage in the United States, 1950–2009. *Sources*: U.S. Bureau of Labor Statistics 2013, n.d.

or unintentionally bankrupted the countryside and generated a continuous exodus of the rural population in the 1990s.

The relation between China's policies toward its rural-agricultural sector and its low manufacturing wage level can be illustrated by contrasting China's rural development with the rural development in Japan, South Korea, and Taiwan, where there were large rural populations and agricultural sectors to start with during their industrial takeoff. In postwar Japan, the ruling Liberal Democratic Party was active in directing resources to the countryside through spending on rural infrastructure, agricultural development financing, outright farm subsidies, tariffs against foreign farm products, and so on (Mulgan 2000). In South Korea, the Park regime launched the New Village Movement (*saemaul undong*) in the early 1970s to divert a large amount of fiscal resources to upgrade rural infrastructure, to finance agricultural mechanization, and to institute rural educational institutions and cooperatives. The success of this movement was phenomenal: it increased rural household income from 67 percent of urban income in 1970 to 95 percent in 1974, virtually obliterating the rural–urban income gap (Lie 1991). In Taiwan, the KMT government pursued similar rural development policies in addition to making a conscious effort to promote rural industrialization in the 1960s and 1970s. The resulting decentralized structure of Taiwan's industry allowed farmers to work in nearby factories seasonally instead of abandoning their farms altogether and migrating to faraway big cities. Improvement in rural-agricultural livelihoods also necessitated export-oriented manufacturers to offer better wages to recruit workers from the countryside (S. Ho 1979; Mellor 1995; Looney 2012). Under these policies, manufacturing wages soared in the relatively early stage of export-oriented industrialization in these economies. The reasoning behind these industrialization choices that balanced rural and urban development in different East Asian economies varied. For the Liberal Democratic Party in Japan, the significance of rural votes to its electoral success explained its attention to rural development. For the right-wing authoritarian regimes in South Korea and Taiwan, promotion of rural-agricultural development was a way to minimize social dislocation that usually accompanied industrialization and to preempt the rise of leftist influences in the countryside. It was also a crucial way to ensure food security in the context of Cold War tension.

In contrast, China's industrial development after the 1980s has been much more imbalanced and the urban bias much more pronounced than in Japan, South Korea, and Taiwan during their takeoff. Since the early 1990s, investment by the Chinese government has been concentrated largely in coastal cities and towns to boost FDI and the export sectors, while attention to rural and agricultural investment has lagged behind. State-owned banks have also focused their effort on financing urban-industrial development, neglecting rural-agricultural financing. The government even deliberately put a brake on rural-industrial growth. In a speech to the central-government agricultural work conference in 1993, Vice Premier Zhu Rongji openly advocated restraining TVE growth so that resources could be freed up for the expansion of the export sector (Zhu R. 2011: 392–93). He also pushed measures to repress grain price in the wake of grain market liberalization in 1993–94 to safeguard urban livelihoods at the expense of the rural-agricultural sector (Zhu R. 2011: 430, 432–45, 493–504).

China's rural-agricultural sector was not only neglected but also exploited in support of urban-industrial growth. A study estimates the direction and size of financial-resource transfer between the rural-agricultural sector and urban-industrial sector in China in 1978–2000 (figure 3.2) (Huang, Rozelle, and Wang 2006; see also Huang P. 2000; Yu 2003; Wen 2005; Zhang 2005). Taking into account the transfer through the fiscal system (via more taxation than government spending in the countryside), the financial system (via more saving deposits from than loans to the countryside), and other means (such as grain marketing and remittance), there was a sustained and ever-enlarging net transfer of financial resources from the rural-agricultural sector to the urban-industrial sector, except for in the years when the urban economy experienced a temporary downturn, such as in the aftermath of the Asian financial crisis of 1997–1998, as shown in figure 3.2. (See also Knight, Li, and Song 2006; Lu and Zhao 2006; Xia Y. 2006; Huang and Peng 2007; Bezemer 2008.)

The emergence of this urban bias in China's development was at least in part caused by the dominance of a powerful urban-industrial elite from the southern coastal regions during China's integration with the global economy. These elites, who germinated after China's initial opening to the world, grew in financial resources and political influence with the export boom and became increasingly adept at shaping the central government's policy in their favor (see Gallagher 2002; Zweig 2002; Kaplan 2006; Kennedy 2008; Shih 2008: 139–88). Their growing leverage in the central government's policy-making process secured the priority given to enhancing China's export competitiveness and the country's attraction to foreign investment in lieu of rural-agricultural development. The urban revolts in 1989 stemming from hyperinflation and deteriorating living standards in the cities only made the party–state more determined to ensure the economic prosperity and stability of big cities at the expense of the countryside in the 1990s and thereafter (Yang and Cai 2003).

The coastal elite's grip on state power can be illustrated by the background of the CCP's top leaders since 1989. Whereas in the 1980s the Politburo Standing Committee—the highest decision-making body in the CCP—had more members with significant prior tenure in inland provinces than members from coastal provinces (excluding those whose entire career was in the central government), in the 1990s and afterward the committee members with coastal backgrounds always outnumbered

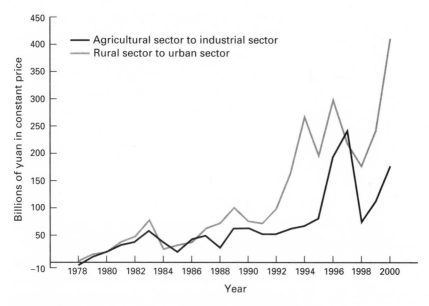

FIGURE 3.2

Total cash transfers from the rural-agricultural sector to the urban-industrial sector, 1978–2001. *Source*: Hwang, Rozelle, and Wang 2006.

those with a rural-inland background, the only exception being the cohorts of 2002 and 2007 (see table 3.4). In particular, two of the three top leaders after 1989, Jiang Zemin and Xi Jinping, served long years in important coastal export-oriented areas—Shanghai and Zhejiang/Fujian, respectively. To be sure, the costal urban background of the top elite is not a guarantee of their pro-coastal urban disposition. But their promotion to the party–state power center definitely increases the leverage of the coastal local elite, many of whom are the top leaders' former protégés and acquaintances, to lobby for policies in their areas' favor.

The consequence of this self-reinforcing urban bias has been the countryside's relative economic decline and the concomitant fiscal stringency in rural local governments in inland provinces. Beginning in the 1990s, the deterioration of agricultural income and rural governance as well as the slowing growth of TVEs, which used to be vibrant employment generators in the early stage of market reform in the 1980s, forced most rural young laborers to leave home for the faraway coastal cities and the meager wages in the export-oriented manufacturing

TABLE 3.4   Number of CCP Politburo Standing Committee Members with
Prior Careers in Either Coastal or Inland Provinces

	1982	1987	1992	1997	2002	2007	2012
Inland provinces	3	3	2	2	5	5	3
Coastal provinces	1	0	3	4	4	4	4

Note: Members who served in both coastal and inland provinces are counted according to
the province where they served the longest tenure.
Source: Data compiled by the author.

sector, creating a vicious cycle that precipitated a rural social crisis and
an accelerating outflow of labor.

Besides unleashing a massive transfer of low-wage labor from the
rural-agricultural to the coastal export sector, central and local governments have also been offering land, tax, and other concessions to export-oriented manufacturers of toys, garments, electronics, and other
goods from Hong Kong and Taiwan to lure them to transfer their production lines to China, bringing with them their technical and management know-how as well as their connections to the overseas consumer
market. This approach to developing the export sector has made private
enterprises prevail and freed them from domination by monopolistic SOEs, as in other sectors.[2] The lack of SOE domination has created
room for domestic private enterprises to grow, many of them becoming
acquainted with Hong Kong and Taiwan exporters through a subcontracting network or competition. The home-grown small and medium
exporters in Wenzhou are good examples of this process (Sonobe, Hu,
and Otsuka 2004; Wei 2009). As shown in table 3.2, both the profit rate
and the aggregate profit of private enterprises and enterprises funded
by Hong Kong, Taiwan, and other foreign investment have been higher
than the profit rate and aggregate profit of state-owned and state-hold-
ings enterprises, although the latter's total industrial assets are much
larger. The central role played by these private enterprises in China's
economy manifests the connection between China's capitalist boom and
the earlier East Asian Tigers as well as the centuries-long development
of Chinese diasporic capital. It also shows that China's capitalist boom,
despite SOEs' continuous domination of its economy, has been driven

primarily by the segment of the economy that is most integrated with the global neoliberal order, which warrants free, transnational flow of capital and trade.

Some may argue that given the weight of fixed-asset investment in GDP (as shown later in figure 3.4), undertaken mostly by SOEs and local governments, the China boom is at least as much driven by the state sector as by the private export sector. But most of the fixed-asset investment in the Chinese economy has been financed by state bank lending, and a large portion of liquidity in the banking system originates from a "sterilization" process in which private exporters surrender their foreign-exchange earnings to state banks in exchange for an equivalent amount of RMB issued by the People's Bank of China, China's central bank. As such, a large part of the increase in liquidity in China's banking system originates from the ballooning trade surplus that the export sector generates as long as the RMB–dollar peg is maintained and China's capital account is closed. At its height in 2007, China's current-account surplus amounted to 47 percent of the increase in money supply, as measured in M2, in the Chinese economy in that year. Likewise, China's foreign-exchange-reserve/M2 ratio throughout the 2000s remained high by international standards, never falling below 20 percent after 2004 and reaching 29 percent at its height in 2007 (see table 3.5).

This monetary expansion, backed by trade surplus and foreign-exchange-reserve growth, is channeled mostly to create bank loans that finance fixed-asset investment by state enterprises and local governments. Had it not been for the large foreign-exchange reserve originating in the thriving export sector, this large-scale expansion in liquidity and credits would have triggered a financial crisis because a small and decreasing foreign-exchange-reserve/M2 ratio is often a precursor

TABLE 3.5   Ratio of Total Foreign Reserves to M2 in China

	2000	2001	2002	2003	2004	2005	2006	2007	2008	2009	2010	2011	2012
Total Reserves/ M2 (%)	10.5	11.6	13.9	16.3	21.3	24.1	24.9	29.2	28.7	27.5	27.2	24.7	22.0

Source: World Bank n.d.

to currency collapse and capital flight, as was the case in many Asian economies on the eve of the Asian financial crisis of 1997–1998 (Sachs, Tornell, and Velasco 1996; Corsetti, Pesenti, and Roubini 1998: 36–39; IMF 2000: 14–15; Kim, Rajan, and Willett 2005). Moreover, because expansion of fixed-asset investment always drives up the import of raw materials and machinery, the absence of an equivalent or faster increase in exports will precipitate balance-of-payment difficulty, as happened in 1992–1993 (Wen 2013: chap. 3, part 4). Viewed in this light, China's thriving export sector constitutes a solid foundation for its aggressive investment growth. It is indeed the mother of the China boom.

From Flying Geese to the Panda Circle

The United States was from the beginning the single most important market for China's exports, as it was for the earlier Asian Tigers, and was surpassed only recently by the European Union as a whole. The rapid expansion of China's export-oriented industries has already made China the biggest exporter to the United States among all Asian exporters, as shown in table 3.6.

As noted earlier, the relatively stagnant manufacturing wages and falling rural living standards have triggered large-scale transfer of rural

TABLE 3.6   China's and Other East Asian Economies' Export Value to the United States and the World (Billion U.S.$)

| | 1985 | | 1995 | | 2005 | | 2013 | |
	U.S.	World	U.S.	World	U.S.	World	U.S.	World
China	2.3	27.3	24.7	149.0	163.3	762.3	369.0	2,210.6
Japan	66.7	117.3	122.0	443.3	136.0	594.9	134.4	714.6
South Korea	10.8	30.3	24.3	131.3	41.5	284.3	62.3	559.6
Taiwan	14.8	30.7	26.4	112.6	29.1	198.4	32.6	305.4
Hong Kong	9.3	30.2	37.9	173.6	46.5	289.5	42.8	459.2
Singapore	4.8	23.0	21.6	118.2	23.9	207.3	24.1	412.2

Source: For 1985, IMF n.d.c. and Taiwan Economic Data Center n.d.; for 1995–2013, Taiwan Bureau of Foreign Trade n.d.

labor into the export sector. The growth of this sector has restrained consumption by worker and peasant households and deepened Chinese manufacturers' dependence on wealthy countries' consumers. This pattern of growth that is highly dependent on external demand is definitely precarious, and I discuss it at more length in chapter 6. But as long as the consumption markets in the United States and Europe continue to expand, as they did under debt-financed hyperconsumerism in most of the 2000s, the stellar growth of China's formidable export engine is guaranteed.

This same reliance on exports, expanding fixed-asset investment, and a low-wage regime that repressed consumption—the key characteristics of China's capitalist boom—could also be observed in the East Asian Tigers' earlier takeoff. But as shown in figures 3.3, 3.4, and 3.5, the Chinese economy's dependence on the export sector and the weight of fixed-asset investment, as measured by total export value and fixed-capital formation as a percentage of GDP, respectively, has been rising and has reached the level that other East Asian economies never attained.[3] However, the weight of private consumption in China's national economy, as

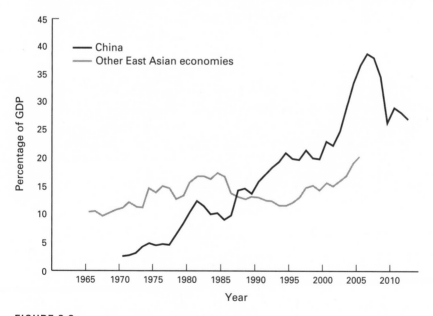

FIGURE 3.3

Export as share of GDP in East Asian economies, 1965–2012. *Sources*: World Bank n.d.; Taiwan Economic Data Center n.d.

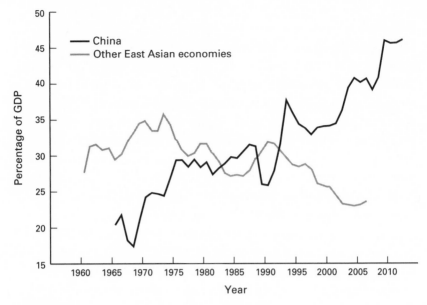

FIGURE 3.4

Fixed-capital formation as share of GDP in East Asian economies, 1960–2012. *Sources*: World Bank n.d.; Taiwan Economic Data Center n.d.

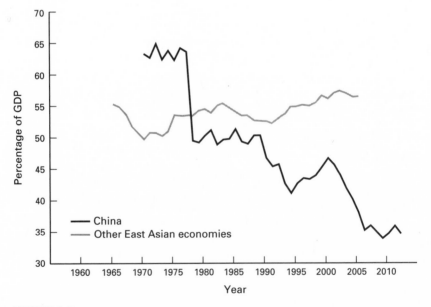

FIGURE 3.5

Private consumption as share of GDP in East Asian economies, 1960–2012. *Sources*: World Bank n.d.; Taiwan Economic Data Center n.d.

measured by household consumption as a percentage of total GDP, has been declining and has dropped well below the level in other Asian exporters during their takeoff.

Besides continuing the East Asian model of export-oriented development, China's capitalist boom also has been reconfiguring the geography of production in East Asia, making earlier East Asian exporters increasingly integrated with China's export engine through the regionalization of the industrial production network. When China had just started to establish itself as the most competitive Asian exporter of products at various levels of technological sophistication in the 1990s, earlier Asian exporters, including Japan and the Four Tigers, together with a group of emerging exporters in Southeast Asia including Malaysia and Thailand, were put under intense pressure to adjust. The export competitiveness from China forced a great amount of export manufacturing to relocate from other Asian economies to China. The *Economist*'s report "A Panda Breaks the [Flying Geese] Formation" in 2001 best describes the challenge that China posed to its neighbors at this time:

> Most of China's neighbors react to the mainland's industrial rise with a mix of alarm and despair. Japan, South Korea and Taiwan fear a "hollowing out" of their industries, as factories move to low-cost China. South-East Asia worries about "dislocation" in trade and investment flows. . . . China is no goose. It does not conform to the . . . stereotype [of a flying goose], because it makes simple goods and sophisticated ones at the same time, rag nappies and microchips. . . . China makes goods spanning the entire value chain, on a scale that determines world prices. Hence East Asia's anxiety. If China is more efficient at everything, what is there left for neighbors to do?
>
> (*Economist* 2001)

Some argue that the erosion of manufacturing profitability under the competition from China was an underlying cause of the Asian financial crisis of 1997–1998 (Krause 1998). Amid the turmoil that the rise of China's manufacturing power raised in the existing export-oriented industrial order in the region, China's neighbors painstakingly restructured their export engine to minimize head-on competition with China and to profit from its rise. In the flying-geese hierarchy of the old industrial order in East Asia, each economy exported specific groups of finished consumer products to Western markets, with Japan exporting the most

TABLE 3.7   Exports to China Versus Exports to the United States as a
Percentage of Total Exports from East Asian Economies

	1985		1995		2005		2013	
	China	*U.S.*	*China*	*U.S.*	*China*	*U.S.*	*China*	*U.S.*
Japan	7.1	37.6	4.95	27.5	13.5	22.9	18.1	18.8
South Korea	0.0	35.6	7.0	18.5	21.8	14.6	26.1	11.1
Taiwan	0.0	48.1	0.3	23.7	22.0	14.7	26.8	10.7
Hong Kong	26.0	30.8	33.3	21.8	45.0	16.1	54.8	9.3
Singapore	1.5	21.0	2.3	18.3	8.6	10.4	11.8	5.8

Source: For 1985, IMF n.d.c. and Taiwan Economic Data Center n.d.; for 1995–2013, Taiwan
Bureau of Foreign Trade n.d.

technologically advanced products, Korea and Taiwan exporting less-so-
phisticated products, and Southeast Asia exporting the least-value-
added ones. The rise of China fomented a new, Sino-centric export-oriented industrial order under which most Asian economies increased
the weight of their export of high-value-added components and parts
(e.g., for Korea and Taiwan) and capital goods (e.g., for Japan) to China,
where these capital goods and parts were employed and assembled into
finished products to be exported to rich countries' markets (Ando 2006;
Baldwin 2006; Haddad 2007).

As table 3.7 indicates, exports from South Korea, Hong Kong, Taiwan,
and Singapore to China surpassed their exports to the United States
during the 1990s and 2000s, and Japan's exports to China rapidly came
to equal its exports to the United States. By the 2000s, the Japan-centered flying-geese model of Asian regionalism had been replaced by a
Sinocentric production network in which China exports most final consumer products to the Western markets on behalf of its Asian neighbors,
which provide China with the parts and machines necessary for the as-
semblage of such products (see figure 3.6).

The regional integration among East Asian exporters is well reflected
in the correlation between the ups and downs of export figures in China
and those of its Asian neighbors. For example, Asia's recovery from the
financial crisis of 1997–1998 and Japan's renewed growth after 2000 are

attributable, at least in part, to the accelerated economic boom in China, which absorbed their manufactured components and capital goods. And when the global crisis unfolded in the fall of 2008 and consumption demand in the United States started to contract sharply, the export value of China's Asian neighbors plunged immediately, but the export value of China itself did not dive to a similar extent until three months later. This lag was caused by the fact that the declining exports of China's neighbors were largely a function of the plunging orders for parts and capital goods by China-based manufacturers in anticipation of plunging orders for the final products from the United States and elsewhere in the months that followed (Setser 2009). The interconnectedness of the Asian network of production also can be illustrated by the manufacturing of the iPhone, which contains key components from Japan and Korea (with Korean components constituting the largest share, 43 percent) and is assembled in China, as shown in table 3.8.

Under this Panda circle of Sino-centric production network and East Asia's increasing dependence on China for export growth, the limits and vulnerability of the Chinese development model, signaled by its overdependence on consumption demand in the rich countries and the

FIGURE 3.6

The Sinocentric and export-oriented network of production in East Asia, c. 1990–present.

TABLE 3.8   Breakdown of an iPhone 4 (Retail Value: U.S. $600)

COUNTRY / COMPANY	COMPONENTS	COST (U.S.$)
South Korea		
LG (or TMD)	Liquid-crystal display	28.50
Samsung	Flash memory chip	27.00
Samsung	Applications processor	10.75
Samsung	DRAM memory	13.80
United States		
Broadcom	Wi-Fi, Bluetooth, GPS chips	9.55
Intel	Radio-frequency memory	2.70
Texas Instruments	Touch-screen control	1.23
Cirrus Logic	Audio codec pack	1.15
Germany		
Infineon	Receiver/transceiver	14.05
Dialog	Power management	2.03
Italy/France		
STIMicroelectronics	Accelerator and gyroscope	3.25
Japan		
AKM	Compass	0.70
Other		
Wintek or TPK Balda	Touch screen	10.00
Not known	Camera, 5 megapixel	9.75
Not known	Camera, video graphics array	1.00
Not known	Battery	5.80
Not known	Other parts	46.25
COMPONENT TOTAL		187.51
ASSEMBLY COST		6.54
MISCELLANEOUS		45.95
PROFIT		360.00

Source: *New York Times* 2010.

relative slow growth of its own domestic market (as examined in detail in chapter 6), are translated into the limits and vulnerability of other Asian economies.

In this chapter, we see how China's capitalist boom originated from both the educated, healthy rural surplus labor in China as a legacy of the Mao period and the export-oriented, labor-intensive manufacturing in the East Asian Tigers. Though the state sector in China, another legacy of the Mao period, is huge, and fixed-asset investment within that sector constitutes a large part of China's economic dynamism, such debt-financed investment is very much grounded in the increasingly large liquidity and foreign-exchange reserve engendered by the export sector. In the latest stage of development, China's export manufacturing has complemented its forward linkages to the export markets in Western capitalist economies with strong backward linkages to components and capital-goods exporters in neighboring Asian economies. The China boom is therefore heavily reliant on the free transnational flow of investment and goods. It would have been impossible without the rise of global free trade since the 1980s. Besides importing components and capital goods from its East Asia neighbors, China has started to be a major buyer of raw materials and energy from other developing countries in Latin America and Africa. It has also started to export its manufactured products and capital to these distant countries in increasing amounts. The next two chapters focus on whether and how China's increasing trade and investment linkages with other developing countries are reshaping the pattern of global inequality, the context of development, and the geopolitical balance of power in the developing world.

PART TWO

Global Effects, Coming Demise

—

FOUR

Rise of the Rest

SINCE THE INCEPTION of the Industrial Revolution, inequality within the world's population has been increasing. Although inequality within individual countries went up and down during the past two centuries, inequality between the wealthy West and the underdeveloped rest continually rose. This trend persisted even after most formerly colonized countries attained political independence and started to industrialize (Maddison 1983; Arrighi and Drangel 1986; Landes 1999; Firebaugh 2000, 2003; Bourguignon and Morrisson 2002).

Many see the rise of China since the 1980s as the beginning of the reversal of this trend. For one thing, the three decades of rapid economic growth in China—the most populous country in the world, constituting "a quarter of humanity" (Lee and Wang 2000)—have made significant contribution to reduction of world poverty at large. The United Nations notes that China is leading the world effort in poverty reduction. In a Millennium Development Goal report published in 2013, the United Nations Development Program lauded China:

> The significant results that China achieved in poverty reduction have made outstanding contributions to the global poverty alleviation effort. According to statistics of the World Bank, from 1990 to 2005, the world's poor population declined from 1.908 billion to 1.289 billion (with USD1.25/

day as the poverty line, constant 2005 PPP). During this period, China's poor population declined from 683 million to 212 million, a decrease of 471 million. A comparison of these statistics shows that between 1990 and 2005, China had achieved the target of halving the poor population ahead of schedule and the decrease of poor population achieved in China accounted for 76.09 percent of the world's total over the same period.

(United Nations 2013: 10)

The closing of the gap between China's average income and the global average, followed by similar processes in other populous developing countries, has spearheaded the reduction in global income inequality. As Branko Milanovic, a former chief economist of the World Bank, noted recently, "The period between the fall of the Berlin Wall and the Great Recession [after 2008] saw the profoundest reshuffle of individual incomes on the global scale since the Industrial Revolution. This was driven by high growth rates of the populous and formerly poor or very poor countries like China, Indonesia and India, and, on the other hand, by the stagnation or declines of incomes in Latin America and post-Communist countries as well as among poorer segments of the population in rich countries" (2014: 78).

These insights notwithstanding, discussions about the China boom's effects on global inequality usually overlook three issues. The first is whether China's contribution to global inequality reduction, which is often measured by assuming everyone in China earns the same average income, will be cancelled out by the rapid increase in inequality *within* China. The second is whether China's contribution to global inequality reduction over the past three decades or so will continue or will diminish and reverse in the future, particularly if China's average income eventually surpasses the world average. The third is whether China's experience of rapid economic growth is replicable in other developing countries and whether the China boom is enhancing or hindering the development of other developing economies. In this chapter, I deal with these three issues to decipher how the China boom is reshaping global inequality in the long run.

China's Great Leap Backward to Inequality

Concomitant with the rise of China as a global economic powerhouse is the spectacular increase in economic inequality within China itself at all fronts. This increase is particularly startling given the obsession with absolute equality in Mao times. Carl Riskin, an expert on the Chinese economy, and his coauthors, Renwei Zhao and Li Shi, are not exaggerating when they remark that with the inception of market reform in China, the country has changed from one of the "world's most egalitarian societies" to one of the world's most unequal ones and that "this retreat from equality has . . . been unusually rapid" (2001: 3; see also Davis and Wang 2008).

In the initial stage of the post-Mao era, whether market reform was enhancing or reducing inequality was a topic of debate among sociologists on China. For example, Victor Nee (1989) claimed that the socialist system under Mao was a highly unequal one because bureaucrats and party members enjoyed vast privileges and monopolized much more resources than common citizens. He also argued, based on rural survey data collected in 1985, that market reform enabled nonprivileged citizens to obtain more resources through market activities. Hence, the reform helped unlock the monopoly of resources by the party–state and reduce inequality. In contrast, Andrew Walder (1995a, 2002a) found in data from an urban survey in 1986 and a rural survey in 1996 that market reform had not reduced inequality and did not unlock the monopoly of resources by the party–state because marketization enabled the politically well connected to convert their power or connections to powerful cadres into economic gains. Therefore, market mechanisms in fact helped reproduce and even exacerbate the preexisting inequality in the original socialist system.

Although the two sides in this debate have not reconciled their differences, it has become increasingly evident in more recent studies that the question of whether bureaucratic privileges in Mao's socialist system have been undermined or reinforced by market reform is related to the changing dynamics of the reform processes in China. As noted in chapter 3, the market reform in its initial phase in the 1980s was mostly about the rejuvenation of the peasant economy, and the economic dynamism at that time was generated mainly by small-scale rural private enterprises and collective enterprises (many of which were private enterprises in disguise). In the 1990s, however, the agricultural sector and rural enterprises were in decline. Large SOEs and the coastal export sector heavily reliant on foreign capital became the new engines of economic growth. The two different dynamics of growth in the 1980s and from the 1990s on must have had different effects on social inequality.

It is noteworthy that Nee's analyses, which find that market-driven inequality was displacing the more rigid inequality based on cadres' power, are based mostly on data collected in rural areas during the earlier period of reform around 1985, whereas Walder's contention about bureaucratic power's persistent influence on shaping income inequality is based on urban data from the 1980s and rural data from 1996. It is plausible that their different conclusions in fact reflect what Huang Yasheng (2008) characterizes as the transition from entrepreneurial capitalism in the 1980s to state capitalism in the 1990s. According to Huang, whereas rural China in the 1980s saw a more decentralized market economy with ample opportunities for ordinary people to thrive on private entrepreneurship, economic opportunities in the 1990s in urban and rural areas alike were more concentrated among the politically well connected and in foreign capital, and opportunities for small entrepreneurs dwindled, particularly in the countryside. More empirical and historical research is needed to test whether this is really the case (see Szelenyi and Kostello 1996).

In the Mao era, stratification in Chinese society did not manifest predominantly as inequality in income but rather as inequality in power. It has been noted that Mao's monthly salary was 404.8 RMB throughout the 1960s and 1970s, and an ordinary worker's monthly salary at the time was about 60 RMB; the former was thus less than seven times greater than the latter, but the difference between Mao's rights and authority and those of the ordinary worker was clearly much more vast (*Xinhua News* 2012c). Most daily necessities were rationed through a coupon system rather than purchased in the market in the period. Differences in income level did not mean much. In this situation, as in other actually existing socialist countries of the time, inequality in power was the most significant form of inequality because the authority that one commanded—as a brigade cadre in the People's Commune, as a party secretary in a town, and so on—was the most significant determinant of one's chances in life and well-being, and the "new class" in the socialist system was marked mostly by excessive authority and the rights it enjoyed (see Andreas 2009). A citizen's political status and label as assigned, many times arbitrarily, by the party–state during political campaigns—such as "landowner," "bourgeois," "petty bourgeois," "model worker," "model peasant," and so on—also determined one's options and material conditions in significant ways. Those labeled as a "class enemy" were forced to perform extra labor, rationed lower-quality food, and discriminated against in allocations for schools and jobs. Mao's China was one of the most egalitarian countries in terms of distribution of income, but it was far from a utopia free of inequality.

The development of a market system after the 1980s turned monetary-income inequality into the increasingly prevalent form of inequality through which other inequalities are expressed. It is true that inequality in power is still important nowadays, but such inequality has also been translated into income inequality—those with more authority or with privileged access to those in power can obtain a higher income. At the same time, the end of the rationing system and privatization of housing, schools, health care, and all other essential aspects of life have made differences in income ever more important in shaping one's opportunities and quality of life. As such, China has been converging with other capitalist societies in that disparity in monetary income has become the most important yardstick to measure all forms of inequality, privilege, and discrimination.

During the past three decades, income inequalities widened along all dimensions of social relations, including class, urban–rural, and interregional divisions. Along class lines, the rising new private entrepreneurs and bureaucratic managers of SOEs constituted the new capitalist elite. Party bureaucrats transformed into, overlapped with (through their own control of SOEs or through kinship networks), colluded with, or appropriated surplus from (through taxes, bribes, and a favor system) these new capitalist classes, and this amalgamated class constitutes the ruling bloc in China. At the bottom of the class hierarchy were the peasants and workers, who in this period were divided into urban workers with an urban household registration and peasants turned migrant workers with a rural household registration and thus denied access to many benefits and opportunities in the urban areas where they lived. In between,

China saw the rise of a middle class made up of highly educated professionals. Though this middle class might be expanding in select prosper-
ing cities such as Shanghai and Beijing, in proportion it still constitutes
only a minuscule part of the population and occupies a place close to the
top echelon of the income-distribution pyramid.

Besides rising class inequality, growing rural–urban inequality has
been the most important force that boosts overall income inequality in
China. In the early phase of reform before the mid-1980s, because most
reform measures, such as the revival of the peasant household economy
and the breakup of the People's Commune, as well as the encouragement
of TVEs, benefited the countryside, while the urban areas were still in the
straitjacket of the state socialist system, rural–urban inequality shrank.
But when market reform advanced in full force in the urban areas during
the 1990s, the rural areas were left behind. The urban bias that exacerbated transfer of resources from the rural-agricultural to urban-industrial sectors only made matters worse, as noted in chapter 3. From then
on, the disparity between urban and rural income continuously expanded,
from a ratio of 1.8 to 1 in 1984 to a ratio of 3.3 to 1 in 2009 (see figure 4.1).

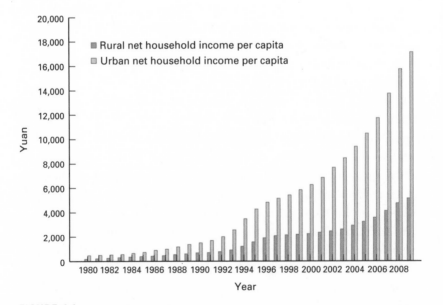

FIGURE 4.1

Urban and rural per capita household income, China, 1980–2009. *Source*: Chinese
National Bureau of Statistics n.d.

Inequality among provinces also has been growing. Since the early 1990s, Chinese economic growth has been driven in large part by FDI and the export sector concentrated in coastal areas, while the growth of inland areas has been stifled. As a result, inequality in the average income in different provinces increased until the central government addressed this issue by directing more investment to the northwestern and southwestern interior beginning in the Hu Jintao era. But any gains made from this interregional redistributive policy have been not large enough to undo the inequality generated in the first two decades of reform.

This interprovincial inequality in income is reflected in the inequality in life expectancy, literacy, and many other human development indicators, as shown in table 4.1. We can also get a clearer sense of how large the inequality has become by comparing the GDP per capita of the richest and poorest provinces in China to the GDP per capita in countries with a similar income profile. As seen in table 4.2, Shanghai's average income, adjusted for its cost of living, has reached the level of a middle-income country such as Cyprus in Europe, whereas Guizhou's average income is about the same level as the average income in the Philippines as of 2010.

Increasing class inequality, urban–rural inequality, and interprovincial inequality combined have generated a rapid rise in overall inequality. The Chinese government rarely discloses overall inequality in the country as measured in gini coefficient, as many other countries do,[1] and the Chinese National Bureau of Statistics has released official gini data for urban and rural areas separately. Estimation of China's overall gini varies, but all those who have studied the figures agree that it has been rising sharply since 1978. One contrast between China's capitalist takeoff and the Asian Tigers' earlier takeoff is that whereas the latter was accompanied by a decline in overall inequality, the former has been marked by a rapid rise in inequality. In this respect, China's pattern of development resembles that of Latin America more than that of East Asia (see table 4.3).

Many scholars see Mao-era China, the most populous nation in the world, as a model for how to reduce national income inequality. This view is not restricted to leftist intellectuals but is also held by mainstream economists and international organizations. For example, Amartya Sen (2005), though pointing out that Mao China's lack of freedom of press

TABLE 4.1   Interprovincial Inequality in China, 2010

	AVERAGE LIFE EXPECTANCY (YEARS)	ENROLLMENT IN SENIOR HIGH SCHOOL (%)	GDP PER CAPITA (CURRENT U.S.$)
Nation as a whole	74.83	82.5	4,430
Shanghai	80.26	91.7	11,012
Beijing	80.18	98.0	10,626
Tianjin	78.89	95.0	10,487
Jiangsu	76.63	96.0	7,776
Zhejiang	77.73	92.5	7,518
Inner-Mongolia	74.44	88.3	6,974
Guangdong	76.49	86.2	6,510
Liaoning	76.38	92.6	6,232
Shandong	76.46	95.0	6,035
Fujian	75.76	83.4	5,894
Jilin	76.18	91.9	4,661
Hebei	74.97	85.0	4,188
Hubei	74.87	87.2	4,118
Chongqing	75.70	80.0	4,058
Shaanxi	74.68	85.3	4,003
Heilongjiang	75.98	87.7	3,995
Ningxia	73.38	84.7	3,943
Shanxi	74.92	86.8	3,803
Xinjiang	72.35	69.1	3,676
Henan	74.57	89.1	3,627
Hunan	74.70	85.0	3,606
Hainan	76.30	70.0	3,511
Qinghai	69.96	67.1	3,540
Sichuan	74.75	76.0	3,155
Jiangxi	74.33	76.0	3,129
Guangxi	75.11	69.0	3,066
Anhui	75.08	80.0	3,065
Tibet	68.17	60.1	2,493
Gansu	72.23	70.0	2,378
Yunnan	69.54	65.0	2,319
Guizhou	71.10	55.0	1,954

Source: United Nations Development Program China and Institute for Urban and Environmental Studies 2013.

TABLE 4.2   Per Capita Income of the Richest and the Poorest Provinces in China and of the Nearest Countries, 2010

PROVINCE / CITY	PROVINCE'S INCOME (IN 2005 INTERNATIONAL DOLLARS)	NEAREST COUNTRY	NEAREST COUNTRY'S INCOME (IN 2005 INTERNATIONAL DOLLARS)
Shanghai	18,070	Cyprus	18,756
Guizhou	3,116	Philippines	3,194

Source: Chinese National Bureau of Statistics n.d.; Heston, Summers, and Aten 2012 (based on China series I).

caused the horrific famine in 1959–1961, acknowledges that China's record in alleviating poverty and improving the living standards of the masses was well ahead of India's and other developing countries' records even before market reform began.

China's rapidly increasing inequality in the post-Mao period, needless to say, has had a conspicuous impact on the pattern of global inequality. But whether China's contribution to global inequality change is a net positive or net negative is not clear yet because China impacts global inequality in two contradictory ways. On the one hand, China's increasing internal inequality is contributing to an increase in overall global inequality. On the other hand, China's rapidly rising average income as a developing country has contributed to the reduction in international inequality since the 1980s. How these opposite effects of the China boom combine to shape the overall pattern of global inequality has been a topic of prolonged scholarly debate: Is the China boom making the world more or less egalitarian?

China and the Reduction in Global Inequality

Social scientists have been debating whether globalization has been reducing or increasing inequality throughout the world. The term *global inequality* refers to the inequality in income among the world's population. Because a real-income survey based on sampling of the entire world population is impossible, many researchers use international inequality—that is, inequality of average income between countries—as

TABLE 4.3   China's Gini Coefficient in Comparative Perspective

YEAR	CHINA	SOUTH KOREA	TAIWAN	BRAZIL	MEXICO
1950					0.53
1953			0.558		
1957					0.55
1960				0.53	
1961			0.440		
1963					0.56
1964			0.360		
1965		0.344			
1966			0.358		
1968			0.362		0.58
1970		0.332	0.321	0.59	
1972			0.318	0.61	
1974			0.319		
1975					0.58
1976		0.391	0.307	0.60	
1978			0.306	0.56	
1980	0.330		0.303		
1982		0.357	0.308		
1984					
1985					
1994	0.400				
1996	0.424				
1998	0.456				
1999	0.457				
2000	0.458				
2003	0.479				
2005	0.485				
2009	0.490				

Note: 0 = absolute income equality, 1 = maximum possible inequality.

Sources: For China 1980–2000, G. Chang 2002; for China 2003–2009, Xinhuanet 2013; for South Korea, Taiwan, Brazil, and Mexico, Haggard 1990.

an approximation of global inequality, assuming income levels within individual countries are relatively homogenous compared with the wide income differences between countries. More sophisticated studies do not make this assumption, however, and instead try to combine both international inequality and inequalities within individual countries— or internal inequalities—to estimate the genuine global inequality of the world's population. Overall global inequality can mathematically be taken as the sum of population-weighted international inequality and population-weighted average internal inequality in the world. These studies point to the centrality of China in determining the trend of global inequality over the past three decades.

A consensus in the literature is that global inequality has been growing continuously since the inception of the Industrial Revolution. It started the great divergence between Europe/North America and the rest of the world, which has struggled to catch up but to little avail (see chapter 1; Maddison 1983; Arrighi and Drangel 1986; Landes 1999; Firebaugh 2000, 2003; Bourguignon and Morrisson 2002). The advent of contemporary globalization, starting around 1980, has triggered a spate of studies with contradictory findings that show that globalization is either perpetuating the increase in global income inequality (Korzeniewicz and Moran 1997; Arrighi, Silver, and Brewer 2003; Wade 2004; Milanovic 2005; Chase-Dunn 2006) or fostering a historic reversal of this trend (Firebaugh 1999; Goesling 2001; Firebaugh and Goesling 2004; Sala-i-Martin 2006). These studies are central to the debate between supporters and critics of globalization. Whereas the former claim that globalization generates shared prosperity that benefits the majority of the world population, the latter argue that this prosperity is concentrated among a privileged few in the rich countries, while most others' livelihoods are becoming relatively worse off.

Few would dispute that under globalization internal inequalities have been increasing in most countries since the 1980s. Rapidly growing inequalities in nations transitioning from centrally planned to market-based economic systems, above all China, are the most notable examples of this trend (Alderson and Nielsen 1999, 2002; Wang and Hu 1999; Cornia and Court 2001; Wade 2004; Gajwani, Kanbur, and Zhang 2006). In contrast, international inequality weighted by each country's population has been decreasing in the same period. The diminishing

TABLE 4.4   Ratio of China's Real Average Annual Income Growth Rate to
the World's Average Income Growth Rate

	1980–1985	1985–1990	1990–1995	1995–2000	2000–2005	2005–2010
China growth rate / world growth rate	10.73	4.20	8.63	3.90	4.30	5.90

Source: Data compiled by the author from World Bank n.d.

income gap between rich and poor countries is attributable mainly to the stellar economic growth of the world's most populous nation, China, which makes up about one-quarter of the world's population and has seen its average income-growth rates consistently reach more than four times the world average growth rate during most of the past three decades, as shown in table 4.4 (see also Firebaugh and Goesling 2004; Berry and Serieux 2006; Bussolo et al. 2007).

If we measure average income in GDP per capita by purchasing power parity (PPP), we see a continuous trend of falling international inequality from 1980 to 2010.[2] But if we take China out of the picture and measure international inequality among the rest of the countries, we see that international inequality generally increased during most of the same period, except after about 2002 (which I discuss later), as shown in figure 4.2. This confirms that the decrease in international inequality from the 1980s through the 2000s has been driven mostly by the rapid growth of GDP per capita in populous China, while in the meantime the rest of the world has been witnessing widening international inequality.

The most contentious issue in the literature is whether the rise in average internal inequality in the world is neutralizing the reduction in international inequality, hence generating a net increase in global inequality. Although consistent and continuous data on international inequality are available, data on internal inequalities across the world are much more uneven, spotty, and sometimes incompatible. Analysts therefore have to approximate average internal inequality by extrapolating whatever scattered data are available, even if data points are many years apart. Different strategies of approximation produce contrasting results. Some researchers discover shrinking global inequality (Sala-i-Martin 2002a, 2002b; Berry and Serieux 2006), but others

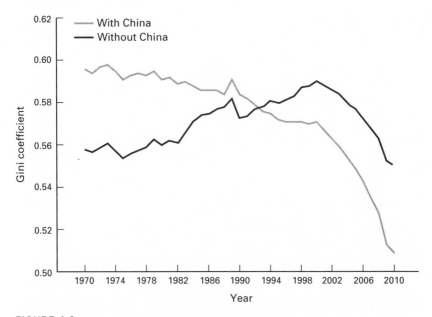

FIGURE 4.2

Change in international inequality with or without China in the calculation, 1980–2010 (0 = absolute income equality, 1 = maximum possible inequality). *Source*: Author's calculation based on Heston, Summers, and Aten 2012.

report the opposite (e.g., Korzeniewicz and Moran 1997; Milanovic 2005). These diverging positions aside, most researchers agree that given the huge population, high growth rate, and rapid expansion of internal inequality in China, whether China makes a net positive or negative contribution to the change in global inequality is the single most important factor in determining what direction overall global inequality has taken and will take. In other words, the key to whether global inequality has been increasing or decreasing under globalization is whether China's rapidly growing internal inequality is larger or smaller than its effect in reducing international inequality.

One way to assess China's net contribution to overall global inequality is to break down China into smaller regional units and treat them as "individual countries" in the calculation of international inequality. Studies show that nearly 90 percent of the increase in internal inequality in China originates from the increase in urban–rural and interprovincial inequalities during the past three decades.[3] It follows that if the

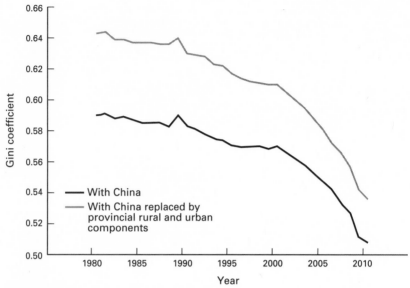

FIGURE 4.3

Determining international inequality by treating the urban and rural population of each of China's provinces as an individual country, 1980–2010 (0 = absolute income equality, 1 = maximum possible inequality). *Source*: Author's calculation based on Heston, Summers, and Aten 2012.

global-inequality-enhancing contribution of China's increasing internal inequality is larger than the international-inequality-reducing contribution of China's average income growth, then the measurement of international inequality when China as a whole is replaced by its rural and urban provincial components will show a net increase in inequality.

Figure 4.3 shows the opposite, however: even taking the vast increase in internal inequality in China into consideration by treating the urban and rural populations of provinces as separate nations, international inequality still decreased from 1980 to 2010, though the inequality level at each point in time became higher. China's overall contribution to the reduction in global inequality is solid. To dissect why this is the case, we can look at the rate of income change in each province during the period. Table 4.5 shows that despite the increasing inequality among these provinces indicated by their diverging rates of income growth, the growth rate of all of these provinces still exceeded growth rate in world average income over the past three decades.

TABLE 4.5   Changes in Real Average Income in Each
Chinese Province Compared with the Change
in the World Average Income, 1980–2010

	% CHANGE IN REAL INCOME PER CAPITA
World	74.09
Chinese Provinces	
Beijing	834.61
Tianjin	951.00
Hebei	1,211.78
Shanxi	1,061.83
Inner-Mongolia	2,462.58
Liaoning	920.41
Jilin	1,287.41
Heilongjiang	662.28
Shanghai	445.46
Jiangsu	1,808.35
Zhejiang	2,045.13
Anhui	1,302.48
Fujian	2,147.21
Jiangxi	1,114.19
Shandong	1,897.89
Henan	1,408.17
Hubei	1,173.99
Hunan	1,223.21
Guangdong	1,717.20
Guangxi	1,322.22
Hainan	1,215.32
Sichuan	1,193.33
Guizhou	1,070.44
Yunnan	1,052.70
Shaanxi	1,474.61
Gansu	711.40
Qinghai	896.13
Ningxia	1,112.02
Xinjiang	1,092.99

Source: Data compiled by author from Chinese National Bureau of Statistics n.d.; Heston, Summers, and Aten 2012.

The same pattern is obtained if we break Chinese provinces down into their urban and rural components. Real income per capita for rural and urban components of all provinces expanded by more than the world average of 74.09 percent. Even rural Heilongjiang, the component witnessing the lowest growth in the period, grew 101.8 percent, which is way higher than the world average growth rate. To put it simply, although the incomes of rich and poor have been polarizing within China in the post-Mao era, even the poorest segment of the Chinese population has been experiencing real-income growth faster than the average-income growth in the world, enabling China to reduce global inequality regardless of the spectacular growth in inequality within its own huge population.

Just as the reduction in global inequality since circa 1980 was largely a function of China's rapid economic growth, the future change in global income inequality will continue to hinge on China's growth performance. Everything else being equal, there are two possible scenarios for the next three decades: China's growth rate significantly slows and becomes closer to or even lower than the world average growth rate, or China continues to maintain its high-speed growth relative to the world average growth rate.

The first scenario is quite likely because the past experiences of rapidly developing countries (such as postwar Japan and the East Asian Tigers in the 1970s and 1980s) suggest that no economy can have breakneck double-digit growth forever. The larger the average income a developing country has attained, the more difficult it is for that country to perpetuate its high growth rate. China will definitely witness diminishing growth rates in the future. Despite the Chinese economy's seeming resilience in the wake of the global economic crisis starting in 2008, it is certain that its growth rate will not return to precrisis levels. With the Great Crash, China's export sector, accounting for much of the country's rapid growth in the past two decades, could no longer roar because the debt-financed consumption spree in the Western markets dramatically slowed. China's investment boom is also set to fade because of rising indebtedness within the system (see chapter 6). We should therefore expect that a long-term slowdown in China's growth rate will reduce China's net contribution to a reduction in global inequality, and China will even start to become a net contributor to the increase in global inequality (see also Winters and Yusuf 2007; Hung 2008, 2009a; Hung and Kucinskas 2011).

Even in the second scenario, in which China maintains its hyper-economic growth in the next few decades, its contribution to reduction in global income inequality will diminish and then reverse after an inflection point, everything else being equal. A rapidly growing economy reduces international inequality only when its per capita income is below the world average. After its average income surpasses the world average, the nation's continuous, faster-than-world-average growth will begin to cause an increase in international inequality. Though China's per capita income is still well below the world average at the moment, its average income is set to surpass the world average in the next three decades. After reaching that point, China will begin to effect a net increase in global inequality.

This second scenario is captured in figure 4.4, which projects the trajectory of change in population-weighted international inequality from 2010 to 2040, as measured by the gini index. The assumptions underlying the graph include: (1) average growth rates of all countries, China included, in 2010–2040 remain the same as in 1980–2010; (2) the population share of all countries remains unchanged; and (3) PPP deflators for all countries remain the same throughout the period.

Figure 4.4 shows that if China maintains its robust average growth rate during 1980–2010 for the next thirty years, international inequality will continue to decrease for a while after 2010. But it will then increase again, ending the temporary retreat of global inequality during the China boom. A comparison of the 2010–2040 projections with and without China shows that China will become a net contributor to global inequality increase after about 2018.

Of course, the simulation in figure 4.4 is much more simplistic than reality. One major complication is how other developing countries will be doing in the future. In the projection, we assume that all the other countries' performances in 2010–2040 are the same as in 1980–2010. Whether this assumption will prove true depends largely on whether China's economic achievement in recent years is an exceptional phenomenon that will not be replicated by others or whether its achievement is a precursor of similarly rapid growth in other populous developing countries.

If China's rise is to be succeeded by the acceleration of economic growth in a significant mass of developing countries through either the

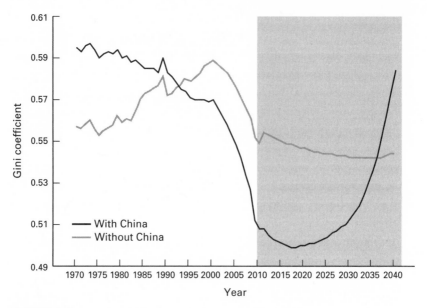

FIGURE 4.4

Projection of international inequality for 2010–2040 (*shaded part*), assuming China's average rate of growth in 2010–2040 is the same as that in 1980–2010 (0 = absolute income equality, 1 = maximum possible inequality). *Source*: Author's calculation based on Heston, Summers, and Aten 2012.

emulation of the successful Chinese model of growth or direct benefits from China's growth, then these countries' contribution to global inequality reduction might exceed China's net contribution to global inequality increase after around 2018. In this case, the reduction in global inequality might continue even after China surpasses the middle-income threshold. Regarding this issue, the 2000–2010 portion of figure 4.2 is telling. It shows that although international inequality without China kept increasing from 1980 to 2000, the increase stalled and then reversed around 2002. This decrease in international inequality without China is not huge, but it suggests that China's rapid economic growth might have already started spreading to other developing countries to the extent that the reduction in international inequality is no longer solely dependent on China. Table 4.6 lists the ten countries that contributed most to the reduction in international inequality besides China for the period 2000–2010.

TABLE 4.6   Real GDP per Capita Growth Rate (2000–2010) and
Population Share of Countries Contributing the Most to
Reduction in International Inequality, Ranked
According to Their Contribution

	CHANGE IN REAL INCOME PER CAPITA (%)	WORLD POPULATION SHARE (%)
World	24.38	100.0
China	152.61	19.66
India	80.93	17.34
Russia	76.81	2.06
Indonesia	44.23	3.59
Vietnam	80.74	1.32
Ukraine	88.81	0.67
Bangladesh	51.05	2.31
Kazakhstan	150.55	0.23
Thailand	42.71	0.98
Azerbaijan	275.76	0.12

Note: Contribution to reduction in international inequality measured in mean log deviation.
Source: Heston, Summers, and Aten 2012.

If these rising stars' economic growth accelerates, and if the growth of internal inequality in these economies, like that in China, is not big enough to offset their international inequality-reducing effect, then it is possible that they will pick up the slack left by China to perpetuate the reduction in overall global inequality in the decades to come. But the core issue is still whether other countries in the developing world can follow in the footsteps of China's prolonged high-speed growth.

In general, two types of countries have the potential to boom ahead and take China's place in bridging the income divide between the West and the rest. The first type of country benefits directly from trade with and investment from China. Such countries include many natural-resource exporters in Latin America and Africa that have thrived under China's mounting demand for their exports. They also usually receive a rising amount of FDI from China in infrastructure construction, resource-extractive industries, and manufacturing. At the same time, however, there is some debate as to whether China's net impact on these countries' development prospects is positive or negative in the long run.

The second type of country is a demographic heavyweight, such as India. As in China, economic growth faster than the world average rate in these countries might have a large impact on global distribution of income, given their large share of the world population. But the question for these countries, India in particular, is whether they have the right conditions for China-like uninterrupted growth. In sum, as China's contribution to the reduction in global inequality is destined to fade and reverse in the years to come, the continued shrinking of global inequality depends on whether China can help elevate other developing countries' economic growth through trade and investment and whether other populous developing countries can replicate the Chinese experience of long-lasting rapid growth.

The Developing World in China's Shadow

During the past decade, China's increasing trade and investment links with other developing countries, particularly in Africa, have attracted increasing attention and triggered debates in both developing and developed regions. In many journalistic and polemical writings on the issues, some see China as a new savior to the developing world that has helped release downtrodden developing countries from the tyranny of Western powers' neocolonialism. Unlike Western countries and international financial organizations dominated by the United States and Europe that often tie aid, loans, investments, and trade agreements with requests for reform and policies that favor Western interests, China putatively acts as an alternative source of trade and investment with no strings attached, thus facilitating more rapid development in the developing world. However, some authors accuse China of being just another neocolonial power that seeks to extract natural resources from other developing countries for its own developmental needs but in the process neglects those countries' long-term development (for more on this topic, see chapter 5). Worse, China is seen as a mercantilist country that aggressively tries to expand its export market at the expense of the manufacturing sector in other developing countries. Some analysts say that China's mounting appetite for resources and its cheap manufactured exports have effectively been deindustrializing many economies in the developing world, pushing them back to a dependence solely on their exports of natural resources.[4]

More serious academic research has been emerging in recent years to address these conflicting claims about China's impact on other developing countries. What these studies find, in fact, is a more complex picture that fails to be captured by politicians' and critical commentators' polemics. In the field of development studies, many works suggest the virtue of diversifying away from natural-resources exports for developing countries. From colonial times to the postindependence era, many developing countries have been locked in a "monoculture" model, under which each of their economies relies on the export of a single or a few agricultural products and raw materials to developed countries. The fluctuations in commodities prices in the world market far beyond these monoculture exporters' control make their developmental path unstable (with the exception of oil exporters). Even if the commodities they export enjoy stable and decent prices, their economies are still vulnerable to the "Dutch disease" or the "resource curse"—that is, the world demand for their exported commodities drives up their currencies and thus curtails the development of their export-manufacturing sectors and encourages conspicuous consumption of luxury imports among the elite. This means that if developing countries want to foment balanced and sustainable growth, they need to contain the natural-resources export sector as well as the vested interests tied to that sector to make room for the growth of other sectors, above all manufacturing (see, e.g., Shafer 1994; Sachs and Warner 1995; Karl 1997; Gallagher and Porzecanski 2010).

In the postwar era, most developing countries have been trying to reduce their reliance on natural-resource exports and to promote industrialization, either through import-substitution industrialization (that is, blocking imports of foreign manufactures to support domestic industries' market share in domestic markets) or through export-oriented industrialization (that is, subsidizing and promoting local industrial products sold on the world market). The China boom has disrupted such endeavors, however. First, the rising demand for oil, raw materials, agricultural products, and the like from China has driven up commodities prices in the international market, generating huge returns to commodities exporters, even though they may not directly export to China. An IMF report confirms that "China is becoming increasingly important for commodity markets. Its role in the market and its impact on world trade and prices varies by commodity; in particular, China has become the dominant importer of base metals and agricultural raw material, with a smaller, but growing role, in food and energy markets" (Roache 2012: 21).

A consequence of rising profits in commodities exporters has been the boom and expansion of mining industries and agribusinesses across the developing world, countervailing the developmentalist efforts to check the expansion of the commodities-exporting sector in many countries. For example, land used for soybean cultivation in Brazil doubled between 1990 and 2005, which led to the vast expansion of farmland deep into the environmentally sensitive Amazon frontier to cater to the demand from China, which constituted 42.7 percent of Brazil's soybean export market (Gallagher and Porzencanski 2010: 31–32; U.S. Department of Agriculture 2004). The copper-mining industry in Chile and other Latin American countries also expanded significantly during the same period. Latin America's total export of copper increased by 237.5 percent between 2000 and 2006, with the increased amount originating mostly from China's demand (Gallagher and Porzencanski 2010: 22, passim). The same happened in Africa. Besides oil-producing countries such as Sudan and Nigeria, countries that are rich in metal ores benefit from China's increasing demand. Zambia's large increase in copper exports driven by China is a case in point.

Yet even while China helps boost raw-materials exporters in developing countries, its efficient, low-cost manufacturing sector has been heightening competitive pressure on the manufacturing sectors in these countries. Some argue that the very genesis of China's export-oriented manufacturing in the mid-1990s is connected to the economic trouble of other Asian exporters such as Malaysia and Thailand and that China did contribute in part to the outbreak of the Asian financial crisis of 1997–1998. The one-off devaluation of the RMB by 33 percent in 1994 ushered in the boom of low-cost and export-oriented manufacturing in China (see chapter 3). It rendered the manufacturing establishment of China's Southeast Asian neighbors, which already suffered from increasing wages and appreciating currencies, less competitive. The ensuing slowdown in economic growth, in addition to loose lending and other forces that shifted these countries farther away from manufacturing and into financial speculation, paved the way for the crisis, as some argue (e.g., Krause 1998).

For Latin American industries, Kevin Gallagher and Roberto Porzecanski have compiled an index to look at how much of a threat Chinese manufactured exports are. It turns out that more than 80 percent of major Latin American countries' manufactured exports are under direct or partial threat from Chinese manufactures (2010: 50) (see table 4.7). Both international and domestic markets for Latin American manufactures have been inundated with Chinese goods.[5]

Taking together the trend of the expanding raw-materials exporting sector and the trend of increasing competitive pressures on domestic industries, we can see that China has created conditions that may lead to deindustrialization and a return to a dependence on natural-resources exports in the developing world. However, whether and how much this change will damage or benefit the long-term developmental prospects of individual developing countries vary and hinge more on each individual country's internal political economies (see Kurtz 2009).

For example, the governments of most Latin American countries regulate or own their mining corporations, so they have at least some

TABLE 4.7   Percentage of Manufactured Exports Threatened by Chinese Exports as of 2006

	DIRECTLY THREATENED (%)	PARTIALLY THREATENED (%)	TOTAL (%)
Argentina	37	59	96
Brazil	20	70	91
Chile	29	53	82
Colombia	15	66	81
Costa Rica	36	60	96
Mexico	70	28	99
All Latin American & Caribbean countries	62	31	94

Source: Gallagher and Porzecanski 2010: 50.

leverage over the pricing and output volume of the materials in demand. They are capable of negotiating with China and other customers to attain deals that maximize their interests. Governments can also establish institutions that direct gains from the booming natural-resources sector to other uses, including long-term investment, support of economic diversification, and poverty alleviation. There are some exceptionally successful cases. For example, the Chilean government has instituted the Economic and Social Stability Fund, which siphons part of the profit from the resource-exporting sector during boom times and spends it on currency-market intervention, investment, and fiscal stimulus during down times. This approach smooths the impact of commodity-price volatility on the economy at large, even though Chile is becoming more dependent on raw-material exports (Gallagher and Porzecanski 2010: 32–37). And the Brazilian government under Luiz Inácio Lula da Silva created a number of efficient redistributive institutions (such as the well-known Bolso Familia conditional cash-transfer program to the poor) just as the Brazilian economy was enjoying a raw-material export boom. These institutions ensure that the profits from the raw-materials bonanza are distributed more evenly and directed to long-term investment crucial to the country's sustainable growth (Anderson 2011; Baiocchi, Braathen, and Teixeira 2013; Campbell and Boodoosingh 2015).

In contrast to Latin America, where many resource-extracting sectors are grounded in companies located within the region or even owned by the state, many African countries lack competitive homegrown mining corporations and have relied on foreign companies to extract their resources. Their increasing export of raw materials to China is without exception accompanied by the investment of Chinese state enterprises in their mining sectors. In many cases, Chinese state companies, together with other transnational mining corporations, own and run the whole commodity chain, from the mining sites to the ports that export the raw materials. Under these circumstances, African governments are in a much less favorable position to negotiate with their Chinese partners (see Haglund 2009; C. Lee 2009; Haroz 2011; also see French 2014; Jiang 2009). It is still debatable whether Chinese companies' practices are worse or better than the practices of Western companies entrenched in the African natural-resources sector. But one thing is for sure: the Chinese companies tend to prioritize their own interests over their host countries' long-term developmental prospect. The copper industry in Zambia—where Chinese mining corporations expand, casualize labor, and collude with the corrupt local government to maximize short-term gains—is a case in point (Haglund 2009; C. Lee 2009).

The impact of the competition from China's manufactured exports likewise varies from country to country, depending on the place in the value chain occupied by each particular country's industrial establishment. Table 4.7 shows that although most industries in most Latin American countries face universal competitive pressure from Chinese manufacturers, some are having a harder time than others. Mexico stands out as the country that has been affected the most because its manufacturing establishment is focused on a very similar range of products exported by Chinese manufacturers. Both Mexican manufacturing and Chinese manufacturing depend heavily on the North American market.

If we take a broader look at the impact of Chinese manufacturing on Asia and on Latin America, we can readily see a more variegated picture. After China's rise as an export-manufacturing powerhouse precipitated the Asian financial crisis, many of China's Asian neighbors adjusted their industrial structure and integrated better with China, as noted in chapter 3. Once China's neighboring economies shifted their focus to products either higher or lower on the value chain than what China produces, they no longer competed head to head with China. Moreover, a large part of China's export sector comprises processing manufacturing, in which China imports components from other manufacturers in Asia and assembles them into final products, which are then exported to the destination market as "made in China" items. As such, a regional network of production has developed within Asia, in which manufacturers supplying China with components and machineries benefit from China's rise as a manufacturing powerhouse. The situation for Latin American and African economies is very different from that of Asian economies because they enter into this Sinocentric global production network as natural-resource providers rather than as component suppliers.

If a sufficient number of developing countries attain long-term high-speed growth by benefiting from their trade and investment link with China, the recent reduction in global inequality will continue even after China turns from a net global inequality reducer to a net enhancer. The reduction in global inequality might also continue if other population giants sustain their high-speed growth independently, as China has done. India, with a population of 1.2 billion, which is nearly 17 percent (as of 2012) of the world's population, is an obvious candidate.

In the 1980s and 1990s, when China started to take off as a new economic powerhouse, India was still often ridiculed for its "Hindu rate of growth," which many analysts attributed to its low-capacity, fragmented state (Chibber 2006). But when the Indian government embarked on economic reform in the aftermath of a financial crisis in 1991, which was in part unleashed by the termination of assistance from Russia when the Soviet Union collapsed, economic growth picked up during the 1990s and 2000s (see Subramanian 2008). This continued growth leads many to see India as an up-and-coming giant on par with China (see figure 4.5).

Owing to the history of geopolitical rivalry between China and India, India's trade and investment link with China has been minimal, and India's takeoff has largely been an independent event not connected to any pull from a rising China. Although some free marketeers would simplistically explain India's rise in terms of its economic liberalization in the

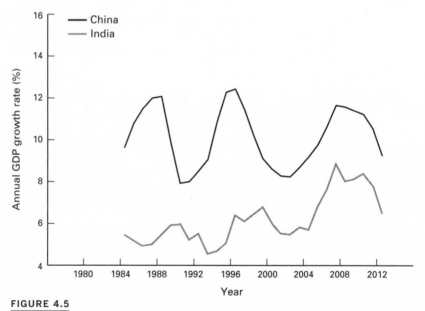

FIGURE 4.5

Annual GDP growth rate of India and China, 1980–2012 (five-year moving average). *Source*: World Bank n.d.

TABLE 4.8   Economic Structures of China and India in the Mid-2000s

	CHINA	INDIA
Household consumption share of GDP (%)	~30–40	~50–60
Fixed capital-formation share of GDP (%)	~40	~30
Export share of GDP (%)	30–40	10–20
Gini coefficient	0.43*	0.33
Agricultural terms of trade with manufacturing	Declining	Improving

* The World Bank estimation is smaller than the figures in table 4.3.
Sources: For the first four rows, World Bank n.d.; for the last row, Bardhan 2010: 46.

1990s, just as they attribute China's economic success solely to marketization, one would readily find a vast difference in the two countries' political economies. As table 4.8 shows, India's economic structure is nearly a mirror image of China's. Whereas China's growth has been driven by exports and fixed-asset investment, India's growth has been driven more by domestic consumption, and the weights of export and investment are far less significant there.

In fact, the strength and weakness of the "Indian model" of development are opposite of those of the "China model." India is plagued by an underdevelopment of infrastructure and a weak current-account surplus, while enjoying strong domestic consumption and lower urban–rural and interregional inequalities. In contrast, China has been characterized by concern about debt-driven overinvestment in infrastructure, an excess trade surplus, a low domestic-consumption share in its economy, and high urban–rural and interregional inequalities. Some see China as the genuine model of sustained high-speed growth and assert that India will have to learn from the Chinese model to achieve long-lasting rapid growth (e.g., Sen 2013). But others use the hare–tortoise competition as an analogy for the China–India competition, arguing that India's path of growth, though slow to start, is more sustainable in the long run because it depends less on foreign demands and debt-financed investment (Huang Y. and Khanna 2003; cf. Bardhan 2012). This projection of future growth in India and China involves the evaluation of the strengths and weaknesses of two different models of political economy, which is too complicated to deal with here. Time will tell whether the Chinese path or the Indian path will prevail or the two paths will eventually meet in the middle point when China and India continue to balance their political economies in opposite directions.

This chapter demonstrates that China made a solid contribution to reduction in global income inequality in 1980–2010, even if we take into consideration the drastic increase in internal inequality in China. But it also shows that this contribution is set to fade or reverse when China's average income level surpasses the world average. The continuation of the historic reduction in global inequality over the past several decades depends on whether other populous poor countries can grow rapidly in the new international context of development precipitated by the China boom. China has surely changed the context of development with its competitive manufactured exports and its huge appetite for raw materials. Whether this context is enhancing or hindering the prospect of development in the developing world varies from country to country. It is therefore uncertain whether the historic reversal of the two-centuries-long trend of polarization between the West and the rest in 1980–2010 will continue into decades to come.

The prospect of economic growth never involves just economic processes. It also depends on the balance of power and relative negotiation advantages and disadvantages among different countries in the international system. We cannot get a full sense of what the future of global inequality will look like unless we seriously consider the influence of geopolitics. Many have claimed that China, making use of its increasing economic influence in the world, has been fundamentally reshaping the global political order by toppling the United States from its position of dominance and that developing countries are empowered politically under the new geopolitical configuration brought about by China's rise. In the next chapter, I show that this perception of China's subversive impact on the global political order is greatly exaggerated.

FIVE

A Post-American World?

MANY ASSERT THAT, accompanying the economic rise of China, the global political center of gravity has been shifting from West to East and from developed countries to developing ones. British writer Martin Jacques's book *When China Rules the World* (2009), discussed in the introduction, is an example of this argument. Roger Altman, a veteran investment banker and former deputy secretary of the U.S. Treasury, published the article "The Great Crash, 2008: The Geopolitical Setback for the West" (2009) in *Foreign Affairs* in the wake of the global financial crisis, arguing that the West's financial distress and China's continuous robust economic performance were accelerating the waning of American's global power and the waxing of China's. Journalist Fareed Zakaria even titled his 2009 best seller *The Post-American World*, seeing the rise of China at the expense of the United States as a global power shift comparable to the rise of the West during the Renaissance and rise of the United States in the twentieth century.

This stipulation of China's rising global power at the expense of the West in general and of the United States in particular is in fact a continuation of the theme of U.S. decline raised since the 1970s. This theme crosses the left–right divide and is shared by conservative, liberal, and radical authors. For example, looking closely at the U.S. defeat in Vietnam and its persistent fiscal, economic, and sociopolitical crises in the

1970s, in conjunction with economic challenges from West Germany and Japan, Marxian world-system analysts reason inductively that the United States had entered a phase of hegemonic decline just as the United Kingdom did in the early twentieth century and as the Dutch did in the eighteenth century (Wallerstein 1979; Arrighi 1994; Arrighi and Silver 1999; Chase-Dunn et al. 2005). Drawing on experiences of past hegemonic transitions from the Dutch to the British and from the British to the Americans, world systemists have for several decades enthusiastically looked for potential candidates for a new hegemon that will provide global leadership and reformulate the world system, with Germany (or a unifying Europe) and Japan topping the list in the 1970s through the 1990s. In more recent years, they have started to see China as a plausible new global leader in the twenty-first century, with Andre Gunder Frank's book *ReORIENT* (1998) spearheading such speculation.

From a different vantage point, Samuel Huntington (1996) also sees the long decline of U.S. and Western power in politicomilitary, demographic, and economic terms. He argues that territories controlled by Western powers have been receding ever since the decolonization movement began in the mid–twentieth century. Demographically, low birth rates have been turning the Western population into a minority in the world. Economically, the "Sinic" world has been roaring ahead and in this view is poised to replace the Western world as the world's economic center. Huntington purports that the Sinic world, empowered by its newfound economic might, is becoming increasingly assertive and is developing an alliance with the Muslim world, which has been predisposed to hate Western civilization. The shift in global power from the West to the East will eventually lead to a showdown between Western civilization and the Sinic–Islamic alliance.

This persistent view of the decline of the West and the concomitant rise of China's global power has become so popular that U.S. politicians have started running campaign commercials accusing their opponents of being responsible for American decline and an imminent Chinese domination of the country.[1] But more sober writers find that the perception of falling U.S. global power and the rise of China as a new subversive superpower may be exaggerated and that China is little more than a status quo power in the international system (see, e.g., Johnston 2003; Shambaugh 2013). The situation is the same as when talk of the rise of Germany and Japan as challengers to the United States back in the 1970s was exaggerated. In this chapter, I discuss how the decline of U.S. dominance in world politics, although true, has been slowed and delayed thanks ironically to support from its supposed challengers, China above all. I also discuss how China has both helped to perpetuate the existing U.S.-centered global neoliberal order and reshaped the balance of power in this order at the same time. The crux of these paradoxes is the U.S. dollar's persistent hegemony in the world economy.

World Power and World Money

After three decades of discussion about a U.S. decline, some scholars have started to find anomalies in this thesis, despite the similarities of this supposed decline to earlier hegemonic declines —that is, the eighteenth-century Dutch decline and the early-twentieth-century British decline. For example, Giovanni Arrighi (1994) notes that the United States, even with the absolute economic supremacy that it once enjoyed in the 1950s and 1960s gone, has managed to maintain a military apparatus that is still far beyond challenge by any other major capitalist power. In particular, Europe and Japan, the two economic powers that at one time posed grave challenges to the United States, have only negligible military capability and depend on the United States for their security needs. This military superiority leads Arrighi to postulate that one possible post-American-hegemony scenario would be a U.S.-centered global empire, which would rest on America's unmatched means of coercion around the world.

Moreover, the economic challenge that Japan and Europe once posed to the United States has been unsustainable. Japan has sunk into an economic quagmire since the 1990s, and Europe's integration encountered huge obstacles when nationalist sentiments against the European Union rose in the 2000s and when the euro crisis erupted after 2008. Moreover, the U.S. share of world GDP has not declined as dramatically as the hegemonic decline thesis suggests, dropping from a height of 39 percent in 1960 to 23 percent in 2010 (figure 5.1) (World Bank n.d.). Leo Panitch and Sam Gindin (2012) even claim that U.S. global power fully recovered from the economic crisis and the setback in Vietnam in the 1970s and reached its zenith by the 2000s, when it successfully imposed the global

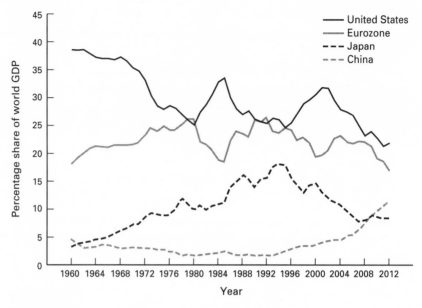

FIGURE 5.1
Share of world GDP in current U.S. dollars, 1960–2012. *Source*: World Bank n.d.

neoliberal order on all corners of the post–Cold War world. The productive and state capacity of the United States has in truth deteriorated
from the 1970s to today, as illustrated by its worsening current account
and fiscal deficits, but the question is how and why it can still hold up its
economic dominance and sustain a formidable military apparatus.

Looking closely, we find that the persisting U.S. economic and military power is attributable largely to the ongoing status of the U.S. dollar
as the most widely used reserve currency and international transaction
currency in the world for the past thirty years. The internationally dominant status of the dollar, which many refer to as the "dollar standard"
(e.g., Bai 2012), allows the United States to borrow internationally at low
interest rates and to print money to repay its debt as a last resort. This
capability to borrow in its own currency has permitted the United States
to solve many instances of domestic economic malaise and to maintain
the most enormous, active war machine in the world through external
indebtedness, while avoiding the kind of debt crises that have wreaked
havoc on many developing economies because they have had to borrow

in creditors' currency (mostly U.S. dollars). Some refer to the exceptional advantage the dollar standard confers to the United States as an "exorbitant privilege" (Eichengreen 2011) or an extreme form of seigniorage, under which all foreign private and public institutions relying on the dollar as the medium of economic activities are effectively paying tribute to the United States. Ironically, the persistence of this exorbitant privilege is now being maintained by the rise of China as the biggest foreign holder of U.S. dollar–dominated assets, mainly in the form of U.S. Treasury bonds. To understand this dynamic, we must first look to the historical trajectory of the dollar's rise to its status as a hegemonic currency and why this hegemonic status was not destabilized by successive economic challenges to the United States from Germany and Japan.

The post–World War II global hegemonic role of the dollar was sealed in the Bretton Woods Conference of 1944, which established the dollar's gold convertibility under the promised rate of thirty-five dollars for one ounce of gold. It also established the pegs of major currencies to the dollar in the capitalist world. The dollar standard was further facilitated by the postwar Marshall Plan, which vastly elevated the dollar's liquidity in the world economy. This arrangement enabled the dollar to complete its replacement of British sterling as the dominant currency in foreign-exchange reserves and international trade around the globe. The stability of the resulting global monetary order in the 1950s and 1960s was warranted by America's enormous gold reserve (two-thirds of the world total), current-account surpluses, and unparalleled competitiveness in the world economy as well as by the rise of London's Eurodollar market, where the abundant offshore dollars in the world economy, including the dollars held by Soviet bloc countries, began to be traded and invested. The dollar standard was not only a reflection of American prowess but also a means through which the United States provided leadership to the capitalist world, securing a stable monetary environment for growth.

The collapse of the Bretton Woods system in 1971 can be traced back to the rising productivity of Europe, West Germany in particular, and of Japan in the 1960s following their full recovery from World War II. Increasing international competition, coupled with the rising wage demand of domestic organized labor and the escalating fiscal and current-account deficits incurred by the troubled U.S. involvement in Vietnam, led to a run on the dollar and the outflow of gold reserves from the

United States. Nixon was left with few choices but to suspend the gold convertibility of the dollar in 1971, forcing other major capitalist economies to undo their currencies' peg from the dollar. The abolition of gold convertibility allowed the United States to attempt to reduce its current-account deficit and to revive its economic competitiveness through dollar devaluation.

Upon the collapse of the Bretton Woods system, many predicted the end of the dollar's hegemony and the rise of a multipolar global economic order grounded on more or less even domination by multiple major currencies such as the yen and the Deutsche mark. Attempts abounded to forecast the trajectory of the dollar's decline by drawing parallels to sterling's decline in the early twentieth century (e.g., Strange 1971). What is puzzling is that this predicted multipolar moment never came, and the dollar's hegemony continued for four more decades, up until today. Even with the formation of the euro as a competitor, the dollar remains the most widely used reserve currency in the world (see figure 5.2).

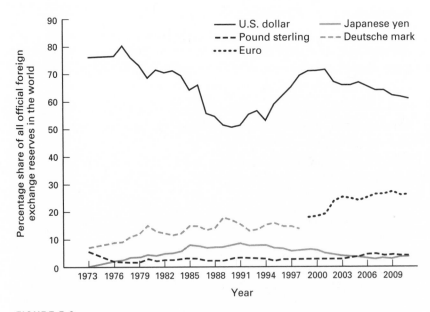

FIGURE 5.2

Shares of currencies in identified official holdings of foreign exchange in the world, 1976–2012. *Source*: International Monetary Fund n.d.c.

TABLE 5.1   Currency Distribution of Global Foreign-Exchange Market Turnover (Percentage out of 200)

	1998	2001	2004	2007	2010	2013
U.S. dollar	86.8	89.9	88.0	85.6	84.9	87.0
Pound sterling	11.0	13.0	16.5	14.9	12.9	11.8
Deutsche mark	30.5					
French franc	5.0					
Japanese yen	21.7	23.5	20.8	17.2	19.0	23.0
Euro		37.9	37.4	37.0	39.1	33.4
Mexican peso	0.5	0.8	1.1	1.3	1.3	2.5
Chinese yuan / RMB	0.0	0.0	0.1	0.5	0.9	2.2

Source: Bank for International Settlement 2014.

The same can be said regarding the use of the dollar in international transactions (see table 5.1). The euro did not in fact gain much ground in comparison to the global use of Europe's national currencies combined before its launch. Although the dollar's hegemony under the Bretton Woods system was a manifestation of overwhelming U.S. economic might, its lingering hegemony after the Bretton Woods collapse was the most significant lifeline that the United States relied on to slow its economic decline. The hegemony of the dollar, as a fiat money since 1971, lasted even longer after Bretton Woods than under Bretton Woods.

The dollar's lasting prowess was first made possible by the exchange between the United States and its military allies during the Cold War period, when the former provided a security umbrella and weapons in exchange for the latter's support of the use of dollars in trade and foreign-exchange reserves. Numerous episodes at the height of the Cold War illustrate well the role of U.S. global military domination in warranting the dollar standard, when the governments of America's European allies were requested to support the dollar by increasing their purchase of dollar instruments and U.S. military supplies, paid for in dollars, under the explicit threat of a reduction of U.S. troops stationed in their countries. Such reduction could have immediately generated a security crisis, forcing those governments to increase military spending to pick up the slack (Gavin 2004; see also Eichengreen 2011: 71). Susan Strange (1980) notes that West Germany has always been the "obedient ally" that pays significant contribution to the maintenance of the dollar standard, which it did even after U.S. gold convertibility was suspended in 1971 (see also Eichengreen 2011: 71). Regarding other countries dependent on U.S. military protection, some analysts even find a positive correlation, which extends far into the post–Cold War era, between the number of U.S. troops deployed in a country and that country's use of dollars (Posen 2008). As shown in column one of table 5.2, before the 1990s countries that purchased the most U.S. Treasury bonds as part of their foreign-exchange reserve mix tended to be the ones that hosted the largest U.S. military bases.

This dollar–security nexus ensured that the dollar would remain the dominant foreign-reserve currency in western Europe and Japan. It also ensured that the monarchial and authoritarian oil-producing states, which needed U.S. protection even more, would invoice their oil exports in dollars. Large-scale governmental purchases of dollar instruments by key capitalist powers and the use of dollars in oil and arms trades

TABLE 5.2   Global Ranking of U.S. Military Base Size in the Top-Five Foreign Holders of U.S. Treasury Bonds

1988		2000		2009	
Top-5 Holders of T-Bonds	Ranking of Military Base Size	Top-5 Holders of T-Bonds	Ranking of Military Base Size	Top-5 Holders of T-Bonds	Ranking of Military Base Size
Japan	3	Japan	2	China	n/a
Germany	1	United Kingdom	5	Japan	3
United Kingdom	4	China	n/a	Brazil	n/a
Canada	n/a	Germany	1	Russia	n/a
Belgium	16	Taiwan	n/a	Taiwan	n/a

Note: Size of U.S. military base measured in total number of military personnel stationed in the country concerned.

Source: Data compiled by the author from U.S. Department of Defense n.d.; U.S. Treasury n.d.

accounted for this currency's vast market liquidity, motivating private enterprises and other governments to use it for their reserves and trade settlement.

This geopolitical support of the dollar's hegemony remained unchallenged until the end of the Cold War in the early 1990s. With the Soviet bloc as a common security threat gone, regional powers used to being held hostage by the U.S. security umbrella tried to break free of the U.S. dollar–security nexus. The Maastricht Treaty of 1992, which presaged the rise of the euro, was an explicit attempt to create a new currency that would rival the dollar. But Europe's continuous dependence on the United States to defend its geopolitical interests, as shown by the Kosovo War in 1999, as well as the lack of a centralized monetary authority and fiscal integration in the eurozone have been undermining the ascendancy of the euro as a true alternative to the dollar (see Gowan 1999, 2004; Krugman 2012; Hung 2013). Some even speculate that one reason for the U.S. invasion of Iraq in 2003 was the need to preempt the realization of an Iraq-Europe pact under which Iraq would denominate its future oil exports in euros in exchange for Europe's support of the lifting of United Nations sanctions against Iraq. This deal, if it had materialized, would have unsettled the dollar's grip on the oil market and enhanced the euro's status as an international currency at the expense of the dollar (Gulick 2005).

With the U.S. global war machine remaining unchallenged and the euro's inability to displace the dollar, the dollar managed to continue its global dominance after the Cold War. Such dominance during and after the Cold War gave Washington unparalleled leeway to adjust the value of the dollar, either in a unilateral way or through twisting the arms of its geopolitical clients, to meet the needs of the U.S. domestic economy.

Figure 5.3 shows that although short-term fluctuations of the dollar's value might have stemmed from developments beyond Washington's control (such as the Iranian hostage crisis in 1979), Washington's initiatives still have a great deal of influence in steering the long-term direction of the dollar's value. These initiatives, even if they did not target currency issues primarily but were devised to solve specific domestic economic problems such as inflation (see Krippner 2011), led to the alternate appreciation or depreciation of the dollar. Such freedom of action enabled Washington to shape the dollar's value, either boosting its value at the price of a deteriorating current-account deficit (as in the

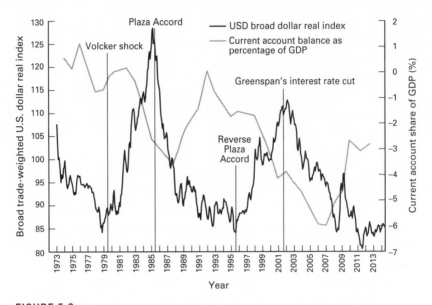

FIGURE 5.3

U.S. dollar trade-weighted currency index and the U.S. current-account balance as a percentage of GDP, 1973–2014. *Source*: U.S. Federal Reserve n.d.; World Bank n.d.

interest-rate hike at the beginning of the first Reagan administration and in the strong-dollar policy adopted by the Clinton administration) or improving the current-account balance at the price of dollar depreciation (as in the Plaza Accord of 1985, when the United States forced Japan and West Germany to appreciate their currencies against the dollar). In this way, Washington has maintained the dollar as a sound currency that is backed up either by an improving U.S. current account balance or by a strong, stable value of the dollar, making the cycle of dollar value and the cycle of current-account balance move in opposite directions. This freedom of action would not have been possible if the United States had not precluded the rise of potentially competing currencies by means of its continuous political-military supremacy in the world (Hung 2014).

But in 2000–2008, the dollar's credibility seemed to be threatened by an unprecedented simultaneous deterioration of the dollar value and of the current-account deficit (see Milesi-Ferretti 2008). This simultaneous deterioration is attributable largely to the rise of China as a formidable low-cost exporter to the United States under a currency peg with the dollar.

China's Addiction to U.S. Treasuries

Chapter 3 noted that the rise of China's export sector was enabled by a series of policy changes in the mid-1990s that precipitated an expanding stream of low-wage rural migrant laborers. This export-oriented path of growth was also facilitated by China's currency peg with the United States that kept Chinese exports competitively cheap. This path is a replication and extension of the earlier export-oriented growth of Japan and other East Asian economies, though on a much larger scale. Japan and the Asian Tigers were loyal allies to the United States during the Cold War because their economic boom was made possible by conscious U.S. policy in their favor to ensure their rise as a capitalist bulwark encircling Communist China. Starting in the 1980s, when the East Asian exporters' tension with China eased and the U.S. fiscal deficit soared as a result of neoliberal tax cuts and escalating military expenditures at the final stage of the Cold War, these exporters, instead of breaking away from the orbit of U.S. hegemony, tightened their ties to the United States by financing its skyrocketing fiscal deficit (see Murphy 1997).

Trade surplus resulting from the export sector and a high savings rate enabled these Asian exporters to accumulate substantial foreign-exchange reserves. They devoted most of these reserves to the purchase of U.S. Treasury bonds, turning themselves into the largest creditors of the United States. Their financing of the U.S. fiscal deficit allowed the U.S. government to expand expenditures while cutting taxes. It also prevented Asian currencies and hence the prices of Asian exports from rising in the U.S. market. It fueled the American appetite for Asian exports, and so the resulting increase in trade surpluses in these Asian economies led to yet more purchases of U.S. Treasury bonds. The two mutually reinforcing processes of increasing Asian exports to the United States and increasing Asian holdings of U.S. public debt continuously deepened East Asia's market and financial dependence on the United States. Asia's massive investment in low-yield U.S. Treasury bonds was tantamount to a tribute payment through which Asia's savings were transformed into Americans' consumption power, prolonging U.S. prosperity but creating a financial bubble in the 1980s and beyond.

China's export-oriented boom is a continuation and escalation of this market and financial dependence on the United States. The Chinese

RMB has been pegged to the dollar since the RMB's 1994 devaluation as an export-boosting measure. After 2001, when the dollar began to weaken following Federal Reserve chairman Alan Greenspan's aggressive interest-rate cuts, China stepped up its purchase of U.S. Treasury bonds to keep the RMB from appreciating against the dollar (Hung 2009c). In 2008, China surpassed Japan as the biggest foreign holder of these bonds (see figure 5.4).

The boom of Chinese exports to the United States under a fixed RMB–dollar exchange rate and the skyrocketing global price of oil, attributable in part to the dollar's depreciation and in part to China's mounting appetite for oil, led to America's deteriorating current-account deficit despite a weakening dollar in 2001–2008. The U.S. current-account balance improved only in the aftermath of the 2008 economic crisis, which forced a contraction in imported consumer goods in the United States. According to one estimation, one-third of the U.S. current-account deficit, which at its height in 2006 amounted to 6 percent of GDP, was due

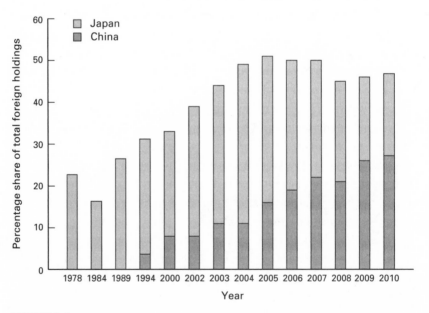

FIGURE 5.4

China's and Japan's holdings of U.S. Treasury bonds as a percentage of total foreign holdings, 1978–2010. *Source*: U.S. Treasury n.d.

to Chinese manufactured imports, and another third was due to petroleum imports (Desai 2007). In 2012, the U.S. trade deficit with China
increased to 43 percent of the total U.S. trade deficit (U.S. Census Bureau n.d.). The part of the U.S. trade deficit originating from oil imports
is also indirectly related to the China boom and not just because China
drives up the price of oil globally. Following the 1970s oil shocks, the U.S.
trade deficit with oil producers did not worsen despite the soaring price
of U.S. oil imports because these imports were balanced by U.S. exports
to many oil-producing countries, including arms exports. This ceased to
be the case in the 2000s, when oil producers' increasing exports to the
United States were no longer matched by their imports from the United
States because their purchase of Chinese manufactured exports rose at
the expense of American goods (Blumenthal 2005; *Economist* 2012b;
Fardoust 2012).

The level of U.S. trade deficit in China's hands far exceeds the level
that all of earlier East Asian exporters had ever attained in total. Many
analysts are alarmed that China's massive exports and credits to the
United States, unlike the earlier exports and credits from Asian allies of
the United States, are posing a threat to the sustainability of the dollar
standard and U.S. economic vitality.[2] They worry that the RMB–dollar
peg and China's growing and unprecedentedly large contribution to the
U.S. current-account deficit have reduced the room for Washington to
strengthen the dollar and improve its current-account balance alter-
nately, hence eroding international confidence in this currency. Most of
all, many fear that China's hoarding of U.S. Treasury bonds makes the
United States increasingly vulnerable to China, which enjoys geopolitical autonomy from Washington and does not rely on U.S. military protection, as earlier leading Asian purchasers of U.S. debt did (see table 5.2
in the previous section). China is theoretically capable of dumping its
dollar assets anytime to induce a run on the currency, financial collapse,
hyperinflation, and fiscal crisis in the United States. If this happens, it
would spell the final disintegration of the global dollar standard.[3]

But upon closer examination, we can see that China's massive purchase of Treasury bonds is not a threat; it is as beneficial to the United
States as earlier East Asian exporters' purchase of U.S. debts was. The
purchase has helped Washington pay for its ever-growing budget deficit, particularly during the ongoing wars in Iraq and Afghanistan. It also

establishes a floor for the dollar's plummet. According to U.S. Federal Reserve chairman Ben Bernanke's "saving gluts" hypothesis and Niall Ferguson's "Chimerica" thesis, large-scale purchase of U.S. Treasury bonds by China as well as by other emerging economies has facilitated prosperity in the U.S. financial and real-estate markets through its bonds-yield-repressing and hence interest-rate-repressing effect (Bernanke 2005; Ferguson and Schularick 2007). And China's low-cost exports, like those from Japan and the Asian Tigers in earlier times, help keep U.S. inflation low despite a diminishing interest rate in the United States. These benefits from China outweigh the damage it generates— that is, a simultaneous deterioration of the dollar value and the U.S. current-account deficit. It is why on the eve of the global financial crisis of 2008, Washington, although it occasionally complained about the RMB exchange rate and China's obsessive focus on exports, never seriously attempted to change the status quo of the U.S.–China economic symbiosis.

China's purchase of U.S. Treasury bonds has become a compulsion generated by its export-led model of development. China's dumping of these bonds owing to its geopolitical rivalry with the United States is unthinkable. The vested interests that propagated export-oriented growth in the 1990s—composed of coastal provincial governments, export manufacturers and their lobbyists, as well as officials from the Ministry of Commerce—were keen on perpetuating this model, preempting China's transformation to a more balanced developmental model driven by domestic consumption and depending less on the United States (see chapter 6). China's entrenched export-oriented growth makes the Chinese economy vulnerable to any major contraction of consumption demand in the United States and Europe. The Chinese government's large incentive to employ its foreign reserves to purchase U.S. debt is a result not only of the vast liquidity of and presumed stability of returns from U.S. Treasury bonds but also of an effort to secure the continuous increase in U.S. demand for China's exports by helping to prevent a freefall of the dollar, uncontrollable inflation, and an interest-rate hike in the United States. Some even contend that China needs U.S. Treasury bonds more than the United States needs to sell them to China (Morrison and Labonte 2013).

China's addiction to U.S. Treasury bonds is attributable to its trade structure, too. Combining the Sinocentric Asian network of production

TABLE 5.3   China (Hong Kong Included) Trade Balance with Different
             Economies (in Billion U.S.$)

	2005	2010
World	92.0	143.3
United States	145.4	201.2
European Union	91.1	154.9
Brazil	−5.1	−13.7
Japan	−34.1	−79.3
Korea	−48.8	−79.5
Middle East	−8.3	−23.2
Africa	−3.3	−5.5
Australia	−3.4	−29.6

Source: IMF n.d.a.

discussed in chapter 3 and China's appetite for raw materials from the
Global South discussed in chapter 4, China has become a nodal point
where raw materials, machines, and components from Asia and other
developing countries are put together into finished consumer goods to
be exported to the United States and Europe. Although China's overall
trade surplus has been growing, it has been running a rising trade deficit
with the whole world if we remove the United States and Europe from
the equation (see table 5.3). This means that the growth in the value of
China's exports to Asia, Latin America, Africa, and other regions has not
caught up with the growth of China's import of manufactured components, machineries, and raw materials from these regions. The United
States and Europe are the two sole sources of China's trade surplus.

China's exports to the United States, needless to say, are settled in
U.S. dollars. Even China's exports to Europe are settled in U.S. dollars
instead of in euros. Right after the Great Crash on Wall Street in 2008,
some Chinese exporters started to shift their settlement currency in
European trade to the euro. But soon thereafter, when the euro crisis
deepened, these exporters shifted back to the dollar (Reuters 2010).
For example, Natutux Apparel Corp., which exported U.S.$1.5 million
worth of fabric for outdoor use to Europe annually, shifted 50 percent
of its settlement to euros in 2009 after the dollar was clouded by the U.S.

financial crisis. But in 2010, when it became clear that the euro was in an even bigger crisis, the company cut back on euro settlement to just 5 percent of its exports. Trade officials from Jiangsu, an export-oriented province, explicitly reminded their exporters that "considering the euro's uncertain future, exports to European countries should be settled in yuan if possible. If the buyers do not agree on yuan settlement, then use the dollar." In the end, more than 80 percent of Chinese exports are paid for in dollars (Reuters 2010). As long as China's rising trade surplus comes mostly in dollars, the Chinese central bank has few choices than to invest these dollars in the most liquid and relatively safe dollar-denominated asset—U.S. Treasury bonds.

There have recently been reports about China's activities in using its foreign-exchange reserves to "buy the world" through outward FDI. Chinese companies' acquisition of Volvo Cars from Ford Motor and Chinese SOEs' inroads into the mining and energy sectors in both developing and developed countries from Zambia to Canada attracts a great deal of media attention. But as Peter Nolan (2012) points out, despite these high-profile cases, China's outward FDI is so far of negligible aggregate size in comparison with other major sources of FDI in the world. As Chinese official statistics show (table 5.4), the stock of China's nonfinancial outward FDI by the end of 2010 amounted to U.S.$298 billion (U.S.$317 billion if financial investment is included). This amount is even smaller than the outward FDI from Singapore, a city-state with a much smaller economy than China.

TABLE 5.4   Stock of China's Nonfinancial Outward FDI in Comparative Perspective (in Billion U.S.$)

COUNTRY	1990	2000	2010
China	4	28	298
Russia	n/a	20	434
Singapore	8	57	300
Brazil	41	52	181
India	0	2	92

Source: Davies 2012: table 1.1.

TABLE 5.5 Geographical Distribution of Stock of China's
Outward FDI to Selected Economies as of 2010

ECONOMY	PERCENTAGE
Hong Kong	62.8
Asia not including Hong Kong	9.1
Cayman Islands and British Virgin Islands	12.8
Africa	4.1
Europe	5.0
Australia	2.5
United States	1.5
Latin America and the Caribbean (excluding Cayman Island and British Virgin Islands)	1.1
Canada	0.8

Source: Chinese Ministry of Commerce 2011.

China's outward FDI looks even more insignificant if we take into consideration that 63 percent of that amount is FDI in Hong Kong (see table 5.5). The stock of China's outward FDI in places other than Hong Kong is less than U.S.$118 billion, which is less than one-tenth of the Chinese holdings in U.S. Treasury bonds, about U.S.$1.2 trillion. After all, no other market except the U.S. debt market has liquidity deep enough to absorb China's mammoth reserves. Paul Krugman (2009) was not exaggerating when he claimed that China has been caught in a "dollar trap," in which it has few choices other than to keep purchasing U.S. Treasury bonds, thus helping to perpetuate the dollar's hegemonic role (see also Prasad 2014).

This symbiosis between China and the United States, despite occasional squabbles over RMB revaluation and China's responsibility for the worsening U.S. current-account deficit, was strengthened in the aftermath of the global financial crisis of 2008. This is illustrated by the twofold increase in China's holdings of U.S. Treasury bonds between 2008 and 2013 despite its frequent complaint about the asset (table 5.6). China has become the biggest holder of U.S. Treasury bonds, only to be surpassed in 2011 by the U.S. Federal Reserve under the aggressive

TABLE 5.6   China's and Hong Kong's Holding of U.S. Treasury Securities Before
and After the Crisis Outbreak in 2008

	CHINA (IN BILLION U.S.$)	HONG KONG (IN BILLION U.S.$)	CHINA AND HONG KONG AS SHARE OF TOTAL FOREIGN HOLDINGS (%)	CHINA AND HONG KONG AS SHARE OF TOTAL OUTSTANDING (%)	FEDERAL RESERVE HOLDING AS SHARE OF TOTAL OUTSTANDING (%)
End of September 2008	618.2	65.5	24.5	11.8	8.3
End of February 2013	1,222.9	143.2	24.1	12.0	15.5

Source: U.S. Treasury n.d.

"quantitative easing" campaign of buying Treasury bonds. China's central bank and the U.S. Fed are now the most important factors in continued U.S. political and economic dominance through supporting the dollar standard.

Though China has the geopolitical autonomy that theoretically enables it to end its dependence on the dollar and even to end the dollar standard, in reality it has been helping perpetuate the standard—and hence U.S. geopolitical dominance—through its insurmountable addiction to U.S. Treasury bonds as the new opium stemming from its export-driven model of growth. The only way that China can cut off this addiction to U.S. debt is to shift away from its export-oriented model, which is not going to happen anytime soon (see chapter 6).

The Chinese government has recently been emphasizing its ambition to internationalize the RMB into a major reserve and international transaction currency as a way to maintain its export-oriented model while reducing its holding of U.S. dollars, hence curbing its addiction to U.S. public debt. But in actuality the Chinese RMB, which is not yet a fully convertible currency, has a long way to go to become a major international currency. Its share in international currency use is minuscule, falling way behind the British pound, the Japanese yen, and even the Mexican peso (see table 5.1). The RMB's rise to the status of a significant international currency will require its full convertibility, which in turn needs China's financial liberalization. This process will take time, even if the reluctant CCP finally agrees to take the very risky step of fully opening up its banking sector to the global economy (see Ma and Xu 2012). This step is far from an easy choice for the party–state because such an opening would be a blow to its command of the economy via its control of credits. Before any such radical shift takes place, all talk about the death of the global dollar standard and U.S. global dominance will remain little more than hot air.

Asia's Two Minds on China

Though China is not subverting and is even supporting the persistence of U.S. global power through its role as the main creditor of the United States, it has been employing its increasing economic clout as the biggest trade partner of many of its neighbors to attempt to establish its regional domination. The "rise of China" in Asia's regional politics is in fact a "resurgence." Throughout history, China had never been a political power with global reach, but the Chinese Empire did exercise hegemony in Asia until the Western imperial powers entered the scene to shatter the premodern Asian international order. Some do see the trajectory of China's rising power in post–Cold War Asia as at least a partial revival of a Sinocentric regional order, which follows a very different logic than the Westphalia international system developed in Europe and based on balance of power between states. To understand how China's political rise is contributing to the reshaping of the Asian political order, we need to take a look at China's relations with its Asian neighbors since imperial times.

According to Japanese historian Takeshi Hamashita (2008), premodern China's view of the world was dominated by a universalism in which the distinction between entities "inside" the empire and those "outside" the empire was not clear cut. The world in China's imperial view was made up of concentric circles, with the emperor at the center, directly governed provinces in the circle around the center, and tribute vassals located in the next circle. This world order diverged from the Western model of empire originating in Roman times and was not grounded on the logic of tributary extractions from the center. Instead, its operation rested on the principle of benevolence from the center and reciprocal loyalty from the periphery. Vassals of the Chinese Empire would send envoys and gifts to the imperial capital in tribute missions. In return, these missions obtained gifts of higher value from the emperor. Under this system, rulers in the tribute states derived their legitimacy from the Chinese emperor's endorsement, and the tribute states' loyalty was instrumental to the empire's border security. At times, the Chinese Empire sent troops to topple rulers of tribute vassals that refused to pledge allegiance to China, and then it installed rulers more subservient to the empire (Kang 2010).

This Sinocentric tributary system consolidated at the height of the Tang dynasty (618–906 C.E.), with Xi'an as the imperial capital that regularly received tribute missions from Central Asia. Into the Song dynasty, when nomadic invasions from the North pushed the empire's center of gravity to the south, official and unofficial Chinese activities in maritime Asia started to grow and culminated in the Ming dynasty (1368–1644 C.E.). With this maritime expansion, the Sinocentric tributary system extended into Southeast Asia and Japan. Concomitant with the growth of private maritime trade in Asia, tribute missions gained not only from the emperor's reciprocal gifts but also from the trading activities conducted by merchants who accompanied the tribute mission to China. With the rise of commerce along with the tribute missions, the Sinocentric tributary system was in fact a tribute–trade system (Hamashita 2008; Kang 2010).

This tribute–trade system was not always peaceful. At times, rising powers in the region sought to challenge Chinese hegemony either by withdrawing from their political economic connection with China or by building up their own tribute–trade networks. For example, after Hideyoshi reunified Japan and ended the country's warring period, he aspired to usurp China's place as Asia's center and invaded Korea in the 1590s. His effort failed with the Chinese army's expulsion of Japan's forces from Korea. His successor, Tokugawa shogun, adopted a seclusion policy that outlawed Japanese trade with China after 1635 (Howe 1996). Japan also established tribute relations with the Ryukyu kingdom, which had been China's tribute vassal. The Ryukyu kingdom was eventually incorporated into modern Japan in the 1870s and became today's Okinawa prefecture of Japan.

According to Hamashita, development of modern international relations in Asia needs to be discerned in light of the transformation of this indigenous tribute-trade system. The disintegration of the Sinocentric tribute-trade system with the rise of nationalism from within the system, such as Vietnam's anti-China movement in the late eighteenth century as well as the advent of Western colonization of China's tribute vassals—such as Burma and Vietnam—in the nineteenth century opened up space for Japan, which successfully industrialized and constructed a modern centralized state with the Meiji Restoration after 1868, to continue its ambition of usurping China's centrality in Asia. The effort to build the Great Asia Coprosperity Circle—which included Japan's colonization of Taiwan and Korea in 1895 and 1905, establishment of a puppet state in Manchuria in 1931, outright invasion of China proper in 1937, and brief colonization of a number of Southeast Asian states during World War II—was in some ways a continuation of the Hideyoshi dream of a Japan-centered Asian order.

After the collapse of the Japanese Empire at the end of World War II, the East Asian international order was replaced with a Cold War order. The United States became the hegemon that took the place of wartime Japan in dominating maritime Asia and in this way providing economic and military security to Japan, Korea, Taiwan, Hong Kong, Singapore, and much of Southeast Asia (Arrighi 1994: epilog). China, turning Communist in 1949, was at first a part of the Soviet bloc. But this Cold War order in Asia was complicated by China's increasing cleavage with the Soviet Union. In the 1950s, though still formally a keen ally of the Soviets, China became a key perpetuator of the nonaligned movement that sought to carve out an autonomous political space for newly independent and developing countries in Asia. After the Sino–Soviet split in the early 1960s, China pursued revolutionary diplomacy and provided financial and military support to revolutionary regimes and movements as in North Korea, Cambodia, and other Southeast Asian states. China's relation with these movements and regimes resembled the patronizing relationship between imperial China and the minidynasties in its neighboring vassal states. During the Cold War, this revival of a Sinocentric tributary order was only partial. China's influence over its neighbors was limited because many of them, such as North Korea, had also succumbed to the Soviet Union. China also patronized guerrilla movements not in power, such as the Communist parties in the Philippines and Malaysia, in addition to the Khmer Rouge, which was in power only briefly in Cambodia in 1975–1979 (see Brautigam 2011: 29–40).

With the end of the Cold War and the advent of China's economic revival, the resurgence of the Sinocentric tribute-trade order became more pronounced. As noted in chapter 3, China has become the biggest exporter of finished manufactured products in Asia, and a regional division of labor has emerged in which China's neighbors specialize in exporting capital goods and components to China, thus generating a Sinocentric network of production. This regional division of labor has made China the biggest trading partner of most Asian countries. In addition to its neighbors' increasing economic dependence on it through trade, China also has been active in providing its poorer neighbors with investments, loans, and other economic assistance (table 5.7) (Lum et al. 2009; Bower 2010). The many infrastructure projects in Cambodia and Myanmar carried out by Chinese state companies or financed by loans from Chinese state banks are a good example of this activity (e.g., see O'Conner 2011; Grimsditch 2012).

When the economic dependence of these Asian countries, rich and poor, on China deepens, China gains more leverage to influence their governments. Though the Chinese government always denies the link, it is believed that the threat of severing economic ties with targeted countries has become a diplomatic weapon available to China. With respect to its territorial disputes with Southeast Asian nations and Japan, China is rarely hesitant to use or threaten to use economic sanctions on whoever is violating its claim of sovereignty (Reilly 2012). For example, when China's territorial dispute with Japan over the Diaoyu/Senkakus Islands escalated in 2012 after Japan's government nationalized the islands, the official newspaper *China Daily* explicitly threatened that "China should use the World Trade Organization's clause of 'security exceptions' to impose economic sanctions on Japan" (*China Daily* 2012). Similar threats were intermittently suggested or even tried in China's territorial disputes with weaker neighbors, such as the Philippines and Vietnam over the Spratly Islands in the South China Sea. It is reported that such unilateral sanctions have so far produced only limited results, though, because the Chinese economy itself is dependent on the intra-Asian network of production and the Chinese government is sensitive to the economic costs of such sanctions (Reilly 2012: 130–31).

TABLE 5.7 Economic Assistance to Southeast Asia from China, the United States, and the World Bank (in million U.S.$)

	CHINA*	UNITED STATES**	WORLD BANK***
2002	36		
2003	644		
2004	1,200		
2005	4,200		
2006	2,000	411	
2007	6,700	452	4,000
2008			4,500
2009			8,200
2010			7,500

* Including all forms of aid, loans, and state-sponsored investment.
** Including only foreign aid.
*** Including only loans.
Source: Weston, Campbell, and Koleski 2011: 12.

China's increasing weight and centrality in Asia are far from a sim-ple replication of the premodern Sinocentric tribute–trade order. For one thing, the premodern Sinocentric tribute–trade order was culturally grounded on Confucianism, which justified the practices of reciprocity between the center and the periphery as benevolence from the center to the periphery and filial loyalty from the periphery to the center. Such a cultural foundation also induced most Asian nations to look up to China as a model of government, economy, and scholarship. Today China's in-creasing centrality in Asia's international order is on the contrary not supported by much cultural ground; it is instead based on no more than naked economic interests and realpolitik. For another thing, whereas China was the only dominating power in the premodern Sinocentric sys-tem, its rising centrality today is countered by the persistent U.S. influ-ence in the region. The lack of a cultural foundation and the competition from the United States constitute big obstacles to the rise of China's re-gional supremacy.

Motivated only by economic interests and lacking cultural admira-tion of China, Asian states' allegiance to China is at best pragmatic and contingent. The protracted U.S. presence also provides an opportunity for these Asian states to play one against another in their dealings with China and the United States. For instance, Myanmar's military junta, which had been supported by Beijing and benefited greatly from its economic ties with China amid sanctions by Western countries beginning in the 1990s, felt increasingly insecure because of its one-sided reliance on Chinese investment. This insecurity, together with the popular discontent regarding some Chinese state-owned mining-investment projects, motivated the junta to attempt political reform in exchange for normalization of relations with the United States and the Western world, starting around 2011. Although the Myanmar government continued its cozy relationship with China, as marked by the 2013 opening of a gas pipeline constructed by the China National Petroleum Corporation that connects the Bay of Bengal to China's Southwest Yunnan province via Myanmar, its relations with the United States warmed to the point that it was invited to be an observer in a U.S.–Thailand military drill in early 2013 (see Haacke 2012). Besides Myanmar, Singapore, Taiwan, South Korea, the Philippines, and many other Asian states strengthen their economic and political-military ties with the United States while enjoying increasing economic ties with China.

The difficulties China has encountered in its rise to political centrality in Asia manifests a contradiction in its geopolitical ascendancy in general: its rising political influence on its neighbors is a direct outgrowth of its increasing economic significance, but that political influence is checked by continuous U.S. dominance, which China ironically perpetuates through its financing of U.S. fiscal deficits. Many Asian countries— such as Japan, Vietnam, and the Philippines— desire a continuous U.S. presence in the region because they feel threatened by China's geopolitical ambitions and have territorial disputes with China. This contradiction is not confined to Asia's geopolitics but also surfaces with respect to China's rising influence in other parts of the developing world.

New Power in the Old World Order

China's practice of extending economic assistance to other developing nations in exchange for their allegiance is not restricted to East Asia. Since at least the 1960s, China has been active in supporting revolutionary movements and governments in other developing regions, Africa in particular, with financial assistance and experts. In the 1960s, such efforts were related to China's competition with the Soviet Union for leadership in the Third World after the Sino–Soviet split. These efforts were also made to win the support and vote of African nations to facilitate Beijing's bid for a United Nations seat in place of the Republic of China in Taiwan (Brautigam 2011: 67–70). After the beginning of economic reform in the 1980s, China abated its attention to Africa but then renewed that attention with greater vigor in the 2000s when rapid economic growth in China urged Beijing to get "back to Africa" as a strategy to secure the supply of oil and other raw materials there. From Beijing's viewpoint, it is important for China to establish its own mining operations in Africa so that it does not become dependent on the natural-resources extraction industries dominated by Western players.

China's general approach to African natural-resources exports is to befriend whoever is in power by means of loans, aid, and infrastructure-investment projects. China has not been discriminate in the type of regime it makes bargains with, and so it courts both democratic and authoritarian governments in the region. In comparison with U.S. investments, Chinese investments in the region are spread more evenly across different countries and carry terms that are more generous from the investment recipients' perspective (see Brautigam 2011). As noted in the previous chapter, China's increasing investment and trade with other developing countries have different socioeconomic effects, depending on local institutions and politics in the host countries. Though the amount of Chinese economic assistance trails the amount offered by traditional Western powers, most of all the United States (see table 5.8), the Chinese assistance generally brings new and positive gains to the continent, creating competitive pressure for other developing and developed countries to offer better terms in dealing with African nations.

China's increasing presence as a new source of financial support and opportunities offers these African countries autonomy to resist political demands from the United States and other Western powers. At the same time, many African states have reciprocated by supporting Beijing in such political issues as the status of Taiwan and the Dalai Lama. In 2011, when fellow Nobel Peace Prize laureate Archbishop Desmond Tutu invited the Dalai Lama to visit South Africa to celebrate Tutu's eightieth

TABLE 5.8   China's Annual Aid to Africa (in Million U.S.$)

	MINISTRY OF FINANCE AID BUDGET	LOANS FROM EXPORT– IMPORT BANK	DEBT RELIEF	CHINA TOTAL	U.S. AID*
2001	250	64	375	689	
2002	266	86	375	727	
2003	278	117	375	770	
2004	242	158	375	775	
2005	273	213	375	861	
2006	309	347	375	1,031	
2007	440	565	375	1,380	4,700
2008	515	921	375	1,811	5,200
2009	600	1,501	375	2,476	

* U.S. data denote official development assistance to sub-Sahara Africa according to the Office of Economic Cooperation and Development definition and is provided for rough comparison only.
Source: China data from Brautigam 2011:170; U.S. data from Lum et al. 2009: 9.

birthday, the South African government did not issue him a visa. The Dalai Lama also had been denied entry to South Africa in 2009. The opposition criticized the government's action as unlawful, saying it was made under pressure from China (*Guardian* 2011).

But just like many of China's Southeast Asian neighbors, which feel insecure with their increasing dependence on China, some African leaders have started to voice their concern about "Chinese colonialism." When the issue of Chinese colonialism in Africa was first discussed among Western critics in the 2000s, it was naturally discredited as hypocritical talk based on Western anxiety of losing influence over the continent to China. In the 2010s, however, discussion of Chinese colonialism emerged from within Africa, when opposition movements across the continent started to capitalize on the growing popular anti-China sentiment by attacking incumbent governments for becoming subordinate to Chinese interests. For example, in the 2011 election in Zambia, the opposition party campaigned on an anti-China platform and successfully ousted the party in power. On the rundown to the BRICS summit in Durban in March 2013, attended by leaders from Brazil, Russia, India,

China, and South Africa, nongovernmental organizations and activists in Africa organized a countersummit and employed the concept of "subimperialism" to refer to the domination of the continent by China and other BRICS countries. Some go as far as to claim that the BRICS enthusiasm in expanding their presence in Africa resembles the "scramble for Africa" among European imperial powers after the 1885 Berlin Conference (Bond 2013). This concern about China's growing influence in Africa has been so powerful and widespread that even sitting governments with close relations to China voice their anxiety about China openly. In March 2013, right before the BRICS summit, the governor of the Central Bank of Nigeria, one of the African countries heavily reliant on Chinese loans for its development, warned in the *Financial Times* that by embracing China Africa is "opening itself up to a new form of imperialism" and asserted that "China takes from us primary goods and sells us manufactured ones. This was also the essence of colonialism" (Sanusi 2013).[4]

China's rising dominance has been checked by the backlash it has generated in both Asia and Africa. The same applies to Latin America, which is wealthier and politically stronger than Africa and is geographically much farther away from China than Asia. For example, in the WTO the United States and Brazil, which is one of the beneficiaries of the resources bonanza driven by China's demand, allied in accusing China of mercantilist trade and currency policies (*Wall Street Journal* 2011).

The limit of China's political influence in other countries ultimately constrains the expansion of China's economic influence. As long as China lacks the will and capability to counteract this backlash with a projection of its political and military hard power, as traditional European imperial powers once did, the talk about China as a rising new dominating power or hegemon in any region or in the world at large will remain an exaggeration. But China's disinterest in projecting its hard power overseas may be ending. A National Defense White Paper in 2013 stated explicitly for the first time that protecting overseas economic interests is now one core goal of the People's Liberation Army: "With the gradual integration of China's economy into the world economic system, overseas interests have become an integral component of China's national interests. Security issues are increasingly prominent, involving overseas energy and resources, strategic sea lines of communication, and Chinese nationals and legal persons overseas" (Chinese

Information Office of the State Council 2013). China has also started to enlist international mercenaries to defend its overseas interests. In 2014, Erik Prince, the founder and former CEO of U.S. security firm Blackwater, which was heavily involved in the Iraq War, became the chairman of a Hong Kong–based logistic and risk-management firm that has close ties to China's biggest state-owned conglomerate, CITIC, and that provides security and transportation services to Chinese companies investing in Africa (*South China Morning Post* 2014).

China will not be a new hegemonic or dominant power in the world anytime soon, but its increasing presence across the developing world is already changing the dynamics of global politics by empowering other developing countries. As many studies have pointed out (e.g., Kentor and Boswell 2003), developing countries' political subjugation to Western, developed countries was not caused by trade with and investment from developed countries per se but rather by Western countries' monopoly role as sources of investment and as major trading partners. Because of the wide competition among developing countries for investment from a limited number of developed countries and their exportation of similar low-value-added products to a limited number of developed countries' markets, developing countries lack bargaining power, which renders them less capable of resisting demands from developed countries in a bilateral setting or in multilateral organizations such as the WTO. With the rising prevalence of China as a new major trade partner and a source of investment alternative to the United States and Europe, many developing countries have become capable of reducing their one-sided reliance on the West for investments and markets. This improves their bargaining position in bilateral and multilateral negotiations.

The rise of the G-20 as a negotiating bloc in the WTO is illustrative. The group was initiated by Brazil, South Africa, and India in the WTO ministerial meeting in Cancun in 2003 with the intention of fostering collective positions in negotiating with developed countries on various key issues. The group collectively resists developed countries' request for further opening of financial markets and urges developed countries to abolish agricultural subsidies to their own farmers (see Hopewell 2012). The inclusion of China in the group constitutes a big boost to the group's share in the world market because China's share in world GDP has surpassed 10 percent and continues to rise. China is now the single-largest economy in the group. Though it is not active in strategizing and organizing, which other members such as Brazil have taken up, its participation has significantly enhanced the group's bargaining power (Hopewell 2014). In the latest Doha round of trade talks, the group's insistence on drastic reduction of government farm subsidies in rich countries in exchange for developing countries' further opening has brought the talks to a standstill. The Doha round has been in limbo since the breakdown of negotiations in 2008. This episode signals that the WTO is no longer a tool that the United States and other rich countries can use to open up developing countries' markets at will while protecting their own markets. It points to how China's rise has contributed to a shift in the balance of power between wealthy countries and developing countries in the latter's favor, even though China has been maintaining its economically subservient role to the United States and has not yet been capable of directly challenging major Western powers head on in global politics.

Though China has altered the global balance of power to its own and other developing countries' advantage, it is still an exaggeration to claim that China is fundamentally transforming the global order. The China boom is in large part driven by the predominantly private export sector, which is closely integrated with the global free market as promoted and warranted by the United States since the 1980s (see chapter 3). China needs the perpetuation of the global neoliberal order to advance its economy through the expansion of its trade and investment ties to the Global North and South. It would be shooting its own feet if it were to subvert this global order, the institutions related to this order, or the U.S. power underlying the order.

In the aftermath of the global financial crisis starting in 2008 and in China's strong rebound in 2009–2010, which helped many of its economic partners in the developing world dodge the worst fallout of the crisis, many claim to see an accelerated shift of power from the United States as the originator of the crisis to China as its solution. They predict further enhancement of China's influence in the developing world at the expense of U.S. power. The next chapter, however, shows that China, far from being a solution to the crisis, is as much an underlying source of the global economic imbalance precipitating the crisis as the United States, given China's export-driven, investment-heavy, and household-consumption-repressing growth model. Its rebound from the crisis is not going to last, and the China boom is set to fade. What China needs to maintain its economic vitality is a difficult economic reorientation, which will inevitably bring growth deceleration. This reorientation will be a necessary part of the global economic rebalancing and the pursuit of a long-term solution to the global crisis.

SIX

Global Crisis

THE CYCLE OF BOOM AND BUST has been perennial to global capitalism. Many works in critical global political economy point out that the contemporary globalization process has been a response to a world economic crisis in the 1970s (e.g., see Wallerstein 1979; Arrighi 1994, 2007; Arrighi and Silver 1999; Brenner 2003, 2004; Harvey 2003, 2005). They suggest that recurrent crises in the capitalist system are always caused by excessive production capacity and demand deficiency, and such crises can bring an intense process of "creative destruction" that wipes out the excesses in the economy through bankruptcies of enterprises, unemployment, and turmoil in financial markets. This process was exactly what many advanced capitalist economies encountered in the 1970s, a decade characterized by ever more disruptive recessions and financial crises as well as by endemic fiscal crisis of the state. These crises unfolded amid the escalating intercapitalist competition starting in the late 1960s, when Europe and Japan recovered from wartime destruction, built up efficient industrial systems, and generated an oversupply of industrial products that eroded the U.S. monopoly in the world market for manufactured goods. Intensifying competition, coupled with the inflating power of organized labor, led to falling profit rates in the manufacturing sector in most core countries (see Brenner 2002, 2004; Arrighi 2007: part II).

One remedy that corporations in advanced capitalist economies employed to rejuvenate profit was to reallocate capital from the manufacturing sector into financial and real-estate sectors, fueling speculative bubbles. Another remedy was to open up and integrate new territories into the world market and to export surplus capital to these territories, where wages were lower and the profit rate was usually higher than that in the home countries. These attempts to fix the system were the origins of the neoliberal and globalization project in the 1980s and 1990s, which was meant to deregulate the capital market and dismantle transnational trade and investment barriers all over the world (Harvey 1982, 2003, 2005; see also Arrighi 1994, 2005). The expansion of the financial and real-estate bubbles in the United States and Europe and the opening of East Asia, above all China, as a dynamic center of growth that would absorb most manufacturing capital after the 1970s constituted key components of these solutions to the global capitalist crisis.

The rise of East Asia and China as a new center of global capital accumulation did not resolve the crisis but only ameliorated it temporarily. As discussed in chapters 3 and 5, China's export-oriented model of development relied on American (and European) overconsumption, which was in turn financed through China's (and other East Asian countries') purchase of U.S. Treasury bonds. The expansion of debt-driven consumption in the United States and other rich countries created transient prosperity in the global system, but this prosperity aggravated the global imbalance characterized by overconsumption, high indebtedness, and financial excess in the United States and Europe, on the one hand, and by underconsumption and overinvestment in China, on the other. Such imbalances were the origins of the global financial crisis in 2008.

Many analysts see the global financial crisis that started in the United States and precipitated a serious debt crisis in the eurozone as well as China's strong economic recovery in 2009–2010 as indications of China's rise to global economic centrality and the final eclipse of the West. This chapter, however, shows that rather than being part of the solution, China is part of the problem that led to the crisis in the first place. China's immediate recovery from the crisis, though impressive and beneficial to its many economic partners, was grounded on a short-sighted boost of debt-financed investment. In the long run, the hangover of such a stimulus will only increase the pain to China when its boom eventually and inevitably fades. The Chinese economy is urgently in need of rebalancing. This internal rebalancing requires a rebalancing of the global economy and vice versa.

The Chinese Source of Global Economic Imbalances

In a report about the state of the global economy written three years before the Great Crash of 2008, the then IMF chief economist Raghuram Rajan (who became the governor of the Reserve Bank of India in 2013) stipulated that the rapid growth of China's export-dependent economy as well as America's debt-financed consumption spree and real-estate bubble constituted two intertwined processes that accounted for nearly half of global economic growth. The report warned that the "excessive dependence of global growth on unsustainable processes in the United States and to a lesser extent in China" had created an alarming imbalance in the global economy. Given that the U.S. current-account deficit and real-estate bubble were clearly unsustainable and that the Chinese economy was increasingly jeopardized by its "excessive investment" and "over dependence on demand from other countries," the report concluded dismally that "the needed transitions to reduce imbalances" were less and less likely to take place smoothly and that "the risks are weighted to the downside" (Rajan 2005). What happened in 2008 and afterward vindicated the report's claims.

In the aftermath of the global financial crash of 2008, much work has been done to support Rajan's diagnosis that the global imbalance leading up to the crash was attributable as much to China's domestic imbalance as to America's financial excess. In one thorough examination of the link between China's imbalance and the global imbalance, Michael Pettis (2013), a professor of finance at Peking University in China and a veteran Wall Street trader, contends that countries running a persistent trade surplus, such as China, are at least as responsible for the global crash as deficit-running countries such as the United States (cf. Rajan 2010). He argues that the financial crisis will likely end the economic miracles of the surplus countries and may lead them into "lost decades" like those Japan experienced after the early 1990s. The only way out of the crisis is a profound rebalancing of the surplus countries (e.g., China) as much as of the deficit countries (e.g., the United States). Pettis shows

that household layman wisdom that sees surplus and saving as more virtuous than deficit and borrowing simply does not apply to global macroeconomics, which follows a very different logic under which excessive
saving is as unhealthy as excessive borrowing.

Pettis sees the global economic imbalance underlying the financial
crisis of 2008 as primarily a product of the consumption-repressing
growth model adopted by the surplus countries, most notably China
(Germany being another example). As a matter of theoretical principle, repression of consumption always brings rise in saving. If saving is
larger than investment, then the excess saving must flow to other countries in the form of net capital exports. In contrast, a country with net
inflow of capital must see larger investment than saving. For China, the
purchase of U.S. Treasury bonds is the predominant channel of capital
exports, whereas for the United States the selling of Treasury bonds to
foreigners constitutes a main channel for capital inflow. The basic rule
of macroeconomics dictates that saving minus investment is also equal
to trade surplus.[1] We therefore have the equation

SAVING − INVESTMENT = CAPITAL OUTFLOW/INFLOW =
TRADE SURPLUS/DEFICIT

This equation means that a country that exports capital will develop
a trade surplus, whereas a country that imports capital will develop a
trade deficit. Because open economies are linked to one another through
trade and capital flow, capital export and trade surplus originating from
a country's underconsumption and high saving must bring capital import and trade deficit as well as overconsumption and low saving to other
countries. Trading partners' domestic imbalances must mirror each
other, generating a global imbalance. In other words, the imbalance in
the United States and the imbalance in China are mutually constitutive.

Pettis points out that China's consumption-repressing model of
growth has nothing to do with its people's culture and habits. China's
high savings rate and low consumption are consequences of the three-
pronged policies of wage repression, undervalued currency, and financial repression, all of which redistribute income from households to the
export and state sectors. First, since the 1990s, the large supply of rural
migrant labors whose rights and services in their location of work were

denied under the *hukou* (household registration) system, as described in chapter 3, has ensured that wages have grown much more slowly than productivity, hence repressing the growth of workers' income and consumption relative to the growth of production. Second, China's central bank has been intervening in the currency market to prevent the RMB from appreciating alongside the growth of trade surplus. The subsequent undervalued currency benefits exporters but makes domestic consumption items more expensive. This currency policy is therefore a hidden tax on household consumers that is transferred to exporters. Third, the low interest rate maintained by state banks for both depositors and borrowers constitutes another hidden tax on households. While ordinary depositors have to put up with a meager or even negative real interest rate, state enterprises and government units can borrow at low interest rates to fuel their orgies of real-estate and infrastructural projects. This is tantamount to a subsidy that household depositors pay to the state sector's excess investment.

Though this model entails high investment, improving infrastructure, and an internationally competitive manufacturing sector, the financial repression involved pushes saving, which is mostly corporate and government rather than household saving, to an even higher level. The saving in excess of investment in China therefore has to be exported overseas in exchange for external demand for its manufactured products. Given the huge liquidity of U.S. assets, Treasury securities in particular, and the size of the U.S. market, most of China's excess saving ends up in U.S. Treasury bonds and much of its manufactured products end up in the U.S. retail market, as noted in chapter 5. To Pettis, the Chinese purchase of U.S. Treasury bonds is a "[trade] policy . . . aimed at generating trade surpluses and higher domestic employment" back in China (2013: 155). For the United States, such "large-scale capital imports [through China's purchase of U.S. Treasury bonds] . . . are usually harmful" because the United States has no choice but to respond to the growing net inflows of capital with higher investment and higher consumption (179). Because the capital inflow is pushing up the dollar, cheapening manufactured imports, and penalizing American manufacturers, "there [is] little incentive for American businesses to borrow and expand production domestically" (157). The expansion of credit brought by the massive inflow of Chinese capital only brings about an expansion

of real-estate investment and debt-financed consumption. Pettis con-
cludes that the U.S. consumption spree and trade deficit are caused by
excessive Chinese investments in U.S. public debt that "*force* Americans
to consume beyond their means" (154, original emphasis).

To Pettis, global imbalance caused by underconsuming countries that
export surplus capital to other economies is not novel in the development
of capitalism. Drawing from insights from John A. Hobson and Vladi-
mir Lenin, he notes that in the late nineteenth and early twentieth centuries underconsumption in industrialized countries, where workers'
demand was repressed as wealth and income were concentrated among
the rich, urged these countries to export capital to their formal or informal colonies, which started to run trade deficits with and be indebted
to the colonial motherland. The main difference between now and then
is that back in the early twentieth century capital-exporting colonizers
"managed the colonial economies and their tax systems, and so they
could ensure that all debts were repaid" (Pettis 2013: 146; see also Austin 2011). Global imbalances could last longer in the age of imperialism
because "large current account imbalances could persist for as long as
the colony had assets to trade [or to be expropriated]" (Pettis 2013: 146).
Many colonies importing capital from their colonizers were underdeveloped economies a century ago, and the imported capital flowed mostly
into extractive industries instead of into financial markets. This highly
territorial form of capital export did not generate the type of volatility
that financial investment in today's deficit countries entails, but it nevertheless drove the capital-exporting imperial powers to aggressively vie
with one another for territories, intensifying interimperial rivalry and
triggering World War I.

Today's capital exporters with large trade surplus, such as China, no
longer enjoy colonial control over major importers of their capital and
goods, such as the United States. Much of their capital export flows into
financial and real-estate bubbles in capital-importing countries. Imbalances in this situation are less sustainable. Once the unstable bubbles in deficit countries deflate or their borrowing capabilities run out,
consumption there will collapse. This is what has been happening in
the United States since 2008. In such a case, trade-deficit countries are
forced to undergo painful rebalancing, which can be achieved through
tax hikes on the rich and on retail sales that restrain consumption and

boost saving. Such rebalancing efforts, however, will be futile if the surplus countries continue to repress consumption, export surplus savings, and maintain a trade surplus with respect to the deficit countries. It is mathematically impossible for the United States to attain a trade surplus and repress consumption if the capital exporters do not shrink their surplus and boost their consumption. In the global economy, someone's surplus must be accompanied by someone else's deficit. A true rebalancing of the global economy is possible only when the deficit countries and the surplus countries rebalance their domestic economies simultaneously through mirroring policies. U.S. policies that restrain consumption and elevate saving have to be accompanied by Chinese policies that stimulate consumption, reduce saving, and reverse the trade balance. Because China's underconsumption is attributable mainly to the squeezing of household income to subsidize export manufacturers and the state sector, the uplifting of consumption there must involve "distributional struggle" (Pettis 2013: 74) in favor of the household sector.

China's rebalancing is not only crucial to the rebalancing of the U.S. and global economy, as Pettis shows, but also essential to preventing a crash of the Chinese economy. The two engines of the China boom—investment and export—are vulnerable. China's infrastructure is becoming excessive relative to its stage of development, and falling returns from the newly constructed infrastructure are exhausting the lending capability of the state sector, which is already overloaded with preexisting bad loans, according to Pettis. In the meantime, U.S. consumption declines, and the concomitant political pressure on China to shrink its trade surplus is mounting. With the investment and export engines under threat at the same time, the increase in household income and consumption becomes all the more important.

The Limits of the Chinese Model

The imbalance of the Chinese economy—characterized by tepid household consumption, excessive investment by the state sector, and reliance on the export sector—is a consequence of China's development model. A rebalancing of the Chinese economy would require a shift from this model and a break from the political institutions and vested interests associated with it. It will not be easy. Chapter 3 points out that what made

China's investment-heavy and export-oriented boom possible was, first, the authoritarian party–state's capacity to repress labor's and peasants' demands in order to keep wages low and, second, the local developmental state's autonomy in single-mindedly promoting local economic growth and competing for investment. These political and social origins of the China boom are double-edged swords. The repression of workers' and peasants' demands constrains the growth of domestic consumption power, while the decentralization of economic governance boosts uncoordinated, redundant, and unprofitable expansion of productive capacity.

This imbalance is particularly notable when China's pattern of growth is compared with that of other Asian Tigers at similar stages of development, also known for their low consumption, high investment, and export dependence. Repression of household consumption in China has been much worse than it was among earlier East Asian exporters during their comparable development phase (see figure 3.5). All East Asian Tigers at the initial stage of industrial takeoff were governed by authoritarian regimes. But these regimes were disciplined by Cold War geopolitics. Just next door to Communist China, they were anxious to root out any plausible socialist influence among the lower classes. They achieved this goal through preemptive redistributive policies such as land reform and provision of free education as much as through eradication of independent labor and peasant organizations. By letting the fruits of economic expansion trickle down to the lower classes, in particular the rural population, these authoritarian regimes became economically inclusive, even though they were highly exclusive politically (Deyo 1987; Haggard 1990: 223–53; see also table 4.3). The reduction in income disparity and rising income among the lower classes helped create sizeable domestic markets in these newly industrializing economies, which buffered them against the vagaries of the world market and provided infant industries with sufficient internal demand before they could compete internationally (Grabowski 1994).

In contrast, China's party–state in the 1990s aggressively pursued rapid economic growth while repressing the laboring classes' wage demands, which brought about rapid social polarization (see chapters 3 and 4). The increasing inequality in income constrained expansion of the mass-consumption market. The decline of the wage share in China's

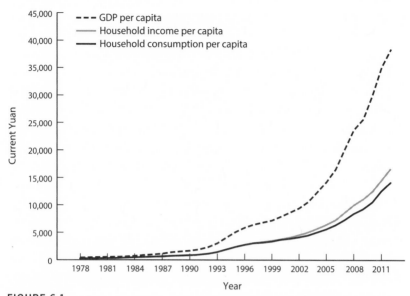

FIGURE 6.1

Growth of household income and consumption as compared with the growth of the Chinese economy at large, 1978–2012. *Source*: Chinese National Bureau of Statistics n.d.

GDP from 53 percent in 1998 to 41.4 percent in 2005 prompted one World Bank study to stipulate that "the declining role of wages and household income in the economy are [*sic*] the key driver behind the declining share of consumption in GDP" (He and Kuijs 2008: 12). The growth of consumption in China is hardly stagnant, but it has not kept pace with the exuberant growth in investment and the economy's expansion at large (Hung 2008: 164). Figure 6.1 illustrates how the rise in average household income and consumption falls far below the rise of GDP per capita. The widening gap between GDP per capita and household income per capita represents rising corporate profits. To be sure, the diagnosis about underconsumption in China sounds counterintuitive in that we all have seen the rapid growth of consumerism in major cities over the past three decades. But what matters here is not the growth in absolute quantity of consumption but the growth in consumption relative to the much more rapid growth in productive capacity and infrastructure.

With wage growth lagging far behind the growth of the economy at large, enterprise profits soar in comparison and are turned into corporate savings and government savings (through direct SOE income and corporate taxes). Corporate and government savings, not household savings, constitute a large and increasing proportion of the aggregate national savings (see figure 6.2). Throughout the 2000s, household saving has made up less than half of total saving in China and is lower than India's level in terms of GDP share. In the meantime, China's corporate saving surpasses Japan's, and its government saving surpasses South Korea's (Ma and Yi 2010: 5–6). These savings deposited in the banks fuel a credit boom that in turn aggravates overinvestment (National Development and Reform Commission of China 2005).

The problem of overinvestment that accompanies worsening underconsumption in China is more severe than it was earlier for the Asian Tigers owing to the decentralized nature of the Chinese developmental state. During the initial economic ascendancy of Japan, South Korea, and Taiwan, central governments played a key role in mobilizing and allocating precious financial and other resources to support the growth

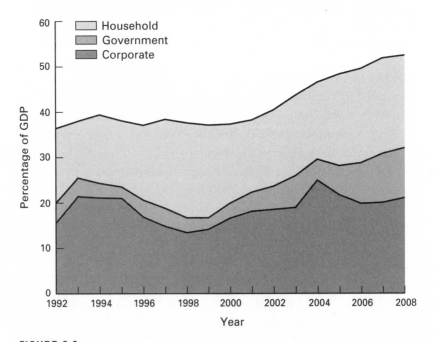

FIGURE 6.2

Composition of China's gross national saving by sector, 1992–2008. *Source*: Ma and Yi 2010: 10.

of strategic industrial sectors. This "pick the winner" process was crucial not only to success in the early stages of industrial takeoff but also to the subsequent industrial upgrading of these economies (Haggard 1990; Wade 1990; Evans 1995). The decentralized economic growth in today's China deviates from the East Asian centralized developmental state model (So 2003). Many local states in China act "developmentally" in that they proactively facilitate growth of selected industrial sectors, and these developmental efforts are often well planned and executed at the local level. The totality of these efforts combined, however, creates anarchic competition among localities, resulting in uncoordinated construction of redundant production capacity and infrastructure. Foreign investors, with the expectation that the domestic and world market for Chinese products will grow incessantly, also race with one another to expand their industrial capacity in China. Though export-oriented foreign investments consistently yield decent profits in the world market, investments made by many domestic-market-oriented enterprises, in particular state-owned ones, become increasingly unprofitable.

Idle capacity in such key sectors as steel, automobile, cement, aluminum, and real estate has been piling up in China ever since the mid-1990s (Rawski 2002). It is estimated that in 2006 more than 75 percent of China's industries were plagued by overcapacity and that fixed-asset investment in industries already experiencing overinvestment accounted for 40 to 50 percent of China's GDP growth in 2005 (Huang Y. 2002; Rawski 2002: 364–65; Rajan 2006; Xie 2006). The buildup of excess capacity was exacerbated by the lack of geographical and intersectoral mobility of domestic enterprises, which increased their propensity to invest in saturated localities and sectors. Many provincial and municipal governments erected protectionist barriers against investment from other provinces and cities. This action created a "one country, thirty-two economies" malaise (Huang Y. 2003: 140–48). One survey found that 85.8 percent of SOEs invested in only a single city and that 91.1 percent invested in only a single province (Keister and Lu 2001: 26). This limited investment was in part due to the underdevelopment of financial markets, which made it difficult for enterprises to divert their savings to investment in other sectors or regions (Rajan 2006, 2010).

Major state-owned banks, rather than discipline enterprises and direct them away from excessive and low-return investments, encouraged these investments through lax lending practices. As the financial arms of the central and local governments, these banks delivered easy credit to insolvent or profligate industrial SOEs, roughly 40 percent of which incurred losses in 2006, according to government figures (Bank for International Settlement 2007: 56). In contrast, private enterprises, even very successful ones, were in a disadvantageous position to obtain financial support from major state banks. These two factors set China apart from the developmental experiences of other East Asian developmental states, whose financial arms "picked the winners" rather than "fed the losers" (Tsai 2002: 29–35; Shih 2004).

The state banks' motivation in extending loans to keep unprofitable SOEs afloat can first and foremost be linked to interpersonal networks and collusion between bank managers and SOE managers. Such loans are often made at the behest of local party bosses, who command overwhelming influence over local branches of state banks and are inclined to fuel local investment booms to lift local growth figures and short-term government revenue gain. The Bank of China even acknowledged in 2006 in the prospectus for its global initial public offering that undisciplined lending at local branches is difficult to avoid because, "[l]ike many other PRC banks, our branches and subsidiaries historically [have] had significant autonomy in their operation and management, and our head office may not be able to ensure that various policies are implemented effectively and consistently across the organization. In addition, due to limitations in our information systems, we [have] not always able to effectively prevent or detect on a timely basis operational or management problems at these branches and subsidiaries" (Bank of China 2006: 30–31). The central government has not discouraged such loans, either, because they help maintain social and political stability by alleviating the social impact of massive layoffs amid SOE reform. However, this practice magnifies the sectoral overinvestment into a generalized risk to the economy through the buildup of NPLs in the financial system (Lardy 1998; Rawski 2002: 364–65; *Economist* 2005). The Bank for International Settlement has long warned that "in China, the principal concern must be that misallocated capital will eventually manifest itself in falling profits, and that this will feed back on the bank system, the fiscal authorities and the prospects for growth more generally. After a long period of credit-fueled expansion, this would be the classic denouement.

Indeed, this was very much the path followed by Japan [before the pro-longed crisis since the 1990s]" (2006).

In theory, the continuous expansion of China's excess capacity and the declining relative consumption power to digest this capacity since the 1990s should precipitate an overproduction crisis that will ultimately lead to a collapse of profit and growth. In reality, this has not yet happened, and the Chinese economy has roared ahead uninterruptedly for more than two decades. This paradox needs to be understood in terms of China's ability to export its excess capacity since the mid-1990s.

From China's Crisis to Global Crisis and Back

Back in the late 1990s, the accumulation of excess industrial capacity, gluts, and relatively sluggish consumption growth precipitated falling prices of finished products in key industrial sectors and falling profit in key industries in China (Fan and Felipe 2005; Islam, Erbiao, and Saka-moto 2006: 149–54; Shan 2006a, 2006b; Hung 2008: 166). The growing economic imbalance and concern about profitless growth led many to question the sustainability of the boom and to anticipate an economic crisis to come. This worry heightened in the aftermath of the Asian fi-nancial crisis of 1997–1998 (Fernald and Babson 1999; G. Lin 2000). The signs of fatigue in the China boom back then included surging NPLs in state banks that started to threaten the stability of the financial system as well as a deflationary spiral (Hung 2008: 165–67).

The fear of a serious economic crisis was soon allayed by a new round of robust economic expansion driven by FDI inflow and export growth after 2000. These upward trends were not unrelated to the heightened optimism about China's export-driven economy at home and abroad, en-livened by China's entry into the WTO, its successful bid to host the 2008 Olympics, and the real-estate bubble and debt-financed consumption spree in the United States and Europe that sustained thriving markets for Chinese exports. The rising state revenue created by the export-led economic boom enabled the state to bail out the state banks and SOEs, as shown in the case of the four AMCs created by the government in 1999 (see chapter 3). The AMCs absorbed 2 trillion RMB of bad loans from the top four state banks under government financial support between 1999 and 2004 (*Economist* 2013b). The reliance on state revenue to bail out the banks further impeded the growth of domestic consumption because it constrained the government's capacity to lower the tax rate or to invest in social programs.

Whenever economic crisis is deferred, China becomes ever more dependent on its export sector to divert the overcapacity problem in the domestic economy. This overdependence can be illustrated by the use of export promotion as a remedy to the alarming excess capacity in the steel sector, as the *Economist* noted in mid-2013:

> After a decade of rapid expansion, Chinese firms are now responsible for half of global [steel] production. Although the government seems determined to cover the entire country with steel and concrete in its drive for growth, the steelmakers have expanded so rapidly that they now suffer from massive overcapacity. Yet more is being added: . . . another 105m tonnes of new capacity is under construction or planned.
>
> China's stated aim of reining back steelmakers and consolidating state-run firms has happened "mostly on paper." . . . The central government wants cheap steel, so it is unwilling to take radical steps to curtail overcapacity. Meanwhile local governments are encouraging more steel mills to set up shop. They are a vital source of direct and indirect employment, and tax revenues. To these enterprises, profits are unimportant.
>
> Since China itself will have little need for this unprofitable steel, it will inevitably add to the country's exports, further depressing world prices. Chinese exports are likely to be 30m–50m tonnes in each of the next few years—a small share of the country's total production of almost 750m tonnes, but an amount that now exceeds the tonnage sold abroad by longer-established exporters such as Japan, South Korea, Ukraine and Russia.
>
> (2013a)

Table 3.2 in chapter 3 showed that the profit rate of large industrial SOEs, despite all the policy favors, subsidies, and low-interest loans from state banks, stood lower than the national average, whereas private industrial enterprises, many of which were foreign-funded and export-oriented, enjoyed profit rates higher than the national average. Ballooning foreign reserves resulting from rapid export growth also fueled a liquidity expansion in the banking sector, because the central bank needed to issue an equivalent amount of local currencies in exchange for the foreign currency surrendered by exporters under the

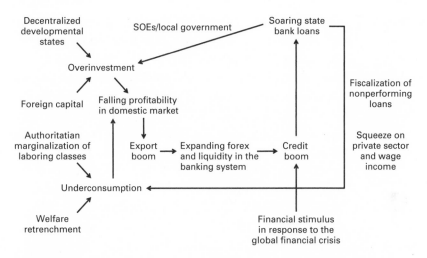

FIGURE 6.3

The cycle of overinvestment, underconsumption, and export surge in the China boom.

government-managed exchange rate (*Washington Post* 2006). The resulting credit boom boosted debt-financed investment further and in
turn exacerbated the buildup of excess production capacity, which in
its turn needed to be countervailed by further export growth. A vicious
cycle of more exports and more inefficient investment ensued. This dynamic of the China boom is summarized in figure 6.3.

Many had doubted since the late 1990s whether China's formidable export engine, so far the economy's single most profitable component as well
as the key force that helped neutralize the risk of an economic crisis, could
last indefinitely. The success of the Asian Tigers' export-led development
strategy rested mainly on the fact that so few small developing economies
were pursuing this strategy at the time of their takeoff. These economies'
exports were easily absorbed in the world market. But when many more
developing countries adopted the strategy in the 1980s and 1990s, the
world market, flooded with cheap manufactured exports, became ever
more volatile. Given its economic size and export volume, China was
exceptionally vulnerable (Mead 1999; Palley 2006). Its export trade depended heavily on the United States and Europe, which relied on unsustainable borrowing to consume. The Great Crash of 2008, which brought
the collapse of the consumer market across the Atlantic Ocean, set off a

free fall of China's export growth rate from 20 percent in 2007 to –11 percent in 2009 (World Bank 2010). It was the worst nightmare coming true.

Subsequent to the collapse of China's export engine at the turn of 2009, the central government attempted to arrest the economy's free fall by introducing a megastimulus package amounting to U.S.$570 billion to revive growth. This fiscal stimulus, announced in November 2008, was accompanied by a loosening of state bank lending. It turns out that local governments as well as local investment entities linked to but not officially under the local authorities obtained most of these new loans and accumulated debt more than three times the fiscal stimulus—that is close to U.S.$2 trillion (Huang Y. 2011; see also Shih 2010). Many initially celebrated this massive stimulus as a precious opportunity to accelerate the rebalancing of the Chinese economy into a more domestic-consumption-driven mode and expected that the stimulus would be made up mainly of social spending, such as financing of medical insurance and social security accounts. To the disappointment of those who advocated the use of the stimulus to rebalance the Chinese economy, the stimulus package in the end carried no more than 20 percent of social spending, and the majority of the spending went into the same old investments in fixed-capital assets, such as high-speed rail, and the expansion of sectors already plagued by overcapacity, such as steel and cement (*Caijing* 2009b, 2009c). Because the stimulus package did not bring much benefit to social welfare institutions and small and medium labor-intensive enterprises, it was not able to generate much increase in the share of disposable income, employment, and domestic consumption in the economy.

The large stimulus did keep the economy roaring with a state-led investment spurt in the short run, however. By the summer of 2009, the stimulus had successfully stalled the free fall of the Chinese economy and induced an impressive economic rebound. But at the same time more than 90 percent of GDP growth in all of 2009 was driven solely by fixed-asset investments (*Xinhua News* 2012b). In 2010, the fixed-asset investment growth rate exceeded 23 percent, but overall GDP grew only at 10.3 percent. Because most of these investments were of low quality and repetitive, with dubious profitability (Pettis 2009), a top Chinese economist criticized this megastimulus program as "drinking poison to quench the thirst."[2]

Many local governments, which became awash with cheap credit from state banks, devoted most of their new loans to building wasteful structures and facilities that could boost short-term local GDP growth but were not profitable in the long run: local government offices of surreal extravagance, repetitive subway lines, redundant airports, and luxury condominiums with scant demand (Kaiman 2012). The craze for construction by local governments or their associated units led to the rise of the infamous "ghost towns" or "ghost shopping malls" in the middle of nowhere that remained mostly empty years after construction. The high-speed rail project, which made a large contribution to the post-2008 rebound and significantly improved long-distance transportation within China under subsidized fares, pushed the Ministry of Railways and Chinese train makers to the brink of bankruptcy and default, when they had to be bailed out by taxpayers' money (*Forbes* 2011; *Wall Street Journal* 2013a).

What the post-2008 stimulus program did, therefore, was to boost fixed-asset investment to pick up the slack of export slump. It has not moved the Chinese economy to become more driven by domestic household consumption, as shown in figure 6.4. In the meantime, as figure 6.5 indicates, new income generated by each unit of fixed-asset investment fell under the investment spree.

It is likely that the fiscal burden, NPLs, and aggravating overcapacity created by the investment-driven stimulus will generate a deeper downturn in China in the future. And to gain the financial resources necessary for bailing out the banks and SOEs, the government will be forced to resort to heavier tax levies, which will further curtail the growth of private consumption. This scenario is increasingly plausible, given the jobless recovery of the U.S. economy from the 2008 crisis as well as the lingering crisis in the eurozone, which have rendered the full recovery of China's export sector challenging. To the fiscal and financial problems that confronted China in the wake of the post-2008 stimulus can be added the NPLs originating in the late 1990s that have not yet been totally resolved, as discussed in chapter 3. China GDP growth slipped to 7.8 percent in 2012 and 7.4 percent in 2014, the lowest rates since 1991. Though pundits and Chinese leaders assert that such a modest growth rate is actually beneficial to China's rebalancing imperative, no one can say for sure whether the Chinese economy will stabilize or continue to

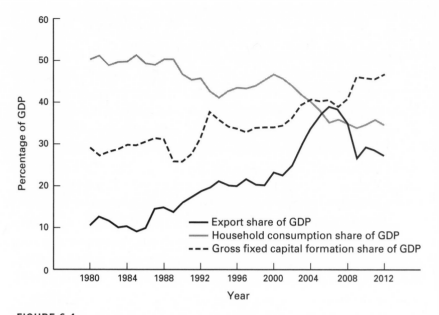

FIGURE 6.4

Export, investment, and domestic consumption share of China's GDP, 1980–2012. *Source*: World Bank n.d.

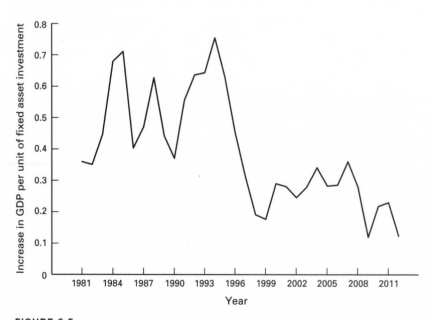

FIGURE 6.5

Increase in Chinese national income generated by one unit of fixed-asset investment, 1981–2012. *Source*: Chinese National Bureau of Statistics n.d.

slide while the investment level tapers off and a new wave of defaults and NPLs by local authorities surfaces. Standard Chartered Bank estimated in mid-2014 that total outstanding debt in the Chinese economy reached 251 percent of its GDP, drastically up from 147 percent in 2008 (*Financial Times* 2014). This figure further soared to 282 percent in early 2015, according to an estimation by the McKinsey Global Institute (2015). This figure is higher than the debt-laden United States and most other developing countries, and it is set to rise further when the economy continues to slow.

China has been the driver of growth for many Asian, Latin American, and African economies in the aftermath of the crash of 2008 because its own investment-heavy recovery drove up the demand for commodities in the developing world. If the current course of China's response to the global crisis continues, China is likely to waste the crisis and cannot be spared a more significant slowdown when fixed-asset investment finally loses steam. Such an inevitable landing, hard or soft, of China's high-flying economy might trigger a new round of global economic turbulence, dragging down the many commodities and capital-goods exporters to China that have so far been unscathed by the global crisis. Only a shift to more balanced growth based on a greater domestic household consumption share can make China's growth sustainable and contribute to the rebalancing of the global economy at large.

The Long Road of Rebalancing

Many policy advisers and scholars in China agree that the key to rebalancing China's export and investment-dependent economy is to boost the consumption power of the laboring classes by redistributing larger portions of income from enterprises to households. Redistributing resources from coastal export-oriented provinces to inland agrarian provinces is crucial as well. But from the 1990s on, the CCP ruling group has been overly represented by the elite with coastal province backgrounds (see table 3.4 of chapter 3). Jiang Zemin, China's president from 1993 to 2003 and the CCP's general secretary from 1989 to 2002, and Zhu Rongji, vice premier from 1993 to 1998 and premier from 1998 to 2003, spent most of their careers in Shanghai before they became national leaders. In the 1990s, the CCP's Politburo Standing Committee, the pinnacle of

China's political power, was overwhelmed by members with coastal province backgrounds. Most policies that favored coastal urban regions and export-oriented sectors were made in this period.

The situation started to change after Hu Jintao, a former local leader in such poor inland regions as Guizhou, Gansu, and Tibet, succeeded Jiang to become the party–state leader in 2002. During his time in office (2002–2012), the number of Politburo Standing Committee members with rural inland backgrounds increased, and in 2002 and 2007 the number of members with rural inland backgrounds surpassed the number of those with urban coastal backgrounds (see table 3.4). The increasing representation of voices from and interests in rural inland provinces coincided with the government's redoubled efforts to reduce rural–urban and coastal–inland inequality during the Hu era.

As an impetus to rebalance China's development, the Hu government tried after about 2005 to foster a takeoff of China's domestic consumption by raising peasants' and urban workers' disposable income, even at the expense of China's export competitiveness. The first wave of such initiatives included the abolition of agricultural taxes, a price increase in the government procurement of agricultural products, and an increase in rural infrastructure investment. Though this attempt to raise the rural living standard was no more than a small step in the right direction, its effect was instantaneous. The slightly improved economic conditions and employment opportunities in the rural-agricultural sector under Hu slowed the flow of rural–urban migration, as shown by the rising share of rural local income (both farm and nonfarm) in comparison with migrant labor remittances in average household incomes (figure 6.6).

A sudden labor shortage and wage hike in the coastal export-processing zones ensued. This tightening of the labor market was reflected in the relatively large increase in Chinese manufacturing wages as a share of U.S. manufacturing wages after 2005 (see figure 3.1). Workers' livelihoods were further protected by the implementation of the new Labor Contract Law in 2008. Even though many local governments did not implement the new law effectively or thoroughly, it became a new weapon that workers could wield in their fight for concessions from employers (V. Ho 2008).

The tightening of the labor market led many social scientists to declare that the "Lewis turning point"—that is, the point at which rural

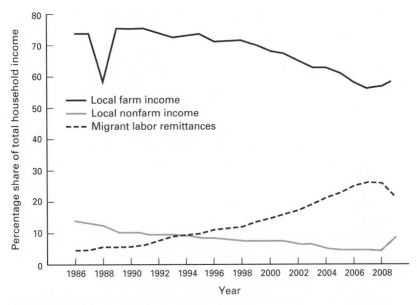

FIGURE 6.6

Percentage share of different sources of total rural household income in China, 1986–2009. *Sources*: Fixed Point Rural Household Survey, Ministry of Agriculture, 2001, 2010.

surplus labor was exhausted—had finally arrived in the Chinese economy (Cai and Du 2009). However, an IMF report indicates that the supply of young labor in China has not run out yet. It is only close to running out, and the Lewis turning point will arrive in 2020–2025 at the earliest (Das and N'Diaya 2013). This projection coincides with recent ethnographic studies showing that there are still plenty of young laborers in the countryside. They are now simply more prone to stay close to their home village because employment opportunities in rural inland areas improved in the wake of Hu's reform (Zhan and Huang 2013). The "labor shortage" and rising wages in the coastal export-processing zone are not indicators of problems in the Chinese economy but signs that the Chinese government's attempt to rebalance the economy has attained some small success.

Despite these initial efforts to rebalance the economy, the economic stimulus measures adopted by the Chinese government after the Great Crash in 2008 were contradictory to such rebalancing efforts because the stimulus's emphasis on debt-financed, fixed-asset investment further repressed consumption. Worse, seemingly horrified by the sudden collapse of the export sector in early 2009, the central government retreated from some rebalancing efforts and expanded a number of export-promotion measures that had already been scaled back, such as the export tax rebate (*Bloomberg* 2012). Vested interests in the export sector even used the crisis to call for a suspension of the Labor Contract Law to ensure the survival of export manufacturers (*Caijing* 2009a). Labor organizations found evidence that the compromises that foreign investors made to the contentious workers under the new Labor Contract Law were in many cases only on paper. These investors instead sought to shift their production to inland areas with harsher labor practices and to exact new deductions from workers' nominally raised salaries to compensate for the losses incurred by the compromises. More unpaid interns from vocational schools were used to cut labor costs (*Financial Times* 2013; Pun, Chan, and Selden forthcoming).

It is still uncertain whether Xi Jinping, who succeeded Hu as head of the party-state in 2012, will continue and deepen the rebalancing policies devised in the Hu era. Xi himself spent the most important part of his prior career in the coastal provinces of Zhejiang and Fujian. His Politburo also revived the larger representation of coastal–urban interests compared to the representation of inland-rural ones (see table 3.4). It is plausible that the imperative to rebalance the economy will force Xi's government to continue the type of rebalancing policies started in Hu's government. But it is also possible that Xi's government, tied more to coastal interests than to inland ones, will part ways with Hu-era policies that favored the rural inland and labor.[3] In any event, the Chinese economy has been slowing down significantly amid the voluntary or reluctant rebalancing because the rebalancing must involve curtailing debt-financed investment, which has accounted for China's continuous hypergrowth since 2008. Whether the debt-infested financial system can withstand such a slowdown is questionable. If the financial system falls under the weight of nonperforming loans, a vicious cycle of defaults/bankruptcy and further slowdown might turn a slowdown into a meltdown. If the central government manages to weather the meltdown through extensive bank bailouts, then the economy will be haunted by myriad lingering "zombie" companies, just as what Japan has faced since the 1990s. The party–state is destined to face some serious dilemma.

To recapitulate, the Chinese economic imbalance, which is a main source of imbalances in the U.S. economy and in the global economy at large, is the result of China's excessive dependence on exports and investment, coupled with the relatively low household consumption that this dependence entails. This model of development, as we have seen, stems from a set of government policies that repress the laboring classes' interests and favor the oligarchic party–state elite. This elite is made up of the costal officials fed by rents from the export sector as well as the neofeudal CCP families that control state companies and siphon benefits from unprofitable investment projects funded by state banks' lax lending. These imbalance-inducing policies include low interest rates and repression of currency appreciation, which force household savers to subsidize the state companies and export manufacturers. They also include the destruction of the rural-agricultural sector that created a large reserve army of labor in the countryside and kept increases in manufacturing wages lagging behind the expansion of the economy at large. It would have been impossible for these policies to take hold in the 1990s had it not been for the consolidation of the capitalist authoritarian state in the aftermath of the 1989 crackdown.

A rebalancing of the Chinese economy and the global economy will therefore require redistributive reforms that would bring significant improvement in the laboring classes' share of economic growth, reduction in urban–rural inequality, a scaling back of state-sector privileges, and so on. But it is impossible to image how these redistributive reforms might be introduced and sustained in the long run in the absence of any democratizing and liberalizing reforms that enhance ordinary citizens' institutional powers to check the privileges of the oligarchic party–state elite. The prospect of global economic rebalancing now depends to a significant extent on the prospect of social and political reforms in China.

After the Boom

IN PART 1 OF THIS BOOK, we saw how capitalism, an economic system driven by the imperative of profit maximization and capital accumulation, developed along a rocky road in China from the nineteenth century to the early twenty-first century. Amid the late-twentieth-century rise of global neoliberalism, under which the United States and Europe shifted to financial expansion, debt-driven consumption, and reliance on imported manufactured goods from low-wage countries, China eschewed central economic planning and absorbed substantial foreign-capital accumulated during the industrial takeoff of its Asian neighbors, particularly those of Chinese diasporic origins, turning itself into a dynamic center of export-driven capitalism.

China had been a geopolitical heavyweight during the Cold War, taking advantage of the U.S.–Soviet rivalry. Now, charged with the energies released by the capitalist boom, China's influence in global affairs rose. In part II, we saw China's uneven impact on the prospect of development in other developing countries. It is apparent that China has no intention of or capacity for transforming the global neoliberal order because the China boom has been relying heavily on transnational free trade and investment flow. China also makes significant contribution to the perpetuation of U.S. global dominance through its addiction to U.S. public debt. But it is also apparent that the China boom is shifting the balance of power within that global neoliberal order in developing countries' favor. And finally, it is clear that because China is a significant source of the global economic imbalances underlying the global financial crisis of 2008, the success of sustained global economic recovery hinges on China's own economic rebalancing, which will require profound social and political reforms.

The Two Myths of Capitalism in China

This book challenges two popular myths about the historical origins and global effects of the development of capitalism in China: that China's capitalist development today is a radical break from its Maoist past and that China's capitalist boom is making it a subversive power within the U.S.-centered global neoliberal order.

Regarding the first myth, many believe that the Communist Party's founding of the People's Republic of China in 1949 and the market reform Deng Xiaoping started in the 1980s constitute two radical breaks that cut the economic development of modern China into three distinct periods: incipient capitalist development around 1850–1949, socialist reorientation in 1949–1978, and capitalist revival from 1978 on. To be sure, the Communists' seizure of power and Deng's reform were important events that triggered significant changes in socioeconomic structure, political order, and government policy. But we should not allow our vision to be clouded by these changes so that we neglect the long rise of capital in China that transcends these watershed events. Chapters 1 and 2 discussed how the Qing state, fearing the social disruptions and unrest that profiteering activities would bring, restrained capital accumulation among the merchant class in eighteenth-century China, even though China had developed the world's most advanced market economy. The merchant class's resulting propensity to move to bureaucratic-official careers instead of continuing a multigenerational accumulation of capital meant that Qing China lacked an entrepreneurial class capable of concentrating the abundant surplus generated in the commercialized agrarian sector to ignite a capitalist-industrial takeoff, as happened in early-modern England. In the meantime, however, some entrepreneurial families moved to European colonial outposts in Southeast Asia, constituting a network of Chinese diasporic capital that persisted into the twentieth century and helped fuel China's capitalist boom at the turn of the twenty-first century.

After the Qing Empire's defeat in the Sino–British Opium War of 1839–1842, China's state elite were confronted with the same challenges faced by their counterparts in all other backward countries in the nineteenth century: how to foster rapid capital accumulation and industrialization to catch up with Europe economically and militarily. Modernizing elites in Germany, Japan, and Russia harnessed centralizing state power to squeeze and channel surplus from the countryside to jump-start capitalist-industrial development. Reformers in the late Qing dynasty followed the same path by initiating a state-sponsored industrialization program. But the Qing state was already in decline before the Opium War, and it simply lacked the capacity to mobilize and concentrate the ample rural surplus effectively. With limited industrial success in comparison with that of other late industrializers, signaled by China's military humiliation at the hands of Russia and Japan, two new industrial powers at the turn of the twentieth century, the decline of the Qing state accelerated, finally leading to the collapse of the empire in 1911.

After the revolution in 1911, the ruling KMT never accomplished its goal of building a strong, centralized state amid local warlordism, military challenges from the CCP's Red Army, and invasion by Japan. The commercialized agrarian economy was still witnessing decent growth despite the social and political chaos of the time, but the state-supported industrialization in the period was far from effective. It was not until the CCP seized power and built a Soviet-style centralized state in 1949 that state-led industrialization really took off.

Many recent studies point out that SOEs and state control of the marketing of agricultural products as a means to speed up rural surplus extraction and industrial capital accumulation began in certain KMT-controlled areas before 1949 (see Kirby 1990, 1995; Cohen 2003; Bian 2005). What the CCP did after 1949 was to expand this state-owned sector to the whole economy and to collectivize agriculture, turning the state into the sole agent of capital accumulation. As a consequence, China managed to build an extensive network of heavy industries and infrastructure despite its international isolation in 1949–1979. It also successfully defended its sovereignty and geopolitical security vis-à-vis both the United States and the Soviet Union. The Mao period in China represented the culmination of a century of the state elite's quest for state-led industrialization.

The continuity between KMT and CCP economic policies across the 1949 divide is also corroborated by recent studies that unveil the comparability of industrialization strategies in the CCP-controlled mainland and KMT-controlled Taiwan after 1949. According to these studies, the expansion of KMT-controlled state enterprises, the successful land reform, and the rise of state-directed rural cooperatives that facilitated agriculture-to-industry surplus transfers in Taiwan can be seen as a mild variation of SOEs and the People's Commune in Mao China (see, e.g., Ka and Selden 1986; Yao 2008). This continuity attests to Immanuel Wallerstein's provocative formulation that "actually existing socialist countries" emerging in the mid–twentieth century were always part of the capitalist world system and that their socialist system has been little more than a strategy of rapid capital accumulation and industrial catch-up under the strong hands of mercantilist states (1984: 86–96).

In retrospect, many Deng and post-Deng reform measures would not have been that successful had it not been for the legacies of the Mao era. The SOEs and infrastructure constructed in Mao times, though moribund and unprofitable at the advent of reform, were important foundations for the capitalist takeoff during the reform period. For example, many foreign companies investing in China did not start from scratch but began as joint ventures with preexisting SOEs. At the same time, many SOEs developed into sizeable transnational capitalist corporations with financial and policy support from the state, though ownership changed from the state by itself to other combinations—for example, public listing but with the government owning a majority share. Most of China's biggest corporations today originated in the Mao era or were built on state assets developed in that era (Nolan 2012). The continuing prevalence of SOEs is inseparable from the long history of the state as the key accumulator of capital. It is not at all surprising that many other formerly socialist countries in Russia and eastern Europe have also witnessed a similar predominance of state corporations (*Economist* 2012a).

Other Mao-era legacies include the restriction of rural–urban migration by means of the household registration system and public investment in rural education and rural health care in the People's Communes. These policies created a generation of literate and healthy rural laborers available in great numbers for private, export-oriented enterprises as well as TVEs from the 1980s on. The self-reliance policy in the Mao period prevented the large-scale external borrowing in the 1970s that many other developing or socialist countries indulged in, thus sparing China from the international debt crisis in the 1980s that brought large setbacks to the developing world and the Soviet bloc.

The emphasis here on the Mao era's legacies in the making of China's capitalist boom is not intended to downplay the significance of the market reform that Deng initiated. Only under such reforms could East Asian industrial capital, which had been thriving since the end of World War II and had inherited the three-centuries-long legacies of Chinese diasporic capitalism, enter China, take advantage of the Maoist legacies and unleash the boom. As a result, China's capitalist boom has been an explosion ignited by the mixing of the Maoist legacies and East Asian export-oriented capitalism, each developing on its separate side of the Cold War in Asia.

The second myth about the rise of capitalism in China is that China is becoming a powerful, subversive, and anti–status quo power, challenging the U.S. political and economic dominance in the world as well as the global free market that the United States has promoted. This perception is often associated with exaggerated accounts of China's intention and capability to subvert the global status quo. Left-leaning authors critical of the existing global neoliberal order are tempted to believe that China will fulfill their wish that an alternative vision of development challenging the free-market orthodoxy will be ushered in. They also expect that China will bring down U.S. global dominance, take the place of the United States, and create a more egalitarian world. In the meantime, many authors on the right are prone to believe that China poses a threat to U.S. global leadership and existing international institutions, a threat that needs to be aggressively contained. In 2003, international politics expert Alastair Iain Johnston argued that China manifested a stronger orientation toward being a status quo power than toward being a revisionist power in the international system. This book shows that after more than a decade of global turbulence and China's continued ascendancy, this characterization remains valid today.

As discussed in chapters 3 and 5, China has not challenged U.S. global dominance despite its leaders' postures and its nationalist press's rhetoric. On the contrary, it has been a key force in helping perpetuate U.S. global dominance. China's SOEs have been transformed into U.S.-style capitalist corporations, many of them with the aid of Wall Street financial firms, and floated in overseas stock markets such as Hong Kong and New York. China's export-oriented growth relies on the United States and Europe, the two biggest markets for its manufactured goods, and China's exports to both places have been paid for mostly in U.S. dollars. The massive flow of U.S. dollars into China in the form of trade surplus impels China to invest addictively in U.S. Treasury bonds as the most liquid and largest US-dollar-denominated store of value. Since 2008, China has replaced Japan as the biggest foreign creditor to the United States, and such financing enables the United States to continue living and fighting beyond its means. This investment in U.S. Treasury bonds in turn facilitates the perpetuation of the global dollar standard, which has been the single most important foundation of U.S. global power. The foreign exchanges brought in by China's export sector have been the foundation of the state banks' profligate creation of liquidity that fuels fixed-asset investment. In short, the China boom relies on the global free market instituted and warranted by the United States. It is thus far from China's interest to undermine the global neoliberal status quo and U.S. leadership in it.

Though China is not likely to terminate U.S. global dominance and the global neoliberal order, it has tipped the global balance of power a bit within that order, enabling other developing countries to obtain better terms in their dealings with the United States and Europe. Throughout the postwar period, developing countries on the U.S. side of the Cold War depended on capital, financial assistance, and credits from the United States and Europe. They also relied on U.S. and European markets for their raw-materials exports. Because of this dependence, the United States or former colonizers was able to interfere with their governments' policies. Beginning in the 1980s, when the Soviet bloc was weakening, and culminating in the 1990s after the bloc's collapse, many developing countries' dependence on the West deepened and widened. Hit by the international debt crisis, many of them were subjugated to the "Washington consensus," a set of radical market-reform as well as trade and financial liberalization policies promoted by the World Bank, the IMF, and the U.S. government. The outcome of the Washington consensus was disappointing if not disastrous because many of these developing countries experienced worsening indebtedness and faltering economic growth in the wake of the reform. Nowadays, even the World Bank and IMF have backpedaled from their fervent pitch for free-market reform in the developing world.

Chapters 4 and 5 show that the capitalist boom in China makes it a new major buyer of energy and raw materials from the developing world. China is also becoming a significant source of FDI in many countries in Africa and Southeast Asia. Accompanying its investment and appetite for natural resources are the aid and loans the Chinese state has offered to its poor economic partners. China's presence in the developing world in general, to be sure, does not yet match the presence of the United States, Europe, or even the former Soviet Union. But it does relieve many developing countries' post–Cold War economic dependence on the West. Although China's presence has not severed developing countries' ties to the developed world, it does increase the plurality of their investors and trade partners, thus enhancing their bargaining power in the world market. It is in this sense that the capitalist boom in China is altering the power relations between the developing world and the developed. But we need to bear in mind that China's investment in these countries and its importing of their natural resources are driven by the same capitalist logic and national interest that drove the expansion of Western powers into the developing world. Its presence in the developing world creates new competition and exploitation, so much so that China is starting to be perceived in some developing countries as a new colonial power that deindustrializes its partners and extracts their resources. China is therefore both a facilitator of developing countries' autonomy from the developed ones and a status quo power that joins hands with traditional core powers to help reproduce a global neoliberal order. Chapter 4 also noted that although China's rapid economic growth is temporarily reversing the long-term trend of increasing global inequality between the West and the rest since the Industrial Revolution, its continuous growth beyond the world average income will bring a revival of rising global inequality. The China boom, therefore, has not altered the capitalist dynamics of world income polarization in the long run.

In response to those who argue that China is the cure for the ongoing global economic crisis, which intensified after 2008, chapter 6 demonstrates that the structural imbalance in China's capitalist development, which has worsened since the 1990s, is in fact one of the sources of the global economic imbalance that precipitated the crisis. A decentralized authoritarian regime of capitalist development emerged in the aftermath of the 1989 crackdown and unleashed rapid export-oriented industrialization and debt-financed investment by the state sector, which led to a deteriorating imbalance between consumption and investment. The relatively slow growth in domestic consumption led to China's increasing reliance on foreign markets, a ballooning trade surplus, and the increasing purchase of U.S. Treasury bonds, which in turn contributed to the expansion of the U.S. debt bubble accountable for the Great Crash of 2008. The expansion of debt-financed overinvestment in China after the 1990s has also created financial and real-estate bubbles within China that are themselves destined to deflate. The rapid rebound of the Chinese economy in 2009–2010 after the initial shock of the Great Crash of 2008 was driven solely by a redoubling of debt-driven overinvestment, which aggravated the economy's structural imbalance. The imminent and inevitable readjustment of the Chinese economy is poised to create significant repercussions throughout the world.

The Many Debts of the China Boom

Any readjustment of the structure of capitalist development in China will have to involve an increase in domestic consumption's share in GDP and a corresponding reduction in export and investment's share. As shown in chapter 6, such restructuring must be associated with a profound redistribution of wealth and income that will let average households share a larger slice of the pie of the expanding economy, reducing the advantages that the state has been offering to the export sector and state enterprises, both of which have been protected by entrenched vested interests in the political process. Such readjustment, coupled with the cleaning up of existing bad debts in the system, will inevitably bring a slowdown in economic growth through either a disorderly hard landing or an orderly soft landing. This slowdown already started in 2013, when China's GDP growth rate dropped below 8 percent, which has happened only two times before in almost three decades, in 1990–1991 and 1999–2000. In 2014, China's GDP growth rate dropped below target to 7.4 percent, hitting a twenty-four-year low point. Although the earlier two slowdowns did not last long, with the economy rebounding strongly amid expanding global free trade that fueled China's export-led prosperity, the latest slowdown is likely to get worse and be more protracted not only because of the dismal state of the global economy but also because of the dangerously high level of the economy's total indebtedness, which has reached a staggering 282 percent of GDP in 2015.

Although such a slowdown is inevitable and normal in the adjustment and rebalancing process, it is unknown whether existing political institutions in China can withstand it. The authoritarian-capitalist state so far has been effective in containing unrest despite escalating social polarization. But this containment has been made possible by a continuously booming economy. Though all types of protests proliferated and intensified from the 1990s to the 2010s (O'Brien 2006; Silver and Zhang 2009; Perry and Selden 2010), the Chinese state, aided by increasing financial and fiscal means resulting from the economic boom, has been able to keep this unrest under control by making concessions to protesters' demands.

For example, in a delayed response to the widespread and increasingly violent tax riots in the countryside during the 1990s, the Chinese government simply abolished agricultural taxes in 2006. The escalating labor unrest in export-processing zones in South China impelled the central government to devise the new Labor Contract Law in 2008, which provided more protection to labor and directed labor to use legal means in defending their rights (Solinger 2009). Of course, these measures were far from providing a solution to the root cause of unrest because the vested interests usually found new ways to get around such measures to reproduce their privileges. Many local governments redoubled their efforts to seize farmland for real-estate development to compensate for revenue loss owing to the abolition of agricultural taxes. Enterprises also increased their use of free vocational labor in place of formal labor protected by the new Labor Contract Law (see Pun, Chan, and Selden forthcoming). Regardless of these limits, these concessions have nevertheless offered an effective temporary containment of unrest.

The booming economy also supports political stability by bestowing the regime with "performance legitimacy" (Zhao 2009), enabling it to claim credit for the continuous prosperity and improvement in livelihoods—either actual or expected. Under this perceived legitimacy of the state, protesters of all stripes will be more prone to restrict their demands to economic ones and not challenge the political system at its core (O'Brien 2006; Whyte 2010; Hung 2011). Another link between economic growth and stability is the availability of a large "stability maintenance fund" to local governments. In the context of the state's ever-improving fiscal position amid the capitalist boom, local governments use this fund to build large networks of surveillance and repression that prevent any incipient protests. Local governments can also use this fund to offer cash compensation to protesters once protest has materialized (C. Lee and Zhang 2013).

All these ways of maintaining stability are connected to the boom in one way or another. Once the economic slowdown continues for a prolonged period, they will no longer be effective. By that time, there might be an uncontained explosion of social unrest that presents a serious challenge to the authoritarian state. The chaos that this unrest might engender would further repress economic growth, creating a downward spiral of deepening economic crisis, worsening social unrest, and possibly even war if the party–state elite were to try to divert popular anger to aggressive nationalism.

Another crisis that feeds into a prospective economic crisis is the environmental crisis, an aggravating factor in most of the past three decades of capitalist boom. In the fierce competition for foreign manufacturing capital, local governments rely on the vast supply of low-wage labor from the countryside and a variety of tax and policy concessions. Their competitiveness also stems from lax implementation of whatever environmental laws and standards exist. The result is that the manufacturing establishment in China has rarely been forced to bear the cost of cleaning up their emission and waste discharges. Industrial pollution to the air, rivers, and underground water has reached deadly levels. It is estimated that the economic costs of environmental degradation around the mid-2000s stood at 8 to12 percent of GDP, mainly in the form of health-care costs and the loss of life (Economy 2010: 91). Such costs are poised to rise as the reckless industrial growth continues.

A related issue is that with the increasing encroachment on farmland by urban and real-estate development, together with the loss of labor power to the urban-industrial sector, growth in agricultural output has been falling far behind growth in demand for three decades. An increasingly meat-heavy diet among the urban population adds pressure on the already dwindling agricultural resources. In the 1980s, when China's capitalist takeoff had just started, China was more than self-sufficient in its food supply. But in 2001, it became a net importer of food. As of 2010, China's trade deficit in agricultural products had passed U.S.$40 billion (Keogh 2013; also see Gale, Hansen, and Jewison 2015).

In 1995, environmentalist and food expert Lester Brown published *Who Will Feed China?*, warning that the rapid economic growth and industrialization of China will eventually generate a food crisis within China and throughout the world. At the time of publication, the book was criticized for "China bashing" because many social scientists argue that improvements in farming technology would catch up with the increasing demand for food in China so that a food crisis would never come (Huang J. et al. 1999). But today, with China's food security being compromised and food prices around the world skyrocketing, Lester Brown's thesis has been reexamined seriously (see, e.g., Bacchus 2011; Brown 2011; Larsen 2012). The pollution of water and soil from urban-industrial growth only makes matters worse as the number of cases of contaminated agricultural land and products rise. Clean, drinkable water is increasingly scarce, leading the World Bank and many other observers to predict a brewing water crisis in China (Zheng et al. 2010; *Economist* 2013c). Some pessimists go as far as to stipulate that the rise of China is pushing the capitalist world economy beyond its environmental limit, and the looming environmental crisis, if not effectively contained, will not only terminate China's economic rise but also threaten the reproduction of the capitalist world system at large (Li M. 2009).

Capitalist development is destined to be plagued by the boom-and-bust cycle. No nation experiencing robust capitalist growth can avoid an outbreak of economic crisis, as demonstrated by the great panic in Britain in 1796–1797; the Great Depression in the United States in the 1930s; and Japan's "lost decade" in the 1990s. The consequences of these crises varied. In some instances, the state, under particular constellations of social and political forces, adopted timely and pertinent reform to rebalance the economy, preparing it for more sustained growth, as in late-eighteenth-century Britain and the early-twentieth-century United States. In other instances, the state failed to respond effectively, and the economy fell into protracted stagnation and crisis, as in late-twentieth-century Japan. It is nearly certain that China will confront this challenge sooner or later, and the social and environmental debts that have been accumulating in the system during its boom years will likely make the readjustment of China's developmental path more challenging. However, economic slowdown and multiple crises might urge China to restart its long-suspended political liberalization, which would foster more inclusive political processes. Political liberalization, if it unfolds smoothly, would enable the Chinese state and society to weather a slowing economy in a more stable manner, making China's rebalancing less painful.

China has come a long way from the eighteenth century. On the road to the capitalist boom at the turn of the twenty-first century, there were imperial disintegration, revolutions, wars, and famines. It is unthinkable that the upcoming crises might be more daunting than the ones that China has weathered over the centuries. In the long run, if China can effectively accomplish the overdue rebalancing of its economy, its robust capitalist development will continue for a long time. Whether it can accomplish such a transition, how long such a transition will take, and how painful it will be to China and to the world depend on a variety of contingent forces inside and outside China. If China successfully weathers intervening crises, it will join the United States, Japan, and Germany as yet another major capitalist power.

In the end, China is far from becoming a subversive power that will transform the existing global neoliberal order because China itself is one of the biggest beneficiaries of this order. It will not be exonerated any time soon for its role in facilitating continued dominance by the United States in the world through its supply of low-cost export and credit to the United States. If U.S. global dominance is going to end, it will not likely be fostered by China but by some other forces. To be sure, China has been reshaping and will continue to reshape the context of development in the developing world, bringing to other developing countries more favorable and competitive conditions for development at the same time. Whether China's net impact will be beneficial or detrimental to development will vary from country to country and will change from time to time. In the short run and from the perspective of specific individual countries, China's capitalist boom might seem like a game changer that will bring new prosperity, empowerment, subordination, or crisis. At the global level and in the long run, nevertheless, China is set to disappoint many who hail or fear the prospect of its challenging the existing global order in any fundamental way.

Notes

PREFACE

1. For these and other quotations of European philosophers' representation of China, see Hung 2003.

ONE. A MARKET WITHOUT CAPITALISM, 1650–1850

1. Before the early-modern period, tea in China was grown principally in Yunan and Sichuan, far inland. When tea exports grew, Fujian gradually replaced the former tea-growing areas.
2. In this analysis, I adopt Ch'u T'ung-tsu's (1962) definition of gentry elite as those who obtained an imperial degree but did not have a bureaucratic career.

THREE. THE CAPITALIST BOOM, 1980–2008

1. See Wang and Hu 1994, 1999: 169–98; and Breslin 1996 for discussion of the central government's falling capacity. See also Zweig 2002 for an interesting discussion of how the globalization of the Chinese economy, once initiated by the central government, has been continuously advanced and shaped by local interests beyond the center's control.
2. For example, the private-enterprise to public-enterprise asset ratio in the textile sector is the highest, at nine to one, as shown in table 3.1.

3. The figures show the weighted average of Japan, Taiwan, and South Korea as "Other East Asian economies"; Hong Kong and Singapore were excluded because of the large share of entrepôt trade in their economies.

FOUR. RISE OF THE REST

1. The gini coefficient is a measurement of inequality that ranges from 0 to 1, in which 0 means absolute income equality, and 1 means maximum possible inequality, in which one person possesses all income in the society. Today, countries' gini coefficients range from about 0.25 to 0.60 across the world.
2. GDP per capita income measured in PPP is the income adjusted for the cost of living and inflation in the country concerned, taking away the effect of diverging and fluctuating exchange rates and making the comparison of per capita income across countries closer to a comparison of living standards. In the data here, GDP per capita in PPP is expressed in the 2005 international dollar.
3. Some studies confirm that rising interregional inequalities are driving the increase in overall inequality in China under recent rapid economic growth and market reform (e.g., Wang S. and Hu 1999; Gajwani, Kanbur, and Zhang 2006; Tsui 2007; Fan and Sun 2008). Some studies dispute this view and argue that at any particular point in time interregional inequality accounts for less than 50 percent of overall inequality in China (see, e.g., Benjamin et al. 2008). But a comparison of *change* in overall inequality and *change* in inequality among the rural and urban components of all provincial units of China shows that the latter accounts for close to 90 percent of the former. For details, see Hung and Kucinskas 2011: table 3.
4. For examples of the debate, see Council on Foreign Relations 2007; BBC Africa Debate 2012.
5. In the calculation, products characterized as under "direct threat" are those where China's market share increases while the markets shares of Latin America and the Caribbean decrease in the world market. Products under "partial threat" are those where the market share of Latin America and the Caribbean increase at a slower rate than China's market share.

FIVE. A POST-AMERICAN WORLD?

1. One example is the "Chinese Professor" ad that ran on the eve of the 2010 midterm election in the United States (http://www.youtube.com/watch?v=OTSQozWP-rM).
2. For example, see *BBC News* 2001.
3. For example, see the widely cited report "China Threatens 'Nuclear Option' of Dollar Sales" (*Telegraph* 2007).

4. Likewise, China's newfound enthusiasm in investing in infrastructure in Central Asia and funding this new initiative by a Silk Road Fund in Beijing and a China-dominated Asian Infrastructure Investment Bank are expected to encounter similar political backlash (Hung 2015).

SIX. GLOBAL CRISIS

1. If Y is national product, C is total consumption, G is government spending, I is total investment, (X – M) is trade balance, and S is saving, we have $Y = C + G + I + (X - M)$, which leads to $Y - C - G - I = S - I = X - M$, as by definition $Y - C - G = S$. Therefore, saving minus investment is equal to trade balance.

2. The comment is from Xu Xiaonian at the China Europe International Business School in Shanghai. See *China Post* 2009.

3. It is noteworthy that right after Xi's assumption of the post of party general secretary in November 2012, the government announced its plan to boost economic growth through urbanization, speeding up the transformation of inland rural residents into urban dwellers. See *Xinhua News* 2012a.

References

Abu-Lughod, Janet L. 1989. *Before European Hegemony: The World System, AD 1250–1350*. New York: Oxford University Press.

Acemoglu, Daron, and James A. Robinson. 2012. "Is State Capitalism Winning?" Project Syndicate. http://www.project-syndicate.org/commentary/why-china -s-growth-model-will-fail-by-daron-acemoglu-and-james-a--robinson.

Aglietta, Michel. 1979. *A Theory of Capitalist Regulation: The U.S. Experience*. London: New Left Books.

——. 1998. "Capitalism at the Turn of the Century: Regulation Theory and the Challenge of Social Change." *New Left Review* 232 (November–December): 41–90.

Aglietta, Michel, and Guo Bai. 2012. *China's Development: Capitalism and Empire*. London: Routledge.

Ahrens, Nathaniel. 2013. *China's Competitiveness: Myth, Reality, and Lessons for the United States and Japan. Case Study: SAIC Motor Corporation*. Washington, D.C.: Center for Strategic and International Studies Hills Program on Governance.

Alderson, Art S., and Francois Nielsen. 1999. "Income Inequality, Development, and Dependence: A Reconsideration." *American Sociological Review* 64 , no. 4: 606–31.

——. 2002. "Globalization and the Great U-Turn: Income Inequality Trends in 16 OECD Countries." *American Journal of Sociology* 107, no. 5: 1244–99.

Allen, Robert C. 1983. "Collective Invention." *Journal of Economic Behavior and Organization* 4 (1983): 1–24.

——. 2009. "Agricultural Productivity and Rural Incomes in England and the Yangtze Delta, c. 1620–1820." *Economic History Review* 62, no. 3: 525–50. http://www.economics.ox.ac.uk/Members/robert.allen/Papers/chineseag.pdf.

Altman, Roger. 2009. "The Great Crash, 2008: The Geopolitical Setback for the West." *Foreign Affairs*, January–February. http://www.foreignaffairs.com/articles/63714/roger-c-altman/the-great-crash-2008.

Amsden, Alice. 1989. *Asia's Next Giant: South Korea and Late Industrialization.* Oxford: Oxford University Press.

Anderson, Perry. 2010. "Sinomania." *London Review of Books*, January 28.

——. 2011. "Lula's Brazil." *London Review of Books* 33, no. 7: 3–12.

Ando, Mitsuyo. 2006. "Fragmentation and Vertical Intra-industry Trade in East Asia." *North American Journal of Economics and Finance* 17:257–81.

Andreas, Joel. 2009. *Rise of the Red Engineers: The Cultural Revolution and the Origins of China's New Class.* Stanford, Calif.: Stanford University Press.

Arrighi, Giovanni. 1994. *The Long Twentieth Century: Money, Power, and the Origins of Our Times.* London: Verso.

——. 1996. "The Rise of East Asia: World-Systemic and Regional Aspects." *International Journal of Sociology and Social Policy* 7:6–44.

——. 2007. *Adam Smith in Beijing: Lineages of the Twenty-First Century.* London: Verso.

Arrighi, Giovanni, and Jessica Drangel. 1986. "The Stratification of the World Economy: An Exploration of the Semiperipheral Zone." *Review* 10, no. 1: 9–74.

Arrighi, Giovanni, and Beverly Silver. 1999. *Chaos and Governance in the Modern World-System.* Minneapolis: University of Minnesota Press.

Arrighi, Giovanni, Beverly Silver, and Benjamin Brewer. 2003. "Industrial Convergence and the Persistence of the North–South Industrial Divide." *Studies in Comparative International Development* 38, no. 1: 3–31.

Atwell, William S. 1977. "Notes on Silver, Foreign Trade, and the Late Ming Economy," *Late Imperial China* 3, no. 8: 1–33.

——. 1982. "International Bullion Flows and the Chinese Economy Circa 1530–1650." *Past and Present* 95 (May): 68–90.

——. 1998. "Ming China and the Emerging World Economy. C. 1470–1650." In Denis C. Twitchett and Frederick W. Mote, eds., *The Cambridge History of China*, vol. 8, no. 2: *The Ming Dynasty*, 376–416. Cambridge: Cambridge University Press.

Austin, Kenneth. 2011. "Communist China's Capitalism: The Highest Stage of Capitalist Imperialism." *World Economics* 12, no. 1: 79–95.

Bacchus, James. 2011. "Chinese Drought Could Cause Global Food Crisis." *Huffington Post*, March 16. http://www.huffingtonpost.com/james-bacchus/chinese-drought-could-cau_b_836565.html.

Baiocchi, Gianpaolo, Einar Braathen, and Ana Claudia Teixeira. 2013. "Transformation Institutionalized? Making Sense of Participatory Democracy in the Lula Era." In Kristian Stokke and Olle Törnquist, eds., *Democratization in the Global South: The Importance of Transformative Politics.* London: Palgrave.

Bai Gao. 2012. "The Dollar Standard and Global Production: The Institutional Origins of the Financial Crisis." Paper presented at the annual meeting of the American Sociological Association, San Francisco, August.

Baldwin, Richard. 2006. *Managing the Noodle Bowl: The Fragility of East Asian Regionalism.* Discussion Paper no. 5561. London: Center for Economic Policy Research.

Bank for International Settlement. 2006. *76th Annual Report.* Basel: Bank for International Settlement.

——. 2007. *77th Annual Report.* Basel: Bank for International Settlement.

——. 2014. "Triennial Central Bank Survey: Global Foreign Exchange Market Turnover in 2013." http://www.bis.org/publ/rpfxf13fxt.pdf.

Bank of China. 2006. *Bank of China Limited Global Offereing.* Hong Kong: Bank of China.

Bardhan, Pranab. 2012. *Awaking Giants, Feet of Clay: Assessing the Economic Rise of China and India.* Princeton, N.J.: Princeton University Press.

Baum, Richard, ed. 1991. *Reform and Reaction in Post-Mao China: The Road to Tiananmen.* London: Routledge.

Baum, Richard, and Alexei Shevchenko. 1999. "The State of the State." In Merle Goldman and Roderick MacFarquar, eds., *The Paradox of China's Post-Mao Reforms*, 334–60. Cambridge, Mass.: Harvard University Press.

BBC Africa Debate. 2012. "China in Africa: Partner or Plunderer?" May 25. http://www.bbc.co.uk/programmes/p00sh19g.

BBC News. 2001. "US Panel Says Yuan Is a Threat to Dollar's Dominance." November 17.

Benjamin, Dwayne, Loren Brandt, John Giles, and Sangui Wang. 2008. "Income Inequality During China's Economic Transition." In Loren Brandt and Thomas Rawski, eds., *China's Great Transformation: Origins, Mechamisms, and Consequences of the Post-Reform Economic Boom.* New York: Cambridge University Press.

Bernanke, Benjamin. 2005. "The Global Saving Glut and the U.S. Current Account Deficit." Sandridge Lecture, Virginia Association of Economists, Richmond, March 10. http://www.federalreserve.gov/boarddocs/speeches/2005/20050414/.

Bernstein, Thomas, and Xiaobo Lu. 2003. *Taxation Without Representation in Contemporary Rural China.* Cambridge: Cambridge University Press.

Berry, Albert, and John Serieux. 2006. *Riding the Elephants: The Evolution of World Economic Growth and Income Distribution at the End of the Twentieth Century (1980–2000).* Working Paper no. 27. New York: United Nations Department of Economic and Social Affairs.

Bezemer, Dirk. 2008. "Agriculture, Development, and Urban Bias." *World Development* 36, no. 8: 1342–64.

Bian, Morris L. 2005. *The Making of the State Enterprise System in Modern China: The Dynamics of Institutional Change.* Cambridge, Mass.: Harvard University Press.

Bix, Herbert P. 1986. *Peasant Protest in Japan, 1590–1884.* New Haven, Conn.: Yale University Press.

Blecher, Marc, and Vivienne Shue. 2001. "Into Leather: State-Led Development and the Private Sector in Xinji." *China Quarterly* 166:368–93.

Bloomberg. 2012. "China Said to Plan Boosting Export-Tax Rebates on Some Goods." September 4.

Blumenthal, Dan 2005. "Providing Arms: China and the Middle East." *Middle East Quarterly* 12, no. 2: 11–19.

Bond, Patrick 2013. "Sub-imperialism as Lubricant of Neoliberalism: South African 'Deputy Sheriff' Duty Within BRICS." *Third World Quarterly* 34, no. 2: 251–70.

Boughton, James M. 2001. *Silent Revolution: The International Monetary Fund, 1979–1989.* Washington, D.C.: International Monetary Fund. https://www.imf.org/external/pubs/ft/history/2001/ch08.pdf.

Bourguignon, François, and Christian Morrisson. 2002. "Inequality Among World Citizens, 1820–1992." *American Economic Review* 92:727–44.

Bower, Ernest Z. 2010. "China's Activities in Southeast Asia and Implications for US Interest." Statement before the U.S.–China Economic and Security Review Commission, February 4, Washington, D.C. https://csis.org/files/100204_bower_testimony.pdf.

Brandt, Loren. 1989. *Commercialization and Agricultural Development: Central and Eastern China 1870–1937.* Cambridge: Cambridge University Press.

Braudel, Fernand. 1992. *Capitalism & Civilization: 15th–18th Century.* 3 vols. San Francisco: University of California Press.

Brautigam, Deborah. 2011. *The Dragon's Gift: The Real Story of China in Africa.* New York: Oxford University Press.

Brenner, Robert. 1993. *Merchants and Revolution: Commercial Change, Political Conflict, and London's Overseas Traders, 1550–1653.* Princeton, N.J.: Princeton University Press.

——. 2003. *The Boom and the Bubble: The US in the World Economy.* London: Verso.

———. 2004. "New Boom or New Bubble? The Trajectory of the US Economy." *New Left Review* 25:57–100.

Brenner, Robert, and Christopher Isett. 2002. "England's Divergence from China's Yangzi Delta: Property Relations, Microeconomics, and Patterns of Development." *Journal of Asian Studies* 61, no. 2: 609–62.

Breslin, Shaun G. 1996. "China: Developmental State or Dysfunctional Development?" *Third World Quarterly* 17, no.4: 689–706.

Brook, Timothy. 1990. "Family Continuity and Cultural Hegemony: The Gentry of Ningbo, 1368–1911." In Joseph W. Esherick and Mary Backus Rankin, eds., *Chinese Local Elites and Patterns of Dominance*, 27–50. Berkeley: University of California Press.

Brown, Lester. 1995. *Who Will Feed China? Wake-up Call for a Small Planet.* New York: Norton.

———. 2011. "The Great Food Crisis of 2011." *Foreign Policy*, November 12.

Bujra, Janet. 1992. "Diversity in Pre-capitalist Societies." In Tim Allen and Allan Thomas, eds., *Poverty and Development in the 1990s*, 219–40. Oxford: Oxford University Press.

Bussolo, Maurizio, Rafael E. De Hoyos, Denis Medvedev, and Dominique van der Mensbrugghe. 2007. *Global Growth and Distribution: Are China and India Reshaping the World?* Policy Research Working Paper. Washington, D.C.: World Bank.

Cai Fang and Du Yang, eds. 2009. *The China Population and Labor Yearbook.* Vol. 1: *The Approaching Lewis Turning Point and Its Policy Implications.* Leiden: Brill.

Caijing. 2009a. "Jiuye xingshi yanjun laodong hetong fa chujing ganga" (Severe unemployment jeopardizes labor contract law). January 4.

———. 2009b. "Siwanyi neiwai" (Inside and outside of the four thousand billion). March 16.

———. 2009c. "Zhongguo GDP zengzhang jin 90% you touzi ladong" (Nearly 90 percent of China's GDP growth was driven by investment). July 16.

Caixin. 2013. "Closer Look: SOEs Can Brag They Are Big—but Not Strong." July 18. http://english.caixin.com/2013-07-18/100557654.html.

Calhoun, Graig. 1994. *Neither Gods nor Emperors: Students and the Struggle for Democracy in China.* Berkeley: University of California Press.

Campbell, Jack, and Avinash Boodoosingh. 2015. "How Can Latin America Overcome Its Dependence on Commodities?" World Economic Forum Agenda. https://agenda.weforum.org/2015/05/how-can-latin-america-overcome -its-dependence-on-commodities/.

Carroll, Patrick. 2006. *Science, Culture, and Modern State Formation.* Berkeley: University of California Press.

Carteier, Michel. 1996. "Lun zhongguo de mianhua shi: gongyi, jinji he shehui tantu" (On the cotton history of China: A technical, economical, and social inquiry). In Li Xueqin, ed., *Faguo hanxue* (French Sinology I), 250–62. Beijing: Qinghua daxue chubanshe.

Chang Chungli. 1962. *The Income of the Chinese Gentry*. Seattle: University of Washington Press.

Chang, G. H. 2002. "The Cause and Cure of China's Widening Income Disparity." *China Economic Review* 13:335–40.

Chao Zhongchen. 1993. "Wenming baiyin dalian liuru ji qi yinxiang" (The massive inflow of silver in late Ming and its influences). *Shixue yuekan* 1:33–39.

Chase-Dunn, Christopher. 2006. "Globalization: A World-Systems Perspective." In Christopher Chase-Dunn and Salvatore J. Babones, eds., *Global Social Change: Historical and Comparative Perspectives*, 79–108. Baltimore: Johns Hopkins University Press.

Chase-Dunn, Christopher, Andrew K. Jorgenson, Thomas E. Reifer, and Shoon Lio. 2005. "The Trajectory of the United States in the World-System: A Quantitative Reflection." *Sociological Perspectives* 48, no. 2: 233–54.

Chen, An. 2002. "Capitalist Development, Entrepreneurial Class, and Democratization in China." *Political Science Quarterly* 117, no. 3: 401–22.

Chen Ciyu. 1982. *Jindai zhongguo chaye de fazhan yu shijie shichang* (Development of the modern Chinese tea business and the world market). Taipei: Academia Sinica.

Chen Donglin. 2004. "Ershi shiji wushi dao qishi niandai zhongguode duiwai jingji yinjin" (China's introduction of external economic assistance from the 1950s through the 1970s). *Shanghai xingzheng xueyuan xuebao*, no. 6: 69–80.

Chen Xuewen. 1991. "Mingqing shiqi minyuetai diqu de zhetangye" (The sugar business of Fujian, Guangdong, and Taiwan in Ming and Qing). In *Mingqing shehua jinji shi yanjiu* (Studies of social and economic history of Ming and Qing), 67–86. Taipei: Hedao chubanshe.

Cheng, Tiejun, and Mark Selden. 1994. "The Origins and Social Consequences of China's Hukou System." *China Quarterly* 139: 644–68.

Chibber, Vivek. 2006. *Locked in Place: State-Building and Late Industrialization in India*. Princeton, N.J.: Princeton University Press.

Chin, Gregory T. 2003. "Building 'Capitalism with China's Characteristics': The Political Economy of Model Joint Ventures in the Automotive Industry." Ph.D. diss., York University, Ontario.

China Daily. 2012. "Consider Sanctions on Japan." September 12. http://www .chinadaily.com.cn/opinion/2012-09/17/content_15761435.htm.

China Data Online. n.d. http://chinadataonline.org/.

China Post. 2009. "China Stimulus Plan Comes Under Attack at 'Summer Davos.'" September 13.

China-Profile. 2011. "Actual Foreign Direct Investment (FDI) by Country of Origin, 1990–2004." December 18. http://www.china-profile.com/data/fig_fdi_3.htm.

Chinese Information Office of the State Council. 2013. *The Diversified Employment of China's Armed Forces.* http://news.xinhuanet.com/english/china/2013–04/16/c_132312681.htm.

Chinese Ministry of Commerce. 2011. *2010 Statistical Bulletin of China's Outward Foreign Direct Investment.* Beijing: Ministry of Commerce. http://english.mofcom.gov.cn/article/statistic/foreigninvestment/201109/20110907742320.shtml.

Chinese National Bureau of Statistics. n.d. *China Statistical Yearbook.* Beijing: Chinese National Bureau of Statistics.

Chiu Peng-Sheng. 2002. "You fangliao dao gongchang: Qingdai qianqi mianbu zihao de jingji yu falu fenxi" (From putting-out system to factory system: A legal and economic analysis of cotton textile workshop in Qing Suzhou). *Lishi yanjiu* 1:75–87.

Ch'u T'ung-tsu. 1962. *Local Government in China Under the Ching.* Cambridge, Mass.: East Asian Research Center, Harvard University.

Cochran, Sherman. 2000. *Encountering Chinese Networks: Western, Japanese, and Chinese Corporations in China, 1880–1937.* Berkeley: University of California Press.

Cohen, Paul A. 2003. "Reflections on a Watershed Date: The 1949 Divide in Chinese History." In Jeffrey Wasserstrom, ed., *Twentieth Century China: New Approaches*, 29–36. London: Routledge.

Collins, Randall. 1997. "An Asian Route to Capitalism: Religious Economy and the Origins of Self-Transforming Growth in Japan." *American Sociological Review* 62, no. 6: 843–65.

Cornia, Giovanni Andrea, and Julius Court. 2001. *Inequality, Growth, and Poverty in the Era of Liberalization and Globalization.* Helsinki, Finland: UNU World Institute for Development Economics Research.

Corsetti, Giancarlo, Paolo Pesenti, and Nouriel Roubini. 1998. *What Caused the Asian Currency and Financial Crisis? Part I: A Macroeconomic Overview.* Working Paper no. 6833. Cambridge, Mass.: National Bureau of Economic Research.

Council on Foreign Relations. 2007. "Is Chinese Investment Good for Africa?" Online debate, February 20. http://www.cfr.org/china/chinese-investment-good-africa/p12622.

Crouzet, Francois. 1985. *The First Industrialists: The Problem of Origins*. Cambridge: Cambridge University Press.

Cumings, Bruce. 1984. "The Origins and Development of the Northeast Asian Political Economy: Industrial Sectors, Product Cycles, and Political Consequences." *International Organization* 38, no. 1: 1–40.

Das, Mitali, and Papa N'Diaye. 2013. *Chronicle of a Decline Foretold: Has China Reached the Lewis Turning Point?* Working paper. Washington, D.C.: International Monetary Fund. http://www.imf.org/external/pubs/cat/longres .aspx?sk=40281.0.

Davis, Deborah, and Wang Feng, eds. 2008. *Creating Wealth and Poverty in Postsocialist China*. Stanford, Calif.: Stanford University Press.

Davis, Ken. 2012. *Outward FDI from China and Its Policy Context, 2012*. Vale Columbia Center Working Paper. New York: Columbia University. http:// www.vcc.columbia.edu/files/vale/documents/China_OFDI_-_FINAL_-_7 _June_2012_3.pdf.

Desai, Nanubhai. 2007. "The Impact of Oil Prices and the Rise of China on US and Global Imbalances." http://globaleconomydoesmatter.blogspot.com/2007/01 /impact-of-oil-prices-and-rise-of-china.html.

Deyo, Frederick C. 1987. "State and Labor: Modes of Political Exclusion in East Asian Development." In Frederick C. Deyo, ed., *The Political Economy of the New Asian Industrialism*, 227–48. Ithaca, N.Y.: Cornell University Press.

Dikotter, Frank. 2006. *Exotic Commodities: Modern Objects and Everyday Life in China*. New York: Columbia University Press.

Duckett, Jane. 1998. *The Entrepreneurial State in China: Real Estate and Commerce Departments in Reform Era Tianjin*. London: Routledge.

Dunstan, Helen. 2006. *State or Merchants? Political Economy and Political Process in 1740s China*. Cambridge, Mass.: Asia Center, Harvard University.

Economist. 2001. "A Panda Breaks the Formation." August 25.

——. 2005. "A Great Big Bank Gamble: China's Banking Industry." October 29.

——. 2012a. "Leviathan as Capitalist: State Capitalist Continues to Defy Expectations of Its Demise." January 21.

——. 2012b. "Petrodollar Profusion." April 28.

——. 2013a. "An Inferno of Unprofitbability." July 6.

——. 2013b. "Lipstick on a Pig: China Is Still Dealing with the Mess Left by Previous Bank Bail-outs." August 24.

——. 2013c. "Water: All Dried Up." October 12.

Economy, Elizabeth. 2010. *The River Runs Black: The Environmental Challenge to China's Future*. Ithaca, N.Y.: Cornell University Press.

Eichengreen, Barry. 2011. *Exorbitant Privilege: The Rise and Fall of the Dollar and the Future of the International Monetary System*. Oxford: Oxford University Press.

Elman, Benjamin. 2000. *A Cultural History of Civil Examinations in Late Imperial China*. Berkeley: University of California Press.

Elvin, Mark. 1973. *The Pattern of the Chinese Past*. Stanford, Calif.: Stanford University Press.

Evans, Peter. 1995. *Embedded Autonomy: States and Industrial Transformation*. Princeton, N.J.: Princeton University Press.

Evans, Peter, and Sarah Staveteig. 2008. "The Changing Structure of Employment in Contemporary China." In Deborah Davis and Feng Wang, eds., *Creating Wealth and Poverty in Post-socialist China*, 69–83. Stanford, Calif.: Stanford University Press.

Fan, C. Cindy, and Mingjie Sun. 2008. "Regional Inequality in China, 1978–2006." *Eurasian Geography and Economics* 49:1–20.

Fan, E. X., and J. Felipe. 2005. *The Diverging Patterns of Profitability, Investment, and Growth of China and India, 1980—2003*. Working paper. Canberra: Center for Applied Macroeconomic Analysis, Australian National University.

Fan Jinmin. 1998. *Mingqing jiangnan shangyede fazhan* (Commercial development in Jiangnan during Ming and Qing times). Nanjing: Nanjing daxue chubanshe.

Fang Xing, Rui Qi Shi, Jian Rui, and Wang Shixin. 2000. "Capitalism During the Early and Middle Qing ." In Xu Dixin Xu and Wu Chengming, eds., *Chinese Capitalism, 1522–1840*, 165–248. New York: St. Martin's Press.

Fang Zhuofen, Hu Tiewen, Jian Rui, and Fang Xing. 2000. "Capitalism During the Early and Middle Qing ." In Xu Dixin and Wu Chengming, eds., *Chinese Capitalism, 1522–1840*, 249–374. New York: St. Martin's Press.

Fardoust, Shahrokh. 2012. "Managing High Oil Prices and Recycling Petrodollars." *International Economic Bulletin*, May 31. http://carnegieendowment.org/ieb/2012/05/31/managing-high-oil-prices-and-recycling-petrodollars/b10a.

Ferguson, Niall, and Moritz Schularick. 2007. " 'Chimerica' and the Global Asset Market Boom." *International Finance* 10, no. 3: 215–39.

Fernald, John G., and Oliver D. Babson. 1999. *Why Has China Survived the Asian Crisis so Well? What Risks Remain?* International Finance Discussion Papers no. 333. Washington, D.C.: Board of Governors of the Federal Reserve System. http://www.bog.frb.fed.us.

Financial Times. 2013. "Foxconn Admits Student Intern Labour Violations at China Plant." October 10.

——. 2014. "China Debt Tops 250% of National Income." *Financial Times*, July 21.

Firebaugh, Glenn. 1999. "Empirics of World Income Inequality." *American Journal of Sociology* 104, no. 6: 1597–630.

——. 2000. "Observed Trends in Between-Nation Income Inequality and Two Conjectures." *American Journal of Sociology* 106, no. 1: 215–21.

———. 2003. *The New Geography of Income Inequality.* Cambridge, Mass.: Harvard University Press.

Firebaugh, Glenn, and Brian Goesling. 2004. "Accounting for the Recent Decline in Global Income Inequality." *American Journal of Sociology* 110, no. 2: 283–312.

Fixed Point Rural Household Survey, Ministry of Agriculture (Nongyebu quanguo nongcun guding guanchadian bangongshi). 2001. *Quanguo nongcun shehui jingji dianxing diaocha shuju huibian, 1986–1999* (National rural social-economic survey data collection, 1986–1999). Beijing: Zhongguo nongye chubanshe.

———. 2010. *Quanguo nongcun guding guanchadian diaocha shuju huibian, 2000–2009* (National village fixed observation point survey data collection, 2000–2009). Beijing: Zhongguo nongye chubanshe.

Forbes. 2011. "Chinese Ministry Saved from Default." October 23.

———. 2014. "China Mobile Racing Ahead of Rivals in 3G & 4G Subscriptions." March 24.

Fortune. 2014. "Fortune Global 500 Ranking 2014." http://fortune.com /global500/.

Frank, Andre Gunder. 1998. *ReORIENT: Global Economy in the Age of Asia.* Berkeley: University of California Press.

French, Howard W. 2014. *China's Second Continent: How a Million Migrants Are Building a New Empire in Africa.* New York: Knopf.

Friedman, Edward. 1999. "Reinterpreting the Asianization of the World and the Role of the State in the Rise of China." In David A. Smith, Dorothy J. Solinger, and Steven C. Topik, eds., *States and Sovereignty in the Global Economy,* 246–63. London: Routledge.

Friedman, Edward, Paul G. Pickowicz, and Mark Selden. 1991. *Chinese Village, Socialist State.* New Haven, Conn.: Yale University Press.

Friedmann, Harriet. 1999. "Remaking 'Traditions': How We Eat, What We Eat, and the Changing Political Economy of Food." In Deborah Barndt, ed., *Women Working the NAFTA Food Chain,* 36–60. Toronto: Second Story.

Gajwani, Kiran, Ravi Kanbur, and Xiaobo Zhang. 2006. *Comparing the Evolution of Spatial Inequality in China and India: A Fifty-Year Perspective.* DSGD Discussion Paper. Washington, D.C.: International Food Policy Research Institute.

Gale, Fred, James Hansen, and Michael Jewison. 2015. *China's Growing Demand for Agricultural Imports.* United States Department of Agriculture. Economic Information Bulletin No. 136. Washington D.C.: U.S. Department of Agriculture, Economic Research Service.

Gallagher, Kevin, and Roberto Porzecanski. 2010. *The Dragon in the Room: China and the Future of Latin American Industrialization.* Stanford, Calif.: Stanford University Press.

Gallagher, Mary E. 2002. "Reform and Openness: Why China's Economic Reform Has Delayed Democracy." *World Politics* 54:338–72.

Gao Wangling. 1995. *Shiba shiji zhongguo de jinji fazhan he zhengfu zhengche* (Economic development and government policies in eighteenth-century China). Beijing: Zhonggu shehui kexue chubanshe.

——. 2005. *Zudian guanxi xinlun: dizhu, nongmin he dizu* (New perspectives on tenant relation: Landlords, peasants, and land rent). Shanghai: Shanghai shudian chubanshe.

Gavin, Francis J. 2004. *Gold, Dollars, and Power: The Politics of International Monetary Relations, 1958–1971.* Chapel Hill: University of North Carolina Press.

Gerschenkron, Alexander. 1962. *Economic Backwardness in Historical Perspective.* Cambridge, Mass.: Belknap Press of Harvard University Press.

Gilboy, George J. 2004. "The Myth Behind China's Miracle." *Foreign Affairs,* July–August. http://www.foreignaffairs.com/articles/59918/george-j-gilboy /the-myth-behind-chinas-miracle.

Goldstone, Jack A. 2000. "The Rise of the West or Not? A Revision to Socioeconomic History." *Sociological Theory* 18, no. 2: 175–94.

——. 2001. "Europe's Peculiar Path: Would the World Be Modern If William III's Invasion of England in 1688 Had Failed?" Paper presented at the conference "Counter-factual History," Ohio State University, February.

——. 2002. "Efflorescence and Economic Growth in World History: Rethinking the 'Rise of the West' and the Industrial Revolution." *Journal of World History* 13, no. 2: 323–89.

——. 2003. "Feeding the People, Starving the State: China's Agricultural Revolution in the 17th/18th Centuries." Paper presented at the Global Economic History Network Conference, London, September.

——. 2004. "Neither Late Imperial nor Early Modern: Efflorescences and the Qing Formation in World History." In Lynn A. Struve, ed., *The Qing Formation in World-Historical Time,* 242–302. Cambridge, Mass.: Asian Center, Harvard University.

Gowan, Peter. 1999. *Contemporary Intra–Core Relation and World System Theory.* London: Verso.

——. 2004. "Contemporary Intra–Core Relations and World Systems Theory." *Journal of World-Systems Research* 10, no. 2: 471–500.

Grabowski, Richard. 1994. "The Successful Developmental State: Where Does It Come From?" *World Development* 22, no. 3: 413–22.

Grassby, Richard. 2001. *Kinship and Capitalism: Marriage, Family, and Business in the English Speaking World*. New York: Cambridge University Press.

Greenberg, Michael. 1951. *British Trade and the Opening of China 1800–42*. New York: Cambridge University Press.

Grimsditch, Mark. 2012. *China's Investments in Hydropower in the Mekong Region: The Kamchay Hydropower Dam, Kampot, Cambodia*. Report. Washington, D.C.: Bank Information Center, World Bank. http://www.bicusa .org/wp-content/uploads/2013/02/Case+Study+-+China+Investments+in +Cambodia+FINAL+2.pdf.

Guardian. 2011. "Dalai Lama Visit Blocked by South Africa to Please China, Says Opposition." September 27.

Gulick, John. 2005. "Rising Intra-Core Rivalry and the US Turn Toward East Asia." In Faruk Tabak, ed., *Allies as Rivals: The US, Europe, and Japan in a Changing World-System*. Boulder, Colo.: Paradigm.

Guo Chengkang. 1996. "The Price Question in 18th Century China and the Government's Remedies." *Qing Studies* (Beijing) 1:8–19.

Guo Yong and Hu Angang. 2004. "The Administrative Monopoly in China's Economic Transition." *Communist and Post-Communist Studies* 37:265–80.

Haacke, Jürgen. 2012. "Myanmar: Now a Site for Sino-US Geopolitical Competition?" In Nicholas Kitchen, ed., *IDEAS Reports—Special Reports*, 53–60. London: London School of Economics and Political Science.

Haddad, Mona. 2007. *Trade Integration in East Asia: The Role of China and Production Networks*. Policy Research Working Paper no. 4160. Washington, D.C.: World Bank.

Haggard, Stephan. 1990. *Pathways from the Periphery: The Politics of Growth in the Newly Industrializing Countries*. Ithaca, N.Y.: Cornell University Press.

Haglund, Dan. 2009. "In It for the Long Term? Governance and Learning Among Chinese Investors in Zambia's Copper Sector." *China Quarterly* 199:627–46.

Hamashita, Takeshi. 2008. *China, East Asia, and the World Economy: Regional and Historical Perspectives*. New York: Routledge.

Hamilton, Gary G. 1999. "Hong Kong and the Rise of Capitalism in Asia." In Gary G. Hamilton, ed., *Cosmopolitan Capitalists: Hong Kong and the Chinese Diaspora at the End of the Twentieth Century*, 14–34. Seattle: University of Washington Press.

——. 2006. *Commerce and Capitalism in Chinese Societies*. London: Routledge.

Haroz, David. 2011. "China in Africa: Symbiosis or Exploitation?" *The Fletcher Forum of World Affairs*. http://www.fletcherforum.org/2011/05/15/haroz/.

Harrell, Stevan, and Elizabeth J. Perry. 1982. "Syncretic Sects in Chinese Society." *Modern China* 8, no. 3: 283–304.

Hartford, Kathleen. 1990. "The Political Economy Behind Beijing Spring." In Tony Saich, ed., *The Chinese People's Movement: Perspectives on Spring 1989*, 50–82. Armonk, N.Y.: M. E. Sharpe.

Harvey, David. 1982. *The Limits to Capital*. Oxford: Blackwell.

——. 2003. *The New Imperialism*. Oxford: Oxford University Press.

——. 2005. *A Brief History of Neoliberalism*. Oxford: Oxford University Press.

He Fengquan. 1996. *Aomen yu putaoya dafanchuan: Putaoya he jindai zaoqi taipingyang maoyiwang de xingcheng* (Macao and the Portuguese Gallean: Portugal and the formation of the early-modern Pacific trade network). Beijing: Beijing daxue chubanshe.

He Jianwu and Louis Kuijs. 2007. *Rebalancing China's Economy—Modeling a Policy Package*. China Research Paper no. 7. Washington, D.C.: World Bank. http://www.worldbank.org.cn/English/Content/253163888224.shtml.

Hesketh, Therese, and Wei Xing Zhu. 1997. "Health in China: From Mao to Market Reform." *British Medical Journal* 314:1540–49.

Heston, Alan, Robert Summers, and Bettina Aten. 2012. "Penn World Table Version 7.1." Center for International Comparisons of Production, Income and Prices, University of Pennsylvania, November. https://pwt.sas.upenn.edu /php_site/pwt_index.php.

Heyer, Hazel. 2008. "Donald Trump Dismayed with the U.S. and the Economy." *Global Travel Industry News*, June 6. http://www.eturbonews.com/2914 /donald-trump-dismayed-us-and-economy.

Hilton, Rodney, ed. 1978. *The Transition from Feudalism to Capitalism*. London: New Left Books.

Hinton, William. 1966. *Fanshen: A Documentary of Revolution in a Chinese Village*. Berkeley: University of California Press.

Ho Ping-ti. 1954. "The Salt Merchants of Yang-chou: A Study of Commercial Capitalism in Eighteenth-Century China." *Harvard Journal of Asiatic Studies* 17, nos. 1–2: 130–68.

——. 1962. *The Ladder of Success in Imperial China: Aspects of Social Mobility, 1368–1911*. New York: Columbia University Press.

Ho, Samuel P. S. 1979. "Industrialization and Rural Development: Evidence from Taiwan." *Economic Development and Cultural Change* 28, no. 1: 77–96.

Ho, Virginia Emily. 2008. "From Contracts to Compliance? An Early Look at Implementation of China's New Labor Legislation." Unpublished manuscript, Indiana University–Bloomington Law School.

Hobsbawm, Eric J. 1952. "The Machine Breakers." *Past and Present* 1:57–70.

Hopewell, Kristen. 2012. "Shifting Power in Global Economic Governance: The Rise of Brazil, India, and China at the WTO." Ph.D. diss., University of Michigan.

——. 2014. "Different Paths to Power: The Rise of Brazil, India, and China at the World Trade Organization." *Review of International Political Economy* 21 (June): 1–28.

Howe, Christopher. 1996. *The Origins of Japanese Trade Supremacy: Development and Technology in Asia from 1540 to the Pacific War.* Chicago: Chicago University Press.

Hsing You-tien. 1998. *Making Capitalism in China: The Taiwan Connection.* New York: Oxford University Press.

Huang Jikun, Scott Rozelle, and Mark W. Rosegrant. 1999. "China's Food Economy to the Twenty-First Century: Supply, Demand, and Trade." *Economic Development and Cultural Change* 47, no. 4: 737–66.

Huang, Jikin, Scott Rozelle, and Honglin Wang. 2006. "Fostering or Stripping Rural China: Modernizing Agriculture and Rural to Urban Capital Flows." *Developing Economies* 44, no. 1: 1–26.

Huang, Philip C. C. 1985. *The Peasant Economy and Social Change in North China.* Stanford, Calif.: Stanford University Press.

——. 1990. *The Peasant Family and Rural Development in the Yangzi Delta, 1350–1988.* Stanford, Calif.: Stanford University Press.

Huang, Philip, and Peng Yusheng. 2007. "Sanda lishixing bianqiande jiaohui yu zhongguo xiao guimo nongye de qianjing" (The conjuncture of three historical trends and the prospect of small-scale farming in China). *Zhongguo shehui kexue* 4:74–88.

Huang Ping. 2000. *Bupingheng fazhan geju xia de nongcun kunjing* (Rural impasses under the structure of uneven development). Hong Kong: University Service Center, Chinese University of Hong Kong. http://www.usc.cuhk.edu .hk/PaperCollection/Details.aspx?id=1786.

Huang Yasheng. 2002. "Between Two Coordination Failures: Automotive Industrial Policy in China with a Comparison to Korea." *Review of International Political Economy* 9, no. 3: 538–73.

——. 2003. *Selling China: Foreign Direct Investment During the Reform Era.* Cambridge: Cambridge University Press.

——. 2008. *Capitalism with Chinese Characteristics: Entrepreneurship and the State.* Cambridge: Cambridge University Press.

——. 2011. "Behind the Veneer of China's Growth." *Forbes*, July 29. http://www .forbes.com/2011/08/03/forbes-india-worrisome-macroeconomic-picture -of-china.html.

Huang Yasheng and Tarun Khanna. 2003. "Can India Overtake China?" *Foreign Policy*, July 1. http://www.foreignpolicy.com/articles/2003/07/01/can _india_overtake_china.

Hughes, Neil C. 2005. "A Trade War with China?" *Foreign Affairs*, July–August 2005. http://www.foreignaffairs.com/articles/60825/neil-c-hughes/a-trade-war-with-china.

Hui, Po-Keung. 1995. "Overseas Chinese Business Networks: East Asian Economic Development in Historical Perspective." Ph.D. diss., State University of New York, Binghamton.

Hung, Ho-fung. 2001. "Imperial China and Capitalist Europe in the Eighteenth-Century Global Economy." *Review* 24, no. 4: 473–513.

——. 2003. "Orientalist Knowledge and Social Theories: China and the European Conceptions of East–West Differences from 1600 to 1900." *Sociological Theory* 21, no. 3: 254–79.

——. 2004. "Early Modernities and Contentious Politics in Mid-Qing China, c. 1740–1839." *International Sociology* 19, no. 4: 478–503.

——. 2005. "Contentious Peasants, Paternalist State, and Arrested Capitalism in China's Long Eighteenth Century." In Christopher Chase-Dunn and E. N. Anderson, eds., *The Historical Evolution of World-Systems*, 155–73. New York: Palgrave.

——. 2008. "Rise of China and the Global Overaccumulation Crisis." *Review of International Political Economy* 15, no. 2: 149–79.

——. ed. 2009a. *China and the Transformation of Global Capitalism*. Baltimore: Johns Hopkins University Press.

——. 2009b. "Introduction: The Three Transformations of Global Capitalism." In Ho-fung Hung, ed., *China and the Transformation of Global Capitalism*, 1–21. Baltimore: Johns Hopkins University Press.

——. 2009c. "America's Head Servant? The PRC's Dilemma in the Global Crisis." *New Left Review*, ser. 2, no. 60. 5–24.

——. 2011. *Protest with Chinese Characteristics: Demonstrations, Riots, and Petitions in the Mid-Qing Dynasty*. New York: Columbia University Press.

——. 2013. "China: Saviour or Challenger of the Dollar Hegemony?" *Development and Change* 44, no. 6: 1341–61.

——. 2014. "Cold War and China in the (Un)Making of the Global Dollar Standard." *Political Power and Social Theory* 27:53–80.

——. 2015. "China Steps Back." *New York Times*, April 5.

Hung, Ho-fung, and Jaime Kucinskas. 2011. "Globalization and Global Inequality: Assessing the Impact of the Rise of China and India, 1980–2005." *American Journal of Sociology* 116:1478–513.

Huntington, Samuel. 1996. *The Clash of Civilizations and the Remaking of World Order*. New York: Simon and Schuster.

Hurst, William. 2009. *The Chinese Workers After Socialism*. New York: Cambridge University Press.

International Monetary Fund (IMF). 2000. *Debt- and Reserve-Related Indicators of External Vulnerability*. Washington, D.C.: Policy Department and Review Department, IMF. http://www.imf.org/external/np/pdr/debtres/debtres .pdf.

——. n.d.a. "Direction of Trade Statistics." http://elibrary-data.imf.org/Query Builder.aspx?key=19784661&s=322.

——. n.d.b. "World Economic Outlook." http://www.econstats.com/weo/CPOL .htm.

——. n.d.c. "Currency Composition of Official Foreign Exchange Reserves." Database. http://data.imf.org/?sk=E6A5F467-C14B-4AA8-9F6D-5A09EC4E62A4.

Islam, Nazrul, Dai Erbiao, and Hiroshi Sakamoto. 2006. "Role of TFP in China's Growth." *Asian Economic Journal* 20, no. 2: 127–59.

Jacques, Martin. 2009. *When China Rules the World: The Rise of the Middle Kingdom and the End of the Western World*. London: Allen Lane.

Jameson, Fredric. 1998. *The Cultural Turn: Selected Writings on the Postmodern, 1983–1998*. London: Verso.

Jiang, Wenran. 2009. "Fuelling the Dragon: China's Rise and Its Energy and Resources Extraction in Africa." *China Quarterly* 199:585–609.

Jing Junjian. 1982. "Hierarchy in the Qing Dynasty." *Social Sciences in China: A Quarterly Journal* 3, no. 1: 156–92.

Johnson, Linda Cook. 1993. "Shangai: An Emerging Jiangnan Port, 1638–1840." In Linda Cook Johnson, ed., *Cities of Jiangnan in Late Imperial China*, 151–82. Albany: State University of New York Press.

Johnston, Alastair Iain. 2003. "Is China a Status Quo Power?" *International Security* 27, no. 4: 5–56.

Ka Chih-ming. 1998. *Japanese Colonialism in Taiwan: Land Tenure, Development, and Dependency*. Boulder, Colo.: Westview.

Ka Chih-ming and Mark Selden. 1986. "Original Accumulation, Equity, and Late Industrialization: The Cases of Socialist China and Capitalist Taiwan." *World Development* 14:1293–310.

Kaiman, Jonathan 2012. "China's Debt Bomb: Half an Hour from Beijing, the Potential Ground Zero of the Chinese Real Estate Meltdown." *Foreign Policy*, August 13.

Kang, David C. 2010. *East Asia Before the West: Five Centuries of Trade and Tribute*. New York: Columbia University Press.

Kaplan, Stephen B. 2006. "The Political Obstacles to Greater Exchange Rate Flexibility in China." *World Development* 34, no. 7: 1182–200.

Karl, Terry Lynn. 1997. *The Paradox of Plenty: Oil Booms and Petro-states*. Berkeley: University of California Press.

Karon, Tony. 2011. "Why China Does Capitalism Better Than the U.S." *Time*, January 20. http://content.time.com/time/world/article/0,8599,2043235,00.html.

Katzenstein, Peter. 2005. *A World of Regions: Asia and Europe in the American Imperium*. Ithaca, N.Y.: Cornell University Press.

Keister, Lisa A., and Jin Lu. 2001. *The Transformation Continues: The Status of Chinese State-Owned Enterprises at the Start of the Millennium*. National Bureau of Asian Research (NBR) Analysis vol. 12, no. 3. Seattle: NBR.

Kennedy, Scott. 2008. *The Business of Lobbying in China*. Cambridge, Mass.: Harvard University Press.

Kentor, Jeffrey, and Terry Boswell. 2003. "Foreign Capital Dependence and Development: A New Direction." *American Sociological Review* 68, no. 2: 301–13.

Keogh, Mick. 2013. *Will China Regain Food Self-Sufficiency or Simply Outsource It?* Surry Hills: Australian Farm Institute. http://www.farminstitute.org.au/_blog/Ag_Forum/post/will-china-regain-food-self-sufficiency-or-simply-outsource-it/.

Kim, Jung Sik, Ramkishen S. Rajan, and Thomas Willett. 2005. "Reserve Adequacy in Asia Revisited: New Benchmarks Based on the Size and Composition of Capital Flows." In Yonghyup Oh, Deok Ryong Yonn, and Thomas D. Willett, eds., *Conference Proceedings, Monetary and Exchange Rate Arrangement in East Asia*, 61–89. Seoul: Korea Institute for International Economic Policy.

Kirby, William. 1990. "Continuity and Change in Modern China: Economic Planning on the Mainland and on Taiwan, 1943–1958." *Australian Journal of Chinese Affairs* 24:121–41.

——. 1995. "China Unincorporated: Company Law and Business Enterprise in Twentieth-Century China." *Journal of Asian Studies* 54, no. 1: 43–63.

Knight, John, Li Shi, and Lina Song. 2006. "The Rural–Urban Divide and the Evolution of Political Economy in China." In James K. Boyce, Stephen Cullenberg, Prasanta K. Pattanaik, and Robert Pollin, eds., *Human Development in the Era of Globalisation. Essays in Honor of Keith B. Griffin*, 44–63. Northampton, Mass.: Edward Elgar.

Kong Xiangzhi and He Anhua. 2009. "Xin zhongguo chengli liushi nianlai nongmin dui guojia jianshede gongxian fenxi" (Analysis of peasants' contribution to national development in the first sixty years of new China). *Jiaoxue yu yanjiu* 9:5–13.

Korzeniewicz, Robert P., and Timothy. P. Moran. 1997. "World Economic Trends in the Distribution of Income, 1965–1992." *American Journal of Sociology* 102, no. 4: 1000–1039.

Krause, Lawrence B. 1998. *The Economics and Politics of the Asian Financial Crisis of 1997–98*. New York: Council on Foreign Relations.

Krippner, Greta. 2011. *Capitalizing on Crisis: The Political Origins of Finance.* Cambridge, Mass.: Harvard University Press.

Krugman, Paul. 2009. "Chinese New Year." *New York Times,* December 31.

——. 2012. "Revenge of the Optimum Currency Area." *New York Times,* June 24. http://krugman.blogs.nytimes.com/2012/06/24/revenge-of-the-optimum -currency-area/.

Kuhn, Philip A. 1970. *Rebellion and Its Enemies in Late Imperial China: Militarization and Social Structure, 1796–1864.* Cambridge, Mass.: Harvard University Press.

——. 1978. "The Taiping Rebellion." In John K. Fairbank, ed., *The Cambridge History of China,* vol. 10, 264–316. Cambridge: Cambridge University Press.

Kuhn, Philip, and Susan Mann Jones. 1978. "Dynastic Decline and the Roots of Rebellion." In John K. Fairbank, ed., *The Cambridge History of China,* vol. 10, 107–62. Cambridge: Cambridge University Press.

Kuo, Huei-ying. 2009. "Agency Amid Incorporation: Chinese Business Networks in Hong Kong and Singapore and the Colonial Origins of the Resurgence of East Asia, 1800–1940." *Review* 32, no. 3: 211–37.

——. 2014. *Networks Beyond Empires: Chinese Business and Nationalism in the Hong Kong–Singapore Corridor, 1914–1941.* Boston: Brill.

Kurtz, Marcus J. 2009. "The Social Foundations of Institutional Order: Reconsidering War and the 'Resource Curse' in Third World State Building." *Politics and Society* 37, no. 4: 479–520.

Lachmann, Richard. 2000. *Capitalists in Spite of Themselves: Elite Conflict and Economic Transitions in Early Modern Europe.* New York: Oxford University Press.

Landes, David. 1999. *The Wealth and Poverty of Nations: Why Some Are so Rich and Some so Poor.* New York: Norton.

Lardy, Nicholas. 1998. *China's Unfinished Economic Revolution.* Washington, D.C.: Brookings Institution Press.

Larsen, Janet. 2012. "Meat Consumption in China Now Double That in the United States." Earth Policy Institute. http://www.earth-policy.org/plan_b _updates/2012/update102.

Lee, Ann. 2012. *What the U.S. Can Learn from China: An Open-Minded Guide to Treating Our Greatest Competitor as Our Greatest Teacher.* San Francisco: Berrett-Koehler.

Lee, Ching Kwan. 2007. *Against the Law: Labor Protests in China's Rustbelt and Sunbelt.* Berkeley: University of California Press.

——. 2009. "Raw Encounters: Chinese Managers, African Workers, and the Politics of Casualization in Africa's Chinese Enclaves." *China Quarterly* 199:647–66.

Lee, Ching Kwan, and Zhang Yonghong. 2013. "The Power of Instability: Unraveling the Microfoundations of Bargained Authoritarianism in China." *American Journal of Sociology* 118, no. 6: 1475–508.

Lee, James, and Cameron Campbell. 1997. *Fate and Fortune in Rural China: Social Organization and Population Behavior in Liaoning, 1774–1873*. Cambridge: Cambridge University Press.

Lee, James, and Wang Feng. 2000. *A Quarter of Humanity: Malthusian Myth and Chinese Reality: 1700–2000*. Cambridge, Mass.: Harvard University Press.

Lee, Philip R. 1974. "Medicine and Public Health in the People's Republic of China: Observations and Reflections of a Recent Visitor." *Western Journal of Medicine* 120:430–37.

Li Bozhong. 1986. "Mingqing jiangnan yu waidi jingji lianxi de jiaqiang ji qi dui jiangnan jingji fazhan de yingxiang" (The strengthening of economic ties between Jiangnan and other provinces and its influences on the economic development of Jiangnan). *Zhongguo jingjishi yanjiu* 86, no. 2: 117–34.

——. 1998. *Agricultural Development in Jiangnan, 1620–1850*. New York: St. Martin's Press.

——. 2000. *Jiangnan de zaoqi gongye hua, 1550–1850 nian* (Early industrialization of Jiangnan, 1550–1850). Beijing: Shehui kexue wenxian chubanshe.

Li, Hongbin, and Scott Rozelle. 2000. "Saving or Stripping Rural Industry: An Analysis of Privatization and Efficiency in China." *Agricultural Economics* 23:241–52.

——. 2003. "Privatizing Rural China: Insider Privatization, Innovative Contracts and the Performance of Township Enterprises." *China Quarterly* 176:981–1005.

Li Huaiyin. 2006. "The First Encounter: Peasant Resistance to State Control of Grain in East China in the Mid-1950s." *China Quarterly* 185:145–62.

Li Linqi. 2002. "Huishang yu qingdai hankou zhiyang shuyuan" (Anhui merchants and the Zhiyang academy in Hankou during Qing times). *Qingshi yanjiu*, no. 2: 87–93.

Li Mingqi. 2009. *Rise of China and the Demise of the Capitalist World Economy*. New York: Monthly Review Press.

Li Peilin, Zhang Yi, Zhao Yandong, and Liang Dong. 2005. *Shehui chongtu yu jieji yishi: dangdai zhongguo shehuimaodun wenti yanjiu* (Social conflicts and class consciousness: A study of social contradictions in contemporary China). Beijing: Shehui kexue wenxian chubanshe.

Li Wenzhi and Jiang Taixin. 2005. *Zhongguo dizhu zhi jingji lun: Fengjian tudi guanxi fazhan yu bianhua* (On China's landlord economy: Development and change in feudal land relations). Beijing: Zhongguo shehui kexue chubanshe.

Lie, John. 1991. "The State, Industrialization, and Agricultural Sufficiency: The Case of South Korea." *Development Policy Review* 9:37–51.

Lieberthal, Kenneth. 1992. "The 'Fragmented Authoritarianism' Model and Its Limitation." In Kenneth Lieberthal and David Lampton, eds., *Bureaucracy, Politics, and Decision Making in Post-Mao China*, 1–30. Berkeley: University of California Press.

Lin, George C. S. 1997. *Red Capitalism in South China: Growth and Development of the Pearl River Delta*. Vancouver: University of British Columbia Press.

——. 2000. "State, Capital, and Space in China in an Age of Volatile Globalization." *Environment and Planning A* 32:455–71.

Lin, Nan. 1995. "Local Market Socialism: Local Corporation in Action in Rural China." *Theory and Society* 24, no. 3: 301–54.

Little, Daniel. n.d. "The Involution Debate: New Perspectives on China's Rural Economic History." http://www-personal.umd.umich.edu/~delittle/new%20 perspectives%20short%20journal%20version.htm.

Lo Yising. 1994. *Mingqing foshan jingji fazhan yu shehui bianqian* (The economic development and social change in Fushan in Ming and Qing). Guangzhou: Guangdong renmin chubanshe.

Looney, Kristen. 2012. "The Rural Developmental State: Modernization Campaigns and Peasant Politics in China, Taiwan, and South Korea." Ph.D. diss., Harvard University.

Lu Ming and Zhao Chen. 2006. "Urbanization, Urban Biased Policies, and Urban–Rural Inequality in China, 1987–2001." *Chinese Economy* 39, no. 3: 42–63.

Lu Xiaobo. 1999. "From Rank-Seeking to Rent-Seeking: Changing Administrative Ethos and Corruption in Reform China." *Crime, Law, & Social Change* 32:347–70.

——. 2000a. "Booty Socialism, Bureau-preneurs, and the State in Transition: Organizational Corruption in China." *Comparative Politics* 32, no. 3: 273–94.

——. 2000b. *Cadres and Corruption: The Organization Involution of the Chinese Communist Party*. Stanford, Calif.: Stanford University Press.

Lum, Thomas, Hannah Fischer, Julissa Gomez-Granger, and Anne Leland. 2009. *China's Foreign Aid Activities in Africa, Latin America, and Southeast Asia*. Report for Congress. Washington, D.C.: Congressional Research Service. http://www.fas.org/sgp/crs/row/R40361.pdf.

Ma Guonan and Wang Yi. 2010. *China's High Saving Rate: Myth and Reality*. Working Paper no. 312. Basel: Bank of International Settlement. http://www .bis.org/publ/work312.pdf.

Ma Jun and Xu Jianjiang 2012. *Renminbi zhouchu guomen zhi lu: Li'an shichang fazhan yu ziben xiangmu kaifang* (Pathway for the internationalization of the renminbi: Development of offshore market and capital account liberalization). Hong Kong: Commercial Press.

Ma, Laurence J. C. 1971. *Commercial Development and Urban Change in Sung China (960–1279)*. Ann Arbor: University of Michigan Press.

Maddison, Angus. 1983. "A Comparison of Levels of GDP per Capita of Developed and Developing Countries, 1700–1980." *Journal of Economic History* 43, no. 1: 27–41.

——. n.d. "Historical Statistics of the World Economy, 1–2008 AD." http://www.ggdc.net/MADDISON/Historical_Statistics/vertical-file_02-2010.xls.

Mahoney, James. 2010. *Colonialism and Development: Spanish America in Comparative Perspective*. New York: Cambridge University Press.

Mann, Michael. 1993. *The Sources of Social Power: The Rise of Classes and Nation-States, 1760–1914*. Cambridge: Cambridge University Press.

Mann, Susan. 1987. *Local Merchants and the Chinese Bureaucracy, 1750–1950*. Stanford, Calif.: Stanford University Press.

Marglin, Stephen A. 1974. "What Do Bosses Do? The Origins and Functions of Hierarchy in Capitalist Production." *Review of Radical Political Economics* 6, no. 2: 60–112.

Marks, Robert B. 1991. "Rice Prices, Food Supply, and Market Structure in Eighteenth-Century South China." *Late Imperial China* 12, no. 2: 64–116.

——. 1996. "Commercialization Without Capitalism: Processes of Environmental Change in South China, 1550–1850." *Environmental History* 1, no. 1: 56–82.

——. 1998. *Tigers, Rice, Silk, and Silt: Environment and Economy in Late Imperial South China*. New York: Cambridge University Press.

Marsh, Robert M. 2000. "Weber's Misunderstanding of Traditional Chinese Law." *American Journal of Sociology* 106, no. 2: 281–302.

Marx, Karl. [1848] 1972. *The Communist Manifesto*. In *The Marx–Engels Reader*, edited by Robert C. Tucker, 331–62. New York: Norton.

McCord, Edward A. 1990. "Local Military Power and Elite Formation: The Liu Family of Xingyi County, Guizhou." In Joseph W. Esherick and Mary Backus Rankin, eds., *Chinese Local Elites and Patterns of Dominance*, 162–90. Berkeley: University of California Press.

McKinsey Global Institute. 2015. *Debt and (Not Much) Deleveraging*. New York: McKinsey & Company. http://www.mckinsey.com/insights/economic_studies/debt_and_not_much_deleveraging.

McMichael, Philip. 2011. *Development and Social Change: Global Perspective*. Thousand Oaks, Calif.: Sage.

Mead, Walter Russell. 1999. "Needed: A New Growth Strategy for the Developing World." *Development Outreach* 1:22–25. http://www-wds.worldbank.org

/external/default/WDSContentServer/WDSP/IB/2001/12/01/000094946_011
11704003241/Rendered/PDF/multiopage.pdf.

Mellor, John W, ed. 1995. *Agriculture on the Road to Industrialization*. Baltimore: Johns Hopkins University Press.

Mertha, Andrew. 2005. "China's 'Soft' Centralization: Shifting Tiao/Kuai Authority Relations." *China Quarterly* 184:791–810.

Milanovic, Branko. 2005. *Worlds Apart: Measuring International and Global Inequality*. Princeton, N.J.: Princeton University Press.

——. 2014. "Winners of Globalization: The Rich and the Chinese Middle Class. Losers: The American Middle Class." *New Perspectives Quarterly* 31, no. 2: 78–81.

Milesi-Ferretti, Gian Maria. 2008. *Fundamentals at Odds? The U.S. Current Account Deficit and the Dollar*. Working paper. Washington, D.C.: International Monetary Fund.

Morrison, Wayne M., and Marc Labonte. 2013. *China's Holdings of US Securities: Implications for the US Economy*. Report for Congress. Washington, D.C.: Congressional Research Service. http://www.fas.org/sgp/crs/row/RL34314.pdf.

Moulder, Francis. 1977. *Japan, China, and the Modern World-Economy: Toward a Reinterpretation of East Asian Development ca. 1600–1918*. Cambridge: Cambridge University Press.

Mulgan, Aurelia George. 2000. *The Politics of Agriculture in Japan*. New York: Routledge.

Murphy, R. Taggart. 1997. *The Weight of the Yen: How Denial Imperils America's Future and Ruins an Alliance*. New York: Norton.

Myers, Ramon H. 1970. *The Chinese Peasant Economy*. Cambridge, Mass.: Harvard University Press.

National Development and Reform Commission of China. 2005. *Zhongguo jumin shouru fenpei niandu baogao* (Annual report of Chinese residents' income distribution). Beijing: National Development and Reform Commission of China.

Naughton, Barry. 1995. *Growing out of the Plan: Chinese Economic Reform, 1978–1993*. Cambridge: Cambridge University Press.

Nee, Victor. 1989. "The Theory of Market Transition: From Redistribution to Markets in State Socialism." *American Sociological Review* 54:663–81.

Nee, Victor, and Sonja Opper. 2012. *Capitalism from Below: Markets and Institutional Change in China*. Cambridge, Mass.: Harvard University Press.

New York Times. 2010. "Inside Your iPhone." July 5. http://www.nytimes.com/imagepages/2010/07/05/technology/20100706-iphone-graphic.html?ref=technology; http://www.nytimes.com/2010/07/06/technology/06iphone.html.

Nolan, Peter. 2012. *Is China Buying the World?* Oxford: Polity.

Nye, Joseph. 2002. *The Paradox of American Power: Why the World's Only Super-power Can't Go It Alone.* Oxford: Oxford University Press.

O'Brien, Kevin. 2006. *Rightful Resistance in Rural China.* New York: Cambridge University Press.

O'Conner, James. 2011. *State Building, Infrastructure Development, and Chinese Energy Projects in Myanmar.* Discussion Paper no. 10. Bangkok: Institut de Recherche Sur l'Asie du Sud-Est Contemporaine, March. http://www.irasec. com/ouvrage.php?id=38&lang=en.

Oi, Jean C. 1999. *Rural China Takes Off: Institutional Foundations of Economic Reform.* Berkeley: University of California Press.

Ozawa, Turotomo. 1993. "Foreign Direction Investment and Structural Transfor-mation: Japan as a Recycler of Market and Industry." *Business and the Con-temporary World* 5, no. 2: 129–49.

Palley, Thomas I. 2006. "External Contradictions of the Chinese Development Model: Export-Led Growth and the Dangers of Global Economic Contrac-tion." *Journal of Contemporary China* 15, no. 46: 69–88.

Panitch, Leo, and Sam Gindin. 2012. *The Making of Global Capitalism: The Polit-ical Economy of American Empire.* New York: Verso.

Perdue, Peter C. 2005. *China Marches West: The Qing Conquest of Central Eur-asia.* Cambridge, Mass.: Harvard University Press.

Perkins, Dwight H. 1967. "Government as an Obstacle to Industrialization: The Case of Nineteenth-Century China." *Journal of Economic History* 27, no. 4: 478–92.

Perleman, Michael. 2000. *The Invention of Capitalism: Classical Political Econ-omy and the Secret History of Primitive Accumulation.* Durham, N.C.: Duke University Press.

Perry, Elizabeth. 1980. *Rebels and Revolutionaries in North China, 1845–1945.* Stanford, Calif.: Stanford University Press.

Perry, Elizabeth, and Mark Selden. 2010. *Chinese Society: Change, Conflict, and Resistance.* New York: Routledge.

Pettis, Michael. 2009. "More Public Worrying About the Chinese Stimulus." China Financial Markets, blog entry, July 24. http://www.mpettis.com/ 2009/07/more-public-worrying-about-the-chinese-stimulus/.

——. 2013. *The Great Rebalancing: Trade, Conflict, and the Perilous Road Ahead for the World Economy.* Princeton, N.J.: Princeton University Press.

Pomeranz, Kenneth. 1997. "'Traditional' Chinese Business Forms Revisited: Family, Firm, and Financing in the History of the Yutang Company of Jining, 1779–1956." *Late Imperial China* 18, no. 1: 1–38.

——. 2000. *The Great Divergence: Europe, China, and the Making of the Modern World Economy.* Princeton, N.J.: Princeton University Press.

Pomeranz, Kenneth, and Steven Topik. 1999. *The World That Trade Created: Society, Culture, and the World Economy, 1400–the Present*. Armonk, N.Y.: M. E. Sharpe.

Posen, Adam S. 2008. "Why the Euro Will Not Rival the Dollar." *International Finance* 11, no. 1: 75–100.

Prasad, Eswar. 2014. *The Dollar Trap: How the U.S. Dollar Tightened Its Grip on Global Finance*. Princeton, N.J.: Princeton University Press.

Pun Ngai. 2005. *Made in China: Women Factory Workers in a Global Workplace*. Durham, N.C.: Duke University Press.

Pun Ngai, Jenny Chan, and Mark Selden. Forthcoming. *Separate Dreams: Apple, Foxconn, and a New Generation of Chinese Workers*. Lanham, Md.: Rowman and Littlefield.

QSL-QL. n.d. *Daqing gaozong shilu* (Veritable record of the Qing at the reign of Qianlong). Beijing: Zhonghua shuju.

Quan Hansheng. 1987. *Mingqing jingjishi yanjiu* (Studies of the economic history of Ming and Qing). Taipei: Lianjing chubanshe.

——. 1996a. "Meizhou baiyin yu shiba shiji zhongguo wujia geming de guanxi" (The relation between American silver and the eighteenth-century price revolution in China). In *Zhongguo jingjishi luncong* (Essays on Chinese economic history), 475–508. Taipei: Hedao chubanshe.

——. 1996b. "Mingqing jian meizhou baiyin de shuru zhongguo" (The inflow of American silver to China in Ming and Qing). In *Zhongguo jingjishi luncong* (Essays on Chinese economic history), 435–50. Taipei: Hedao chubanshe.

——. 1996c. "Qing yongzheng lianjian (1723–35) de mijia" (The rice price in the reign of Yongzheng [1723–35]). In *Zhongguo jingjishi luncong* (Essays on Chinese economic history), 547–66. Taipei: Hedao chubanshe.

——. 1996d. "Qing zhongye yiqian jiangzhe mijia de biandong cuishi" (The trend of the change of rice price in Jiangsu and Zheijiang before mid-Qing). In *Zhongguo jingjishi luncong* (Essays on Chinese economic history), 509–16. Taipei: Hedao chubanshe.

——. 1996e. "Yapian zhanzheng qian Jiangsu de mian fangzhiye " (The cotton textile history in Jiangsu before the Opium War). In *Zhongguo jingjishi luncong* (Essays on Chinese economic history), 625–50. Taipei: Hedao chubanshe.

Rajan, Raghuram G. 2005. *Global Imbalances: An Assessment*. Report. Washington, D.C.: Research Department, International Monetary Fund. http://www.imf.org/external/np/speeches/2005/102505.htm.

——. 2006. "Financial System Reform and Global Current Account Imbalances." Paper presented at the American Economic Association Meeting, Boston, January 6.

——. 2010. *Fault Lines: How Hidden Fractures Still Threaten the World Economy*. Princeton, N.J.: Princeton University Press.

Ramo, Joshua C. 2004. *The Beijing Consensus*. London: Foreign Policy Centre.

Rawski, Thomas G. 1989. *Economic Growth in Prewar China*. Berkeley: University of California Press.

——. 2002. "Will Investment Behavior Constrain China's Growth?" *China Economic Review* 13:361–72.

Reddings, S. G. 1991. "Weak Organizations and Strong Linkages: Managerial Ideology and Chinese Family Business Networks." In G. G. Hamilton, ed., *Business Networks and Economic Development in East and Southeast Asia*, 30–47. Hong Kong: Center of Asian Studies, University of Hong Kong.

Reilly, James. 2012. "China's Unilateral Sanctions." *Washington Quarterly* 35, no. 4: 121–33.

Reuters. 2010. "Chinese Exporters Ditch Wounded Euro for Dollars." June 4. http://www.reuters.com/article/2010/06/04/china-economy-euro-idUSTOE 64R05420100604.

Riskin, Carl, Renwei Zhao, and Li Shi. 2001. "Introduction: The Retreat from Inequality. Highlights of the Findings." In Carl Riskin, Renwei Zhao, and Li Shih, eds., *China's Retreat from Equality: Income Distribution and Economic Transition*, 3–24. Armonk, N.Y.: M. E. Sharpe.

Roache, Shaun K. 2012. *China's Impact on World Commodity Market*. Working paper. Washington, D.C.: International Monetary Fund. http://www.imf.org /external/pubs/ft/wp/2012/wp12115.pdf.

Rose, Mary B. 2000. *Firms, Networks, and Business Values: The British and American Cotton Industries Since 1750*. New York: Cambridge University Press.

Ross, Heidi. 2005. *Where and Who Are the World's Illiterates? China Country Study*. Global Monitoring Report submitted to UNESCO. portal.unesco.org /education/en/files/...China.../Ross_China.doc.

Rowe, William T. 1998. "Domestic Interregional Trade in Eighteenth-Century China." In Leonard Blusse and Gaastra Femme, eds., *On the Eighteenth Century as a Category of Asian History: Van Leur in Retrospect*, 173–92. Aldershot, U.K.: Ashgate Press.

——. 2001. *Saving the World: Chen Hongmou and Elite Consciousness in Eighteenth-Century China*. Stanford, Calif.: Stanford University Press.

——. 2002. "Social Stability and Social Change." In Willard J. Peterson, ed., *The Cambridge History of China*, vol. 9, 473–562. Cambridge: Cambridge University Press.

Sachs, Jeffry, Aaron Tornell, and Andres Velasco. 1996. *Financial Crises in Emerging Markets: The Lessons from 1995*. Working Paper no. 5576. Cambridge, Mass.: National Bureau of Economic Research.

Sachs, Jeffrey D., and Andrew M. Warner 1995. *Natural Resource Abundance and Economic Growth*. Development Discussion Paper no. 517a. Cambridge, Mass.: Institute for International Development, Harvard University.

Saich, Tony. 1990. "When Worlds Collide: The Beijing People's Movement of 1989." In Tony Saich, ed., *The Chinese People's Movement: Perspectives on Spring 1989*, 25–49. Armonk, N.Y.: M. E. Sharpe.

Sala-i-Martin, Xavier. 2002a. *The Disturbing "Rise" of Global Income Inequality*. Working Paper no. 8904. Cambridge, Mass.: National Bureau of Economic Research.

——. 2002b. *The World Distribution of Income*. Working Paper no. 8933. Cambridge, Mass.: National Bureau of Economic Research.

——. 2006. "The World Distribution of Income: Falling Poverty and Convergence, Period." *Quarterly Journal of Economics* 121, no. 2: 351–97.

Sanusi, Lamido. 2013. "Africa Must Get Real About Chinese Ties." *Financial Times*, March 11.

Sargeson, Sally, and Jian Zhang. 1999. "Reassessing the Role of the Local State: A Case Study of Local Government Interventions in Property Rights Reform in a Hangzhou District." *China Journal* 42:77–99.

Schurmann, Franz. 1966. *Ideology and Organization in Communist China*. Berkeley: University of California Press.

Segal, Adam, and Eric Thun. 2001. "Thinking Globally, Acting Locally: Local Governments, Industrial Sectors, and Development in China." *Politics and Society* 29, no. 4: 557–88.

Selden, Mark. 1993. *The Political Economy of Chinese Development*. Armonk, N.Y.: M. E. Sharpe.

——. 1997. "China, Japan, and the Regional Political Economy of East Asia, 1945–1995." In Peter J. Katzenstein and Takashi Shiraishi, eds., *Network Power: Japan and Asia*, 306–40. Ithaca, N.Y.: Cornell University Press.

Sen, Amartya. 2005. "What China Could Teach India, Then and Now." Citigroup and Asia Society Global Issues Series. http://asiasociety.org/business/development/amartya-sen-what-china-could-teach-india-then-and-now.

——. 2013. "Why India Trails China." *New York Times*, June 19.

Setser, Brad. 2009. "This Really Doesn't Look Good." Council on Foreign Relations, blog entry, January 11. http://blogs.cfr.org/setser/2009/01/11/this-really-doesnt-look-good/.

Shafer, D. Michael. 1994. *Winners and Losers: How Sectors Shape the Developmental Prospects of States*. Ithaca, N.Y.: Cornell University Press.

Shambaugh, David. 2013. *China Goes Global: The Partial Power*. New York: Oxford University Press.

Shan Weijian. 2006a. "China's Low-Profit Growth Model." *Far Eastern Economic Review* 169, no. 9: 23–28.

——. 2006b. "The World Bank's China Delusions." *Far Eastern Economic Review* 169, no. 7: 29–32.

Shen Daming. 2007. *Daqing luli yu qingdai de shehui kongzhi* (Qing legal code and social control in the Qing). Shanghai: Shanghai renmin chubanshe.

Shevchenko, Alexei. 2004. "Bringing the Party Back in: The CCP and the Trajectory of Market Transition in China." *Communist and Post-Communist Studies* 37:161–85.

Shiba, Yoshinobu. 1970. *Commerce and Society in Sung China*. Translated by Mark Elvin. Ann Arbor: Center for Chinese Studies, University of Michigan.

——. 1983. "Sung Foreign Trade: Its Scope and Organization." In Morris Rossabi, ed., *China Among Equals: The Middle Kingdom and Its Neighbors, 10th–14th Centuries*, 89–115. Berkeley: University of California Press.

Shih, Victor. 2004. "Dealing with Non-performing Loans: Political Constraints and Financial Policies in China." *China Quarterly* 180:922–44.

——. 2008. *Factions and Finance in China: Elite Control and Inflation*. New York: Cambridge University Press.

——. 2010. "Looming Problem of Local Debt in China—1.6 Trillion Dollar and Rising." February 10. http://chinesepolitics.blogspot.com/2010/02/looming -problem-of-local-debt-in-china.html.

Shirk, Susan L. 1993. *The Political Logic of Economic Reform in China*. Berkeley: University of California Press.

Shiue, Carol H., and Wolfgang Keller. 2007. "Markets in China and Europe on the Eve of the Industrial Revolution." *American Economic Review* 97, no. 4: 1189–216.

Shue, Vivienne. 1980. *Peasant China in Transition: The Dynamics of Development Toward Socialism, 1949–56*. Berkeley: University of California Press.

Silver, Beverly, and Zhang Lu. 2009. "China as a New Epicenter of World Labor Unrest." In Ho-fung Hung, ed., *China and the Transformation of Global Capitalism*, 174–87. Baltimore: Johns Hopkins University Press.

Smith, Paul J. 1988. "Commerce, Agriculture, and Core Formation in the Upper Yangzi, 2 A.D. to 1948." *Late Imperial China* 9, no. 1: 1–78.

Smith, Thomas C. 1959. *The Agrarian Origins of Modern Japan*. Stanford, Calif.: Stanford University Press.

So, Alvin Y. 2003. "Rethinking the Chinese Developmental Miracle." In Alvin Y. So, ed., *China's Developmental Miracle: Origins, Transformations, and Challenges*, 3–28. Armonk, N.Y.: M. E. Sharpe.

——. 2005. "Beyond the Logic of Capital and the Polarization Model: The State, Market Reforms, and the Plurality of Class Conflict in China." *Critical Asian Studies* 37, no. 3: 481–94.

Solinger, Dorothy. 2009. *States' Gains, Labor's Losses: China, France, and Mexico Choose Global Liaisons, 1980–2000*. Ithaca, N.Y.: Cornell University Press.

Somers, Margaret R., and Fred Block. 2005. "From Poverty to Perversity: Ideas, Markets, and Institutions Over 200 Years of Welfare Debate." *American Sociological Review* 70, no. 2: 260–87.

Sonobe, Tetsushi, Dinghuan Hu, and Keijiro Otsuka. 2004. "From Interior to Superior Products: An Inquiry Into the Wenzhou Model of Industrial Development in China." *Journal of Comparative Economics* 32, no. 3: 542–63.

South China Morning Post. 2014. "Blackwater Founder Erik Prince to Help Chinese Firms Set Up Shop in Africa." July 6.

Stallings, Barbara, ed. 1995. *Global Change, Regional Response: The New International Context of Development.* New York: Cambridge University Press.

Strange, Susan. 1971. *Sterling and British Policy: A Political Study of an International Currency in Decline.* Oxford: Oxford University Press.

——. 1980. "Germany and the World Monetary System." In Wilfrid Kohl and Giorgio Basevi, eds., *West Germany: A European and Global Power*, 45–62. Lexington, Mass.: Lexington Books.

Subramanian, Arvind. 2008. *India's Turn: Understanding the Economic Transformation.* New York: Oxford University Press.

Sun Liping. 2002. "Zhongti xing ziben yu zhuanxing qi jingying xingcheng" (Formation of general capital and elite formation during the transition period). *Zhejiang xuekan*, no. 3. http://www.usc.cuhk.edu.hk/PaperCollection/Details .aspx?id=3337.

Szelenyi, Ivan, and Eric Kostello. 1996. "The Market Transition Debate: Toward a Synthesis?" *American Journal of Sociology* 101, no. 4: 1082–96.

Taiwan Bureau of Foreign Trade. n.d. "Trade Statistics." http://www.trade.gov.tw /english/Pages/List.aspx?nodeID=94.

Taiwan Economic Data Center. n.d. AREMOS database. http://www.aremos.org .tw/.

Telegraph. 2007. "China Threatens 'Nuclear Option' of Dollar Sales." August 8.

——. 2010. "WikiLeaks: China's Politburo a Cabal of Business Empires." December 6.

Thompson, E. P. 1971. "The Moral Economy of the English Crowd in the Eighteenth Century." *Past and Present* 50:76–136.

Thun, Eric. 2006. *Changing Lanes in China: Foreign Direct Investment, Local Governments, and Auto Sector Development.* New York: Cambridge University Press.

Tilly, Charles. 1975. "Food Supply and Public Order in Modern Europe." In Charles Tilly, ed., *The Formation of National States in Western Europe*, 380–455. Princeton, N.J.: Princeton University Press.

Tsai, Kellee S. 2002. *Back-Alley Banking: Private Entrepreneurs in China.* Ithaca, N.Y.: Cornell University Press.

———. 2007. *Capitalism Without Democracy: The Private Sector in Contemporary China*. Ithaca, N.Y.: Cornell University Press.

Tsui, Kai-yuen. 2007. "Forces Shaping China's Interprovincial Inequality." *Review of Income and Wealth* 53:60–92.

Unger, Jonathan, ed. 1991. *The Pro-democracy Protests in China: Reports from the Provinces*. Armonk, N.Y.: M. E. Sharpe.

United Nations. 2013. *China's Progress Towards the Millennium Development Goals: 2013 Report*. Beijing: Chinese Ministry of Foreign Affairs and the United Nations.

United Nations Development Program China and Institute for Urban and Environmental Studies. 2013. *China Human Development Report*. Xiamen: Institute for Urban and Environmental Studies. http://www.undp.org/content/china/en/home/library/human_development/china-human-development-report-2013/.

U.S. Bureau of Labor Statistics. n.d. "International Labor Comparison." Database. http://www.bls.gov/fls/#compensation.

U.S. Bureau of Labor Statistics. 2013. "International Comparisons of Hourly Compensation Costs in Manufacturing, 2012." http://www.bls.gov/fls/ichcc.pdf.

U.S. Census Bureau. n.d. "US Trade in Goods by Country Data." http://www.census.gov/foreign-trade/balance/#W.

U.S. Department of Agriculture (USDA), Production Estimates and Crop Assessment Division. 2004. *Brazil: Soybean Expansion Expected to Continue in 2004/05*. Washington, D.C.: Foreign Agricultural Service, USDA. http://www.fas.usda.gov/pecad/highlights/2004/08/brazil_soy_files/index.htm.

U.S. Department of Defense. n.d. *Base Structure Report*. Washington, D.C.: U.S. Department of Defense. http://www.defense.gov/pubs/.

U.S. Federal Reserve. n.d. "USD Board Dollar Real Index." http://www.federalreserve.gov/releases/h10/summary/.

U.S. Treasury. n.d. "Major Foreign Holders of U.S. Treasury Securities." Database. http://www.treasury.gov/resource-center/data-chart-center/tic/Pages/ticsec2.aspx.

Vermeer, Eduard B. 1982a. "Income Differentials in Rural China." *China Quarterly* 89:1–33.

———. 1982b. "Rural Economic Change and the Role of the State in China, 1962–78." *Asian Survey* 22, no. 9: 823–42.

Vlastos, Stephen. 1986. *Peasant Protest and Uprising in Tokugawa Japan*. Berkeley: University of California Press.

Von Glahn, Richard. 1996. *Fountain of Fortune: Money and Monetary Policy in China, 1000 to 1700*. Berkeley: University of California Press.

Vries, P. H. H. 2001. "Are Coal and Colonies Really Crucial? Kenneth Pomeranz and the Great Divergence." *Journal of World History* 12, no. 2: 407–45.

Wade, Robert. 1990. *Governing the Market: Economic Theory and the Role of Government in East Asian Industrialization.* Princeton, N.J.: Princeton University Press.

——. 2004. "Is Globalization Reducing Poverty and Inequality?" *World Development* 32, no. 4: 567–89.

Walder, Andrew G. 1995a. "Career Mobility and Communist Political Order." *American Sociological Review* 57:524–39.

——. 1995b. "Local Governments as Industrial Firms: An Organizational Analysis of China's Transitional Economy." *American Journal of Sociology* 101:263–301.

——. 2002a. "Markets and Income Inequality in Rural China: Political Advantage in an Expanding Economy." *American Sociological Review* 67, no. 2: 231–53.

——. 2002b. *Privatization and Elite Mobility: Rural China, 1979–1996.* Asia Pacific Research Center Paper Series. Stanford, Calif.: Stanford University. http://APARC.stanford.edu.

——. 2003. "Elite Opportunity in Transitional Economies." *American Sociological Review* 68, no. 6: 899–916.

——. 2004. "The Party Elite and China's Trajectory of Change." *China: An International Journal* 2, no. 2: 189–209.

Wallerstein, Immanuel. 1974. *The Modern World-System.* Vol. 1: *Capitalist Agriculture and the Origins of the European World-Economy in the Sixteenth Century.* New York: Academic Press.

——. 1979. *The Capitalist World-Economy.* Cambridge: Cambridge University Press.

——. 1984. *The Politics of the World-Economy: The States, the Movements, and the Civilizations.* New York: Cambridge University Press.

——. 1990. "Antisystemic Movements: History and Dilemmas." In Samir Amin, Giovanni Arrighi, Andre Gunder Frank, and Immanuel Wallerstein, ed., *Transforming the Revolution: Social Movements and the World-System,* 13–53. New York: Monthly Review Press.

Wall Street Journal. 2011. "Debate on Yuan Manipulation Moves to WTO." November 16.

——. 2013a. "China to Transfer Railway Ministry Debt." March 14.

——. 2013b. "SAIC Motor's Profit Climbs 6%: China's Largest Auto Maker Reports Lower-Than-Expected 6% Increase on Tough Competition." August 29.

Walter, Carl E., and Fraser J. T. Howie. 2011. *Red Capitalism: The Fragile Financial Foundation of China's Extraordinary Rise.* New York: Wiley.

Wang Feiling. 2005. *Organizing Through Division and Exclusion: China's Hukou System*. Stanford, Calif.: Stanford University Press.

Wang, Gungwu. 2002. *The Chinese Overseas: From Earthbound China to the Quest for Autonomy*. Cambridge, Mass.: Harvard University Press.

Wang Hui. 2003. *China's New Order: Society, Politics, and Economy in Transition*. Cambridge, Mass.: Harvard University Press.

——. 2006. "Gaizhi yu zhongguo gongren jieji de lishi mingyun: Jiangsu tongyu jituan gongshi gaizhi de diaocha baogao" (Transition and the historical destiny of the Chinese working class: A survey report on the Jiangsu Tongyu Corporation ownership transition). *Tianya* 1:52–72.

Wang Shaoguang. 2000. "The Social and Political Implications of China's WTO Membership." *Journal of Contemporary China* 9, no. 25: 373–405.

Wang Shaoguang and Hu Angang. 1994. *Zhongguo guojia nengli baogao* (A report of China's state capacity). Hong Kong: Oxford University Press.

——. 1999. *The Political Economy of Uneven Development: The Case of China*. Armonk, N.Y.: M. E. Sharpe.

Wang Zhenzhong. 1996. *Mingqing huishang yu Huaiyang shehui bianqian* (Anhui merchants and social change in Huaiyang area in Ming and Qing times). Beijing: Sanlian shudian.

Washington Post. 2006. "Foreign Currency Piles Up in China." January 17.

Weber, Max. 1958. *The City*. New York: Free Press.

——. [1930] 1992. *The Protestant Ethic and the Spirit of Capitalism*. London: Routledge.

Wei, Yehua Dennis. 2002. "Beyond the Sunan Model: Trajectory and Underlying Factors of Development in Kunshan, China." *Environment and Planning A* 34:1725–47.

——. 2009. "China's Shoe Manufacturing and the Wenzhou Model: Perspectives on the World's Leading Producer and Exporter of Footwear." *Eurasian Geography and Economics* 50, no. 6: 720–39.

Wen Tiejun. 2000. *Zhongguo nongcun jiben jingji zhidu yanjiu: Sannong wenti de shiji fansi* (A study of the fundamental economic institutions of Chinese villages: A centennial reflection on the "three rurals" problem). Beijing: Zhongguo jingji chubanshe.

——. 2004. *Women daodi yao shenme* (What do we want?). Beijing: Huaxia chubanshe.

——. 2005. *Sannong wenti de shiji fansi* (Rural China's centenary reflection). Beijing: Sanlian Shudian.

——. 2013. *Baci weiji: Zhongguode zhenshi jingyan 1949–2009* (Eight crises: The real experience of China, 1949–2009). Beijing: Dongfang chubanshe.

Westney, Eleanor D. 1987. *Imitation and Innovation: The Transfer of Western Organizational Patterns to Meiji Japan*. Cambridge, Mass.: Harvard University Press.

Weston, Jonathon, Caitlin Campbell, and Katherine Koleski. 2011. "China's Foreign Assistance in Review: Implications for the United States." U.S.–China Economic and Security Review Commission Staff Research Backgrounder, September 1. http://origin.www.uscc.gov/sites/default/files/Research/9_1_%202011_ChinasForeignAssistanceinReview.pdf.

Whyte, Martin. 2010. *Myth of the Social Volcano: Perceptions of Inequality and Distributive Injustice in Contemporary China*. Stanford, Calif.: Stanford University Press.

Williamson, Jeffrey G. 2008. *Globalization and the Poor Periphery Before 1950*. Cambridge, Mass.: MIT Press.

Winters, Alan L., and Shahid Yusuf, eds. 2007. *Dancing with Giants: China, India, and the Global Economy*. Washington, D.C.: World Bank.

Wong, Bin R. 1997. *China Transformed: Historical Change and the Limits of European Experience*. Ithaca, N.Y.: Cornell University Press.

World Bank. 2010. *China Quarterly Update*. March. Beijing: Beijing Office, World Bank.

——. n.d. *World Development Indicator Database*. http://databank.worldbank.org/data/views/variableSelection/selectvariables.aspx?source=world-development-indicators.

World Health Organization. 2008. "China's Village Doctors Take Great Strides." *Bulletin of the World Health Organization* 86, no. 12: 909–88. http://www.who.int/bulletin/volumes/86/12/08-021208/en/.

Wright, Tim. 1981. "Growth of the Modern Chinese Coal Industry: An Analysis of Supply and Demand, 1896–1936." *Modern China* 7, no. 3: 317–50.

Wu Chengming. 2000. "Introduction: On Embryonic Capitalism in China." In Xu Dixin and Wu Chengming, eds., *Chinese Capitalism, 1522–1840*, 1–22. New York: St. Martin's Press.

Xia Ming. 2000. *The Dual Developmental State: Development Strategy and Institutional Arrangements for China's Transition*. Brookfield, Vt.: Ashgate.

Xia Yongxiang. 2006. "Gongyehua yu chengshi hua: Chengben tanfen yu shouyi fenpei" (Industrialization and urbanization: Division of cost and distribution of benefits). *Jianghai xuekan* 5:84–89.

Xie, Andy. 2006. "China: What Next?" Global Economic Forum, Morgan Stanley, February 3. http://www.morganstanley.com/GEFdata/digests/20060203-fri.html.

Xinhuanet. 2013. "Gini Coefficient Release Highlights China's Resolve to Bridge Wealth Gap." January 21. http://news.xinhuanet.com/english/china/2013-01/21/c_132116852.htm.

Xinhua News. 2012a. "China to Advance Urbanization Next Year." December 16.

——. 2012b. "Investment Contributes More Than 90% to China's GDP Growth: NBS." February 2. http://news.xinhuanet.com/english2010/business/2010-02 /02/c_13160274.htm.

——. 2012c. "Zhongguo jidai lingdao ren yuexin jiemi" (Unveiling the salary of several generations of Chinese leaders). December 16. http://news.xinhuanet .com/comments/2012-12/16/c_114042076.htm.

Xu Maoming. 2004. *Jiangnan shishen yu jiangnan shehui, 1368–1911* (Gentry and society in Jiangnan, 1368–1911). Beijing: Shangwu yinshu guan.

Xu Tan. 1999. "Qingdai qianqi shengpin liutong geju de bianhua" (The change in the pattern of commodity circulation in early Qing). *Qingshi yanjiu* 3:1–13.

Xu, Xinwu. 1992. *Jiangnan mianbu shi* (A History of Jiangnan Indigenous Cloth). Shanghai: Shanghai shehui kexue yuan chubanshe.

Yang, Dali L. 1996. *Calamity and Reform in China: State, Rural Society, and Institutional Change Since the Great Leap Famine*. Stanford, Calif.: Stanford University Press.

Yang, Dennis Tao, and Cai Fang. 2003. "The Political Economy of China's Rural–Urban Divide." In Nick Hope, Dennis T. Yang, and Mu Yang, eds., *How Far Across the River? Chinese Policy Reform at the Millennium*, 389–416. Stanford, Calif.: Stanford University Press.

Yao Zhaoyu. 2008. "Nongcun hezuo yundong yu nongye jishu de zhiru: Yi minguo shiqi Jiangsu sheng weili (1927–1937)" (The cooperative movement of rural areas and the implantation of agricultural technique: Take Jiangsu Province during the Republic of China [1927–1937] as an example). *Zhongguo nongshi* 27, no. 4: 28–34.

Ye Xianen. 1980. "Shilun huizhou shangren zibende xingcheng yu fazhan" (On the formation and development of Huizhou merchant capital). *Zhongguo shi yanjiu*, no. 3: 391–409.

——. 1982. "Huishang de shuailuo jiqi lishi zuoyong" (The decline of Anhui merchants and their historical legacy). *Jianghuai luntan* 3:57–63.

Ye Xianen and Tan Dihua 1984. "Mingqing zhujiang sanjiaozhou nongye shangyehua yu xushide fazhan" (The Commercialization of Agriculture and Town Development of the Pearl River Delta in Ming and Qing). *Guangdong shehui kexue* 84, no. 2: 73–90.

Yu Jianrong. 2003. "Nongcun hei'e shili yu jiceng zhengquan tuihua: Xiangnan diaocha" (Mafia in the village and regression of local governments: A survey of southern Hunan). *Zhanlue yu guanli* 5. http://www.usc.cuhk.edu.hk/Paper Collection/Details.aspx?id=2725.

Yuan, Tsing. 1979. "Urban Riots and Disturbances." In Jonathan D. Spence and John E. Wills, eds., *From Ming to Ch'ing*, 277–320. New Haven, Conn.: Yale University Press.

Zakaria, Fareed. 2009. *The Post-American World*. New York: Norton.

Zelin, Madeleine. 1984. *The Magistrate's Tael: Rationalizing Fiscal Reform in Eighteenth-Century Ch'ing China*. Berkeley: California University Press.

Zelin, Madeleine, Jonathan K. Ocko, and Robert Gardella, eds. 2004. *Contract and Property in Early Modern China*. Stanford, Calif.: Stanford University Press.

Zhan Shaohua and Huang Lingli. 2013. "Rural Roots of Current Migrant Labor Shortage in China: Development and Labor Empowerment in a Situation of Incomplete Proletarianization." *Studies in Comparative International Development* 48, no. 1: 81–111.

Zhang Yulin. 2005. *Litu shidai de nongcun jiating: Mingong chao ruhe jiegou xiangtu zhongguo* (The rural family in the age of migration: How the tide of peasant labor outmigration is deconstructing rural China). Hong Kong: Chinese University of Hong Kong University Service Center. http://www.usc .cuhk.edu.hk/PaperCollection/Details.aspx?id=4638.

Zhao, Dingxin. 2001. *The Power of Tiananmen: State–Society Relations and the 1989 Beijing Student Movement*. Chicago: University of Chicago Press.

——. 2009. "The Mandate of Heaven and Performance Legitimation in Historical and Contemporary China." *American Behavioral Scientist* 53 (November): 416–33.

Zheng, Chunmiao, Jie Liu, Guoliang Cao, Eloise Kendy, Hao Wang, and Yangwen Jia. 2010. "Can China Cope with Its Water Crisis? Perspectives from the North China Plain." *Ground Water* 48, no. 3: 350–54.

Zhou Xiaoguang. 1996. *Shijiu shiji wushi dao liushi niandai zhongguo shehuide zhanluan yu Huizhou shangbang de shuailuo* (China's civil war in the 1850s and 1860s and the decline of Huizhou merchants). Hefei: Huangshan shushe.

Zhu Jieming. 2004. "Local Developmental State and Order in China's Urban Development During Transition." *International Journal of Urban and Regional Research* 28, no. 2: 424–47.

Zhu Rongji. 2011. *Zhu Rongji Jianghua Shilu* (A veritable record of speeches of Zhu Rongji). Vol. 1. Beijing: Renmin chubanshe.

Zweig, David. 2002. *Internationalizing China: Domestic Interests and Global Linkages*. Ithaca, N.Y.: Cornell University Press.

Index

U.S. Treasury bonds, xxiii, 11–12, 146; China's addiction to, 125–33, *127*; dollar in, 119; exports and, 128, 148; Great Crash and, *132*; Japan and, *127*; military and, *122*; quantitative easing campaign with, 132; top-five holders of, *122*

Vietnam War, 52, 117, 119
Voltaire, xiii, xiv

wages: in manufacturing, 69–70, *70*, 71, 74–75, 164; profit and, 154; repression of, 152–53
Walder, Andrew, 89, 90
Wallerstein, Immanuel, 6–7, 34
Walter, Carl, 63
Washington consensus, 59
water pollution, 179
wealth accumulation, 8. *See also* capital accumulation
Weber, Max, 5–6
weifu buren (rich but not benevolent), 27
Wen Jiabao, 66
westernization, xiv

What the U.S. Can Learn from China: An Open-Minded Guide to Treating Our Greatest Competitor as Our Greatest Teacher (Lee), 1
When China Rules the World (Jacques), 2, 115
White Lotus Rebellion, xx, 32–33, 35–36
Who Will Feed China? (Brown), 179
WikiLeaks, 66
workshop of the world, 61, 68
World Trade Organization (WTO), xxiii, 55, 157; Brazil and, 141; Diaoyu/Senkakus Islands and, 136; G-20 in, 142–43; U.S. and, 141, 143

Xi Jinping, xxiv, 73, 166, 185n3

yumin (stupid people), 29

zaibatsu (private corporate conglomerates), 38
Zakaria, Fareed, 115
Zambia, 108, 140
Zheng He, 15
Zhu Rongji, xxiii, 59, 63, 71, 163
zombie companies, 166